HOW TO RIDE THE HORSE
You Thought You Bought

*All You Need
to Know Exactly What to Do
Every Time You Get in the Saddle*

ANNE BUCHANAN

Trafalgar Square
North Pomfret, Vermont

First published in 2025 by

Trafalgar Square Books
North Pomfret, Vermont 05053

Copyright © 2025 *Anne Buchanan*

All rights reserved. No part of this book may be reproduced, by any means, without written permission of the publisher, except by a reviewer quoting brief excerpts for a review in a magazine, newspaper, or website.

Disclaimer of Liability
The author and publisher shall have neither liability nor responsibility to any person or entity with respect to any loss or damage caused or alleged to be caused directly or indirectly by the information contained in this book. While the book is as accurate as the author can make it, there may be errors, omissions, and inaccuracies.

Trafalgar Square Books encourages the use of approved safety helmets in all equestrian sports and activities.

Trafalgar Square Books certifies that the content in this book was generated by a human expert on the subject, and the content was edited, fact-checked, and proofread by human publishing specialists with a lifetime of equestrian knowledge. TSB does not publish books generated by artificial intelligence (AI).

Library of Congress Cataloging-in-Publication Data
Names: Buchanan, Anne (Writer on horsemanship), author.
Title: How to ride the horse you thought you bought : all you need to know exactly what to do every time you get in the saddle / Anne Buchanan.
Description: North Pomfret, Vermont : Trafalgar Square Books, 2024. | Includes bibliographical references and index.
Identifiers: LCCN 2023043527 (print) | LCCN 2023043528 (ebook) | ISBN 9781646012053 (paperback) | ISBN 9781646012060 (epub)
Subjects: LCSH: Horsemanship. | Horses--Training.
Classification: LCC SF309 .B8825 2024 (print) | LCC SF309 (ebook) | DDC 798.2--dc23/eng/20231107
LC record available at https://lccn.loc.gov/2023043527
LC ebook record available at https://lccn.loc.gov/2023043528

Excerpt from the USDF Glossary of Judging Terms (Appendix I) reproduced with permission of USDF ©2018 United States Dressage Federation (USDF). All rights reserved. Reproduction without permission is prohibited by law. USDF is not responsible for any errors or omissions in the publication or for the use of its copyrighted material in an unauthorized manner.

Excerpt from *The Miniature Guide to Critical Thinking*, Eighth Edition, by Richard Paul and Linda Elder, published by The Foundation for Critical Thinking © *Linda Elder 2020*,'reproduced by arrangement with The Rowman & Littlefield Publishing Group.

Photos by: *Fennells.com* (1.4); *Anne Buchanan* (3.6 A–D, 6.3 A & B, 6.4 B, 6.5 A & B, 6.6, 6.13 A & B, 6.14 A & B, 6.15 A & B, 7.4 A & B, 7.5 A & B, 7.7 A & B, 8.2); *Paige Metcalfe* (3.8 A & B); © *Wendy Wooley/Equisport Photos peepsandpaws.com* (4.6, 7.6 A & B, 7.6, 7.8 A & B, 8.7 C, 8.9); *Varian Arabians* (4.7); *Correct Connect LLC* (6.7); *Linda Grandia* (6.17); *Shelley Smith Giacomini* (10.4)

Illustrations by *Taylor Sterry, Cindy Sither, Stacy Rector,* and *Emilie Goddard (p. 270)*

Book design by *Katarzyna Misiukanis–Celińska (misiukanis-artstudio.com)*
Typefaces: *Noto Serif, Domus, Brushberry* and *Roboto*
Cover design by *RM Didier*
Index by *Andrea Jones (JonesLiteraryServices.com)*

Printed in China
10 9 8 7 6 5 4 3 2 1

**This book is dedicated
to** *Sheila Varian, Michelle Peck Williams,*
and *Sharon Vander Ziel*

Contents

Foreword	**VIII**
Introduction	**XII**
Who Am I?	3
This Book's Objectives	3
What to Expect in the Pages Ahead	4
Keep in Mind	13
Study Guide: Overview	14

PART ONE: GROUND RULES ... 18

Who Is Your Horse? Building a Relationship from the Ground Up	21
Study Guide: Lesson Plans	23

Chapter / 1 /: Space Bubble ... 30

Space Bubble 1: Teach Your Horse to Respect Your Space	33
Space Bubble 2: Turning	36
★ Caveats	37
Study Guide: Rephrasing	39

Chapter / 2 /: Tap Tap ... 42

The Foundation Exercise of Groundwork	45
Study Guide: Reflection	47

Chapter / 3 /: Longeing ... 50

Tap Tap on a Circle—AKA Longeing	53
★ Caveats	59
★★ Extensions	65
Study Guide: Thinking About Your Thinking	67

Chapter / 4 /: Moving Body Parts ... 74

Moving Body Parts Independently of the Rest of the Body	77
★ Caveats	83
Study Guide: Self-Perception	86

PART TWO: NON-NEGOTIABLES ... 88

Study Guide: Create Your Own Non-Negotiables	92

Chapter / 5 /: Go — 94

    Aids Inform the Horse—They Are *Not* the Moving Force — 97

    The Effect of Balance on the Horse — 101

    ★ Caveats — 104

    ★★ Extensions — 110

    Study Guide: Applying Intellectual Standards to Riding Terminology — 113

Chapter / 6 /: Get Connected — 116

    Connection Theory: The Circuit — 119

    Connection, Shifting Weight, and Balance — 125

    Connection Isn't Automatic…or Easy — 127

    Establishing Contact — 129

    The Key to Connection? Patience — 132

    The Kinesthetic Conundrum: Being Sure You Know What Contact and Connection Feel Like — 133

    Connection Takes Practice and Time — 147

    ★ Caveats — 153

    ★★ Extensions — 155

    Connection in Closing — 161

    Study Guide: Clarity/State, Elaborate, Illustrate, and Exemplify (SEIE) — 162

Chapter / 7 /: Stay Connected — 164

    Contact and Connection: Now You Have It, Now You Don't — 167

    Maintaining Connection: It's Not Just Reins! — 168

    Improving Connection — 175

    ★ Caveats — 179

    ★★ Extensions — 181

    There Isn't "One" Connection — 186

    Using Connection: It's All About the Outside Rein — 186

    …And Also About the Inside Rein…and Leg! — 187

    ★ Caveats — 190

    ★★ Extensions — 194

    Study Guide: Craft an X Post — 197

Chapter / 8 /: Transitions — 200

    Remaining Connected Through Transitions — 203

    Keys to Clear Transitions — 210

Downward Transition to Walk	213
Canter Transitions	215
★ Caveats	216
★★ Extensions	218
Study Guide: Prior Questions	225

Chapter / 9 /: Flexion 228

Flexion Is Kryptonite for Tension and Resistance	233
The Role of Flexion in Connection	234
To the Outside Rein, Not Through It	235
Establishing Correct Flexion	242
★ Caveats	249
★★ Extensions	254
Study Guide: Summarizing Excerpts	256

Chapter / 10 /: Half-Halt 258

The Universal Tool	261
Half-Halts Are Part of Your "Horse Code" Language	261
Why Call Them Half-Halts?	262
The Role of Flexion in Half-Halts	262
Timing of the Half-Halt	263
Aids for the Half-Halt	264
Examining the Ingredients	265
Half-Halt Stages	268
Consistent Connection Is Critical	270
How Can You Tell If the Half-Halt Worked?	271
★ Caveats	272
★★ Extensions	274
Study Guide: Fundamental and Powerful Concepts	276

Conclusion	**278**
Appendix I: Glossary of Terms	**282**
Appendix II: Foundation for Critical Thinking Intellectual Standards	**288**
Appendix III: Circle Templates for Dressage Arenas	**289**
Acknowledgments	**290**
Bibliography	**292**
Index	**294**

Foreword

Anne was one of my first students when I moved to Kentucky, and I have enjoyed helping her navigate through the different methods of training horses for over 12 years. I have coached her on several horses that varied in breed, training, age, and conformation.

Anne's quest to leave no stone unturned led her to focus on dressage, which to me is the science of gymnastic training for the horse. A dedicated student, Anne always takes notes and thinks about the lesson plan for the next lesson; she is determined to make sure she understands every detail of the exercise. Anne also is one of the few people willing to take whatever time it takes to have the horse accept the concept. That could be 45 minutes at walk or ending a ride after eight minutes of great work.

When you educate a horse, you help that horse. When you educate the rider, you help every horse that person rides, and all the people that rider may help along the way. This describes my years with Anne perfectly. It is fun to see her pass on many of the theories and sayings that were passed on to me from the great horsemen who helped me over the last four decades. *How to Ride the Horse You Thought You Bought* is a great step in that direction; it will help many people have a better relationship with their horses, which in turn tends to keep horses in happy homes.

It is the rider's responsibility to do the best for the horse you are on. Use the information in this book to help you do that. Enjoy learning to communicate clearly with your horse, which will allow you to put the horse in the position where he can do the work you are asking of him. Most of all, enjoy the process—and put the horse first.

– SHARON VANDER ZIEL –

Judge Curriculum Manager
United States Dressage Federation
Dressage Instructor for Over 40 Years

"Go after whatever it is that you are seeking to find

with all of the ability that you have to find it."

David Goggins, Retired US Navy SEAL,
New York Times Bestselling Author, Endurance Athlete

Introduction

Whether it's for speed, power, jumping, or moving in intricate harmony with another creature, when people set out to ride horses, they are eager to experience the sensations generated by the beautiful animals performing underneath. Often, however, the realization quickly follows that horses don't operate like an automatic transmission in a car, and you probably won't be able to accomplish everything you envisioned on the first ride. Or, you accept what a horse feels like at face value, not realizing how much more smooth, intuitive, and connected the experience can be. But what makes riding horses fascinating is the challenge of learning to communicate with your horse in a way that enables you to achieve your desired goals. Like so many things, riding is about discovery and the lessons learned along the way. There is great joy and satisfaction in achieving a hard-earned goal and developing a partnership with your horse. The objective of this book is to equip you with tools for understanding and working with your horse's responses, so that you can eventually achieve your goals with him. And, although your horse (probably) has been trained, it (probably) was done by someone else. This book teaches you how to build a relationship with your horse from the ground up, ensuring a common understanding for harmonious interactions going forward.

We yearn for the sensations that we observe others achieving with their horses and strive to emulate them. How do they do it? This book offers practical tools that are applicable to the majority of horses, allowing horse and human to develop a mutual understanding. This, in turn, enables every rider to make progress toward an objective.

Who Am I?

Why did I write this book? I have a voracious appetite for learning and have immersed myself in a variety of disciplines (dressage, jumping, reining, racing, halter, and saddle seat, to name just a few), and breeds (Arabians, Warmbloods, Saddlebreds, Quarter Horses, Thoroughbreds, and Akhal-Tekes) over the course of a half century. I was fortunate to have learned from numerous notable individuals in each field and have compiled useful guidance from each here. I have ridden hundreds of horses, enabling me to discern which techniques are universally effective with an array of equine temperaments. Lastly, I am an educator. I spent my entire career devising ways of making baffling science concepts relatable, meaningful, and useful. Such experience grants me a cumulative and nimble point of view and, from this context, I harvested a few key points:

- Doing something is hard when you don't know how to do it.

- Doing something is fun and easy when you DO know how to do it.

- Achievement makes people feel good.

- There are things (the *Four Stages of Competence* introduced by Gordon Training International employee Noel Burch in the 1970s) that:

  - You know you know (*conscious competence*).

  - You know you don't know but want to learn (*conscious incompetence*).

  - You don't even know that you don't know (*unconscious incompetence*).

  - You can do because of innate talent, although you can't articulate what you do (*unconscious competence*).

  - You think you know, but you actually *don't* (false self-assurance, which can be very harmful).

The awareness to know that you must distinguish amongst these when riding and working with horses is powerful, and that is one of the things I hope to teach you.

This Book's Objectives

This book endeavors to reveal what lies between the lines of conventional horsemanship instruction, pulling back the curtain on knowing *exactly* what you need to do each ride. The goal is to make the implicit explicit by elaborating (providing more information), exemplifying (giving examples) and illustrating (offering analogies) for better comprehension. I want you to know that you *can* ride "the horse you thought you bought," *but you must create it*. And after reading and implementing the material from this book, you will be more capable of having the horse "you thought you bought" (whether you literally bought a horse or are just working with one and a set of expectations) because you are empowered to do so.

For any activity I've described in the pages ahead, there are four components that are addressed: "what," "how," "why," and "how well." A useful learning tool would be to obtain four different color highlighters and mark each of these four

I.1 Active Reading. A reader gains significantly more knowledge from a text when she thoughtfully and actively interacts with its content. To engage in such a dialogue with the text, one must read with a purpose: searching for specific concepts, such as "what," "why," "how," and "how well," requires a reader to think critically, generate a response to the text, and evaluate whether it meets needs. Color-coding makes it possible to connect "what" with "how" and "why" and to determine what "how well" means. Understanding the how and why of a task makes determining "what to do" much clearer. A second advantage of highlighting is the ability to quickly locate useful information in the future. ●

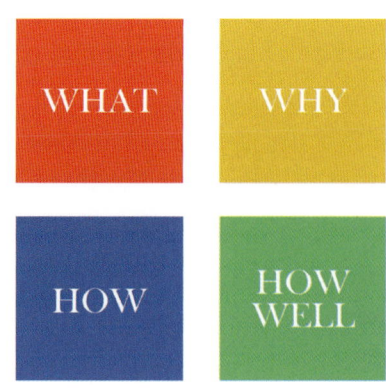

concepts in a particular color throughout this book in order to cement these ideas in your mind. Understanding why something happens or why something ought to be done is compelling knowledge that improves learning (fig. I.1).

It also helps to be aware that, frequently, horse training doesn't look like the finished product, and that's okay. Sometimes, you need to do things in whatever way necessary for your horse to understand what you want. That may mean that you need to break conventional rules of equitation for a moment (for example, look down at your horse or watch your hands). Once he understands, you can refine your movements and return to accepted norms. Be prepared to be patient. Too many people are in a rush. Time invested on the front end waiting for a horse to become solid in his understanding is well worth the effort. His subsequent learning curve will be much faster as a result, and you will reap the benefits of your patience. Your horse will be substantially happier, and this is of great value all around. Force without comprehension isn't the quickest, safest, or most successful way in the long game of riding.

What to Expect in the Pages Ahead

This book addresses the question, "How do I know what to do on my horse today?" This text assumes that you already ride in a basic fashion (walk, trot, and maybe canter independently), that you are working with a horse that has already been backed (albeit is perhaps not well-trained or well-behaved), and that you desire to "be productive" with your horse. What do I mean by the latter? In my experience working with more than a thousand individuals, I have come to the realization that people purchase horses with specific intentions in mind.

So in this context, "being productive" refers to making progress toward that specific intention, whether competing at a certain level or going for a trail ride with friends.

My students generally have come to me because they are unable to communicate with their horse, particularly at a fundamental level, and there is a significant disparity between their aspirations (those intentions I just mentioned) and the harsh realities of their "situation." This book serves as a conduit between what you may have believed your horse to be (either due to assumptions, unrealistic expectations, naivety, or misinformation) and the resources needed to realize your aspirations. I provide practical tools that are suitable for nearly *all* horses, enabling the horse and human to establish a shared understanding. We get to the nitty-gritty of the skills that I wish had been taught from the outset, elusive concepts that few articulate in depth. I want to help you understand what to do *to get what you expect from your horse.* This begins with fundamental preliminary experiences, what I call the "Non-Negotiables," designed to teach you how to ride your horse in a way that achieves predictable, repeatable results. You will learn to distinguish between correct and incorrect responses. When your horse performs well, you will want to replicate that; good feelings are gratifying and reinforcing. This is how progress is made. The more you understand the interdependence of the Non-Negotiables, and become

Learning on Your Own

While having eyes-on-the-ground feedback is the real-time, horse-specific way to learn to ride, I have successfully learned from a "remote" teacher through means other than in-person lessons. Learning from media *does* work; but you must approach learning differently than the traditional form of receiving passive instruction. In some ways, it's actually better because you must be an active, deliberate participant in your learning, rather than outsourcing your brain and letting someone else do the problem-solving for you: you must learn to objectively assess yourself and seek ways to identify, articulate, clarify and resolve what you don't understand.

Discovery learning, or solving a problem on your own (with guidance), is a powerful experience because you are compelled to be self-reflective and independent. This notion is illustrated by Mortimer Adler in his book *How to Read a Book* (Touchstone, 1972), where he asserts that "books are absent teachers:"

> **There is good reason to place primary emphasis on reading, and let listening become a secondary concern. The reason is that listening is learning from a teacher who is present—a living teacher—while reading is learning from one who is absent. If you ask a living teacher a question, he'll probably answer you. If you are puzzled by what he says, you can save yourself the trouble of thinking by asking him what he means. If,**

Learning on Your Own

however, you ask a book a question, you must answer it yourself… [the book] answers you only to the extent that you do the work of thinking and analysis yourself.

Lessons learned this way, on one's own, tend to be more deeply internalized and open the door to further insightful thinking processes.

Because horseback riding is a diagnostic and problem-solving activity, it is conducive to self-study. The more attuned you are to recognizing when something is amiss, systematically experimenting with how to address it, and remembering what worked and what didn't, the better rider you become. This means you will be able to assist a horse, more like a trainer, rather than simply "pushing buttons" and hoping for the best. Moreover, you will develop the feel, timing, and methodology of riding, which are all essential components of horsemanship (treating horses with respect and understanding), as opposed to focusing solely on correct equitation. This is also advantageous when you are alone and encounter a difficult situation.

Let me share an example from my own experience.

Dr. Thomas Ritter *(ArtisticDressage.com)* has hundreds of fascinating and meaningful exercises to ride. They are purposeful, effective, and well-explained with regard to what, why, how, when, and where to use them. But one of the more basic ones just plain eluded *me*. It seemed straightforward, proficient in their application, the more sense each will make.

Repetition

Several concepts are intentionally repeated throughout the book. This has been done for the following reasons:

❖ Sometimes a notion isn't understood in its entirety on first reading.

❖ It is presented slightly differently as applied in a new, more refined or advanced context.

❖ When described in a slightly new way, you come to see more sense to it.

❖ It's something that people persistently forget to implement while riding.

❖ It's important enough to warrant repetition in order to remain in the forefront throughout the book.

This technique, referred to as "spiraling the curriculum," revisits topics while progressively deepening the material as learning advances. When you encounter a concept that has been repeated for these reasons and your mind says, "Yes, yes, I know"—and you can correctly project what it will say before you finish reading the sentence—then I have achieved my goal! Only when one has internalized a concept can one build on prior knowledge.

Note that everyday concepts ("heels down") are not ascribed to any specific author, whereas unique concepts—or those that I have only ever heard once—are cited. This book further seeks to overtly define and contextualize equestrian jargon so the reader isn't obliged to guess what a descriptor means. Indeed, the United States Dressage Federation (USDF) recently created a glossary of terms to standardize the use of terminology for riders, trainers, and judges to ensure that everyone using the same word means the same thing. These terms can be found in Appendix I (p. 282).

Organization

This book is structured so that the bulk of what needs to be said about "how" to do something is addressed in the initial body of the text. Then, because every horse is different, and many variables can occur, a list of caveats (cautionary elements) follow at the end of most sections. These alert you to common and expected behaviors or reactions you may encounter, enabling you to be prepared and not surprised by their occurrence; you are not alone in facing them. They aren't listed in any specific order. Here are a few examples as pertain to this book and working with horses in general:

★ Caveats

❖ Many people don't realize how much **training** horses need, or that they learn in small increments.

but it didn't click in my brain for some reason. So, I just kept revisiting it. It's called "Stopping into All Four Feet" and "it creates a connection from the rider's weight through each leg of the horse to the ground," says Dr. Ritter. "Stopping into a leg improves the horse's permeability for the aids, his balance, his body awareness, his back activity, his suppleness, and his rein contact."

Here is how Dr. Ritter explains the exercise on his website (note I have transcribed it exactly):

1. *Ride walk to halt transitions into each leg.*

2. *Start with the outside front leg, followed by the outside hind leg, etc.*

3. *If you want to stop into an outside leg, apply a pressure with the outside rein when an outside leg is on the ground. If you want to stop into an inside leg, apply a pressure with the inside rein when an inside leg is on the ground.*

4. *Ride each transition in with 3 half-halts in consecutive strides. The first 2 half-halts are announcements for the horse so that he can prepare himself for the upcoming transition. The 3rd half-halt executes the transition.*

5. *When you ride the transition, count in your head: half-halt, half-halt, halt.*

6. *When you ride a down transition into a specific leg, you send your weight through this leg into the ground, creating a connection between your weight and*

Learning on Your Own

the ground. This connection can only be established when the horse opens himself up to the aids and allows the aids to travel through this part of his body. If there are muscle blockages in and around this leg, the aids won't be able to go through. The horse will then drop his back and brace with his body against the half-halts.

I couldn't quite fathom stopping "into a leg." I didn't *believe* that I could specifically control each of the horse's legs and I was, frankly, intimidated to even give it a go. I finally just decided to *try* stopping into each leg and see if *doing* it helped my understanding. The first time I tried on the ground, walking a well-trained horse wearing a bridle in-hand so that I could watch his legs to get a feel for it. It turned out to be easy and worked like a charm. The next morning, I tried it riding on a green and unbalanced four-year-old. Same result.

But I still couldn't see the value or the power of the exercise. It was only when I tried it on a horse that was a runaway with a history of abuse that I understood the full impact of the value of this concept! When I tried to stop either front leg, the horse just plowed on through. There was no stopping her. Then, I was surprised when I tried stopping the horse on the hind legs because that turned out to be easy! She stopped immediately, with no question or resistance.

Up until this point, I must have been habitually trying to stop her with a front leg and didn't even realize that I was doing that, because I could *never* stop or slow this horse.

❖ Expecting horses to act like dogs is unrealistic. Horses are **prey animals**, while dogs are predators. These opposing points of view affect how they react to their surroundings and stimuli.

❖ Because horses are convinced that doing something they have never done before is impossible, they **need time** to adjust to new ideas; they need you to "show them the way." Knowing what to expect reduces anxiety, allowing them to focus attention to you.

❖ **Introduce new arena exercises in walk,** so the horse can see the work space and become familiar with the task. Familiarity will help when he's moving faster and covering more ground. Walking is also beneficial for the rider because it allows you to **assess** the exercise and plan and strategize: Are you on the intended path, for example, a true 20-meter circle, or is your horse crooked? Is the exercise easy or hard for the horse, or for a specific part of the horse's body?

❖ When riding, do not wander aimlessly. **Ride a predetermined course,** such as a circle, straight line, or serpentine. Not only will your horse be able to sense your intent, but such arena exercises are informative because they reveal both horse and rider's strengths and weaknesses. Furthermore, other riders are able to anticipate your path to avoid collisions.

- A horse cannot be expected to meet complex training goals for months. Like their human counterparts, horses **need time to develop** their bodies and understanding before they can do a task without strain or difficulty.

- People tend to assume that horses have some level of permanent fitness, just by virtue of being a horse. However, horses are biological beings, just like humans, and they must also become fit. **Treat the horse's body with the consideration** with which you would treat your own.

- **You are not just a passenger on your horse;** he is not the only athlete in the equation. You are participating in a sport in which your muscles are also engaged to maintain your posture and balance in the saddle for an extended period of time, so you need to be physically fit as well.

- Horses don't actively consider how many legs they have or where they put them, so walking a straight line can be challenging. Riding in a straight line while slightly flexing the horse's head to the left or right may seem simplistic, but riders quickly discover how difficult this is! As the horse swerves and leans, the rider realizes that **horses are not automatic**.

- Horses must first **learn to balance** themselves before negotiating the added weight and movement of a rider. It is even more difficult when the rider is

Now that I *knew* which legs were out of control, I changed my strategy to utilize the hind legs and began working methodically to get the front legs to respond. Using the rein on the same side as a front leg turned out to be useless, but using the rein on the *opposite* side did work. So, then, I had a tool to use to help control this horse.

From this experience, I learned that, when something didn't work with a horse, to look at the situation like the game show *Wheel of Fortune* in which contestants guess letters of the alphabet to solve hangman-like puzzles. The most commonly used letters in the English language are R, S, T, L, N, and E, so the producers give those letters to contestants automatically to force them to try something different. Sometimes, we have to stop using "R, S, T, L, N, and E"; try the "rest of the alphabet" to freshen up our horses' responses.

Dr. Ritter's exercise turned out to be diagnostic, giving me a powerful means of evaluating what the fundamental issue was preventing a rider from being able to stop this horse. It definitely took a couple of weeks of intentional riding to consistently get this horse to come back on a half-halt on the front legs, but the exercise removed her anxiety, gave her a clear understanding of what I wanted, and improved communication drastically. It was life changing! I had no one around to help me, but just by trying the exercise and paying attention, I was able to figure it out.

Doing this exercise was extremely valuable in itself, but it also opened a whole new world of feel and awareness for me: I discovered that I was more attuned to the timing of aids and could feel whether the horse's legs were underneath him or stepping away from his body. I could use my seat, legs, or reins to put them back. It also taught me how to control the movement of his shoulders and keep them beneath the withers, providing new levels of control and stability.

In Mortimer Adler's *How to Read a Book*, he states:

> *Getting more information is learning, and so is coming to understand what you didn't understand before. To be informed is to know simply that something is the case. To be enlightened is to know, in addition, what it is all about…. This distinction is familiar in terms of the differences between being able to remember something and being able to explain it. If you remember what an author says, you have learned something from reading him. But, you have gained nothing but information if you have exercised only your memory. You have not been enlightened. Enlightenment is achieved only when, in addition to knowing what an author says, you know what he means and why he says it…. The point, however, isn't to stop at being informed.*

Enlightened riding then, is knowing "how" and "why" something is done, as opposed to just "what."

unstable (see next bullet); the horse cannot predict where or when the rider's weight will shift from stride to stride.

❖ Try standing on two scales that are placed adjacent to one another. Observe 1) whether your **weight is evenly distributed** on each scale and 2) the degree to which your weight varies when you lean from side to side. Even a seemingly insignificant shift in weight can represent 30 to 40 pounds that your horse must compensate for. And when you stand on the two scales and intentionally sway from side to side, you will note that your weight can shift 50 pounds or more! The front end of the horse is already burdened by the weight of his head and neck, so this extra weight shift is not only extremely challenging for him to balance, it can impact his health and soundness.

❖ Horses aren't born knowing what aids mean, or the horse you ride might not know *your* cues. Take time to assess your horse's understanding and **teach him what you mean**. Clarity and consistency are essential.

❖ "Don't get greedy" is good advice. If your horse is doing well, **don't drill**. Repetition increases the chance that you'll do it slightly differently each time and muddy the waters. Get what you want, stop, and reward for performing the exercise correctly. Let him relax. Revisit tomorrow.

- When your horse does everything right the first time, *get off*! Quality is more important than quantity! **Give your horse the confidence** of knowing he did well. Although you would have liked to ride longer, it's always okay to stop riding early. This doesn't happen often. And since horses usually offer up what they did well the day before, your next ride should be more successful.

- **Your horse gets tired.** Once he exhibits signs of fatigue, especially when introducing new content, avoid overworking him. He won't perform as well if he's tired, sore, too hot/cold, or if the footing is bad. Tomorrow is another day. Moreover, if he's working incorrectly because he's tired, he'll develop *incorrect* muscle memory and physique.

- The ideas presented in this book may encourage the reader to undergo a **paradigm shift**, or a shift from one way of thinking to another, which can be unsettling. Misconceptions about horses and riding abound, and there is a strong desire to cling to beliefs or habits even when logic contradicts them. It can be disconcerting to come across concepts you didn't even know you didn't know. You may believe you know how to ride, only to discover that your body is doing something difficult to recognize or change.

- Accept the journey! For example, if you lean forward, simply sitting vertically can make you feel like you're leaning too far back until you get used to the improved posture. Don't let frustration, the **"weirdness" of a new sensation**, or discouragement stand in the way of progress.

- The purpose of this book is to help you discern the logic of your discipline **and learn how to think like an equestrian**. It encourages your curiosity and perception, enabling you to identify and articulate questions you have as a rider.

★★ Extensions

An extension activity extends the learning of a lesson. Extension tasks provide additional or alternative forms of practice. When they appear in the pages ahead, they aren't presented in any order. Incorporate them as may be applicable. As with the Caveats, here are some sample Extensions that apply to the book in general:

❖ Work through this book with a friend; it is a book you *do*. **Read and discuss the text** *one paragraph, or section, at a time*, even rephrasing one *sentence* at a time. Take turns explaining it to each other; working together gives you the opportunity to experience the old adage, "to teach is to learn twice." Scheduled discussion:

  •• Creates accountability.

  •• Encourages you to listen to what you are saying and see if that's really what you mean.

  •• Causes you to think about what you're doing while riding.

  •• Causes you to refine your understanding of a subject as you explain it to others.

  •• Brings notions into focus that may not have occurred to you.

  •• Further extends your understanding.

❖ Ride, then revisit the topic to see what insights have surfaced as a result of the implementation of the material. **Reviewing the text a second time after riding** may prove eye-opening and valuable: because of your experience, you will "hear" the material "with new ears," thus enabling you to perceive the deeper meanings in what was presented. Reading the book again later may even feel like you are reading a different book because, what you need to know *now* will be what you focus on but, as your skill and experience grow in the future, *other* sections will stand out with new significance. Because your capacity for a more complete understanding develops, you will gain a more refined comprehension of what you need at this moment. This is how learning about riding works.

❖ Explore the **Feldenkrais Method,** which teaches people how to be more aware of their bodies to improve function. Becoming aware of what your body does is crucial for riding success. For example, many people think they are sitting upright when, in fact, they are leaning forward, back, left or right. Feldenkrais activities can assist you in changing your perception of where you are in space.

Keep in Mind
Opportunity: A Book is an Absent Teacher

This book is designed to behave somewhat like a nerve cell: nerve cells convert an *electrical* impulse into a *chemical* signal. In a similar fashion, this book endeavors to translate the *experience* of riding into *words* so that you can think like good riders think; feel what good riders feel, do what good riders do. It will get you on a road that makes sense and is doable, even if you don't always have an instructor. You will develop confidence as you learn to recognize what is working, what isn't, what you need to do, whether you achieve it, and whether success is replicable. And, most importantly, it will help you recall what to do while riding so you don't flounder.

Learn from Your Horse

Your actions have direct effects on your horse's behavior. If the same error keeps occurring, analyze the situation and determine the relationship between your actions and the horse's behavior. Dr. Thomas Ritter points out in his YouTube Artistic Dressage "Rider Revolution" series that a horse's responses show the rider exactly how she is influencing him. He clarifies that "there are mainly two options for anything you want to try: go forward or back, left or right, more pressure on one seat bone or the other, etc.… There are a very limited number of options and the horse will either get better or worse every time you change something…note where the horse seems the happiest, roundest and softest." He recommends experimenting with doing things alternatively and compare what you get for doing "this," or for doing "that." If you only have to choose between "this" or "that," it's not that hard to do. Then, you intentionally keep what you like and eliminate what you don't. In this way, your *horse* can serve as a very effective teacher…The trick is to *remember* to maintain doing what you do want.

The Right Equipment and Attitude

The following will help you get the most out of this book:

- If using a bridle and bit, use a mild bit like a snaffle (I recommend using an anatomical shape made of salox or aurigan so that it has neutral taste, warms readily, and encourages salivation). Bitless options are also acceptable.

- Practice the material until it works (usually takes three days for success).

- Have patience and self-reflection; think about what you are doing.

- Mirrors, video, and eyes on the ground help a lot.

Study Guide

Overview

When I was teaching, I told my students that science was hard only because they didn't know how to do it… *yet*. To illustrate this point, I showed them the number 13511214385171341683 for five seconds. Then, I asked them to write the number down immediately for a quiz grade, which created a lot of anxiety because that was "hard." When they couldn't do it, I said to them, "What if I told you to start with the first number in the sequence and use the formulaic pattern "times 2 plus 1, times 2 minus 1?" Thus:

❖ Multiply the first number by 2, **add one:** 1x2= 2, 2+1= 3

❖ Take that result and multiply that by 2, then **subtract 1:** 3x2= 6, 6-1= 5

❖ Alternate the pattern of "times 2 *plus* 1, times 2 *minus* 1" to figure out the rest of the numbers in the sequence.

❖ Therefore:
5x2= 10, 10+1= 11
11x2= 22, 22-1= 21 (now you have generated 135121….)
And so forth

Once my students could see the pattern, they were able to generate the number on demand any day for the *rest of their lives* because they

Study Guide

Overview

understood how to do it. Once they comprehended the pattern, it was *no longer hard* and they eagerly retook the quiz, fully confident that they would get 100 percent. This set the tone for the class from the first day: *Anything is easy when you know how to do it*.

Further, taking a page from "Marketing 101"—*perceived need drives consumer desire for a product*—I purposefully created a need in the students so that they were eager to learn how to memorize that number. Likewise, you're probably reading this book because horses create powerful needs—for friendship, for safety, or for a deep yearning to ride your horse in a certain way or at a certain level.

As with the number sequence quiz and my students, this book guides you to understand patterns of horse behavior that govern riding so that it becomes easy for you to solve, too. The study guide sections, like this one, appear at the end of each chapter and serve as "formulas" that you can use to reconstruct the material for yourself at any time. Instead of using math as in my example here, I introduce *cognitive structures*—mental tools the brain uses to make sense of information—to help you actively engage with the material (how much effort and focused attention are you willing to invest in learning the task at hand?), rather than merely being a passive spectator to words on a page. The activities in the Study Guides are intellectually stimulating and were selected because of their high appeal and capacity for producing the desired result with students. The Study Guides will:

❖ *Familiarize you with the terminology, concepts, and skills you will need for riding.*

❖ *Give you confidence for implementing these concepts and skills through explaining, in detail, when, why, and how to do these things, what to expect from the horse and what the rider's role is in the horse's response.*

❖ *Give you strategies for grappling with, distilling, and organizing the information for yourself in order to internalize, retain, apply, and modify it.*

❖ *Help you develop day-to-day and long-range plans.*

Study Guide

Overview

❖ Apply what you have learned to new situations or problems you will encounter.

❖ Encourage you to reflect on what you have learned and sort out what "you know you know" and what "you know you don't know"...yet.

To share these tried-and-true structures, I turned, in part, to *criticalthinking.org* and to best-selling author and communications guru Carmine Gallo, author of Talk Like TED (St. Martin's Press, 2015). (TED is a nonprofit organization devoted to spreading ideas in the form of short, powerful and memorable presentations on the topics of Technology, Entertainment and Design, thus "TED.") In his book, Gallo shares with readers that "in order to force the brain to see things differently, you must find new and novel ways to help the brain perceive information differently. The brain must be provided with something it has never before processed to force it out of predictable perceptions." Gallo continues, in the section of the book entitled, "Teach Me Something New," that things are "more interesting if you share ideas from fields that are much different from your own." As an example, he noted that Apple, the technology company, visited Ritz-Carleton Hotels to learn more about customer service. It's a new way of looking at your world.

Through the Study Guide presented at the end of each chapter, I want to help you look at the world of riding horses through the fresh lenses of structures like critical thinking and TED strategies to stimulate your brain in order to internalize the content in ways that are meaningful to you. What you generate, you know. This is important because, the more facile you are with this information, the more diagnostic you can be—for both you and your horse—while you are riding. While you will find the Study Guides at the end of particular chapters, all of them can be utilized with any topic, or you can reuse one that works particularly well for your learning style. It is invaluable to work through these exercises so that you actively engage with the text to discern how well you truly understand the material I'm sharing with you. Riding is an intellectual endeavor, and the more you dissect it, the more success and satisfaction you will find. You need to practice the thinking as much as you need to practice the riding! *Riding is a thinking game.* ●

Your notes

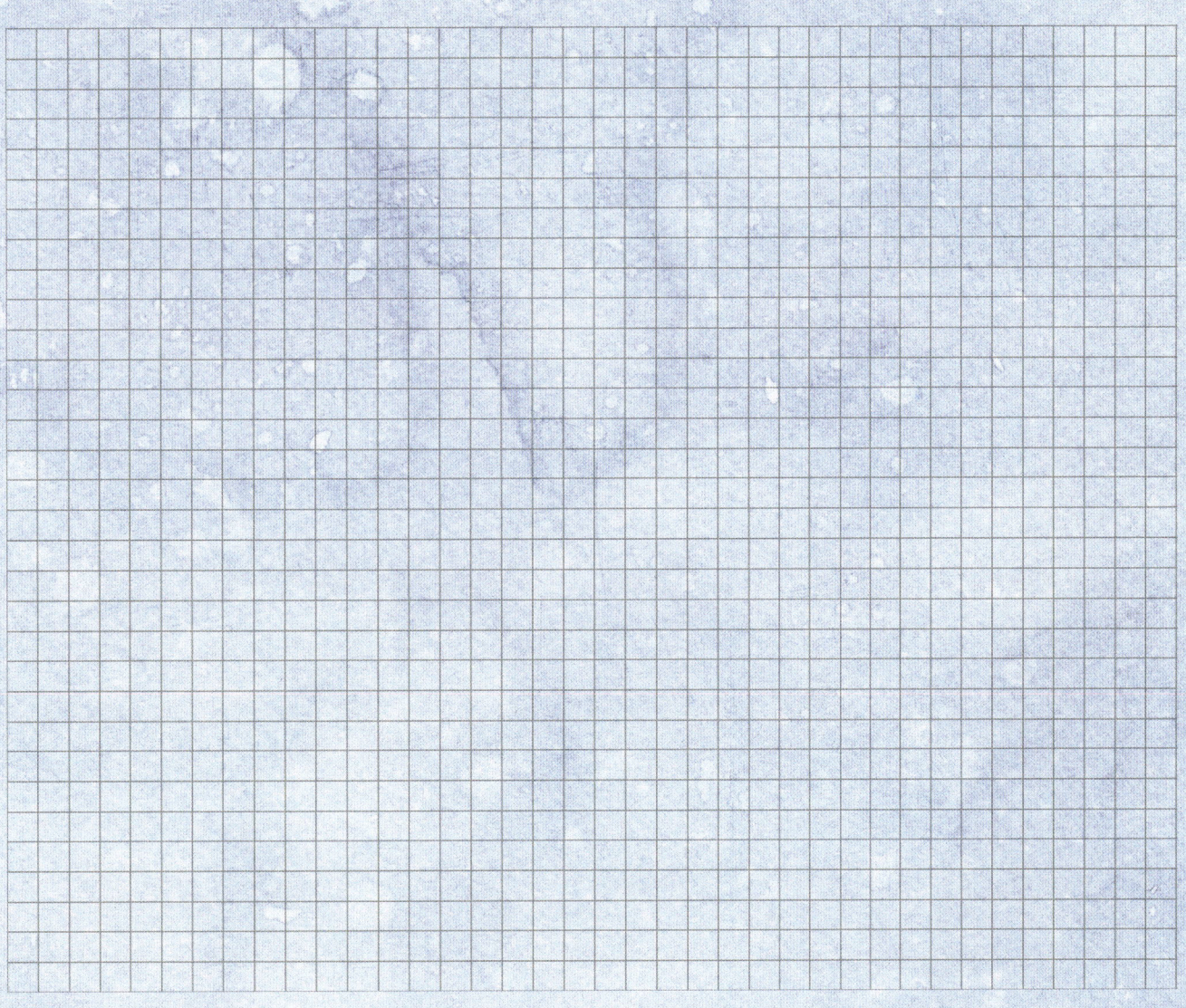

Part One

GROUND RULES

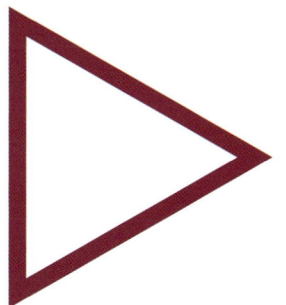

P1.1 Displacement. When you don't teach your horse to respect your space, he will crowd you. This is not safe.

Working with your horse on the ground is beneficial in many ways:

- When *you* are nervous, groundwork allows you to get to know your horse and work with him until *you* feel confident and relaxed.

- When *your horse* is nervous, groundwork will help him establish a familiar routine until *he* feels confident and relaxed.

- You will learn to control your horse's body on the ground so that you will know what to do when you ride.

- You will learn to identify what is going well or not going well; whether your horse is sore; how to predict what he will do; and whether his gaits, shape, movement, and alignment are correct.

- It prepares the horse for riding and enables you to see what is going on beneath you when you ride.

Groundwork and riding are two inseparable sides of the same coin.

Who Is Your Horse? Building a Relationship from the Ground Up

Horses are big and physical. Therefore, before you start riding, it is highly beneficial to get a good grasp of who your horse is and how he reacts. By being observant, you can see how horses communicate in their language (body language) and use this to your advantage.

Horses innately utilize a technique referred to as *displacement*, which means that they use their bodies and body language to compel another individual to move their feet, to move away (fig. P1.1). They may pin their ears, bump you with their shoulder, swing their head or hindquarters toward you, lean into you, or plow past you. They will continue to manage the space around themselves and you if you don't recognize this is happening and do something to correct it. Since horses are hierarchical herd

P1.2 Good Relationship. Your horse will feel secure once he recognizes and accepts your leadership. You can only make progress with a horse when he is calm and trusting. When his mind is relaxed, his muscles can relax. •

animals, establishing yourself as a "leader" makes them less inclined to displace you. They should be respectful and make space for you.

In this section you will learn to use human tools of displacement to communicate with your horse in ways that he more easily understands. This lets you win his respect on *his* terms and predict his behavior. In turn, he learns what to expect from you. Your horse starts to understand the concept of training; that your signals mean that you want him to respond. As he learns to consistently repeat behaviors on command, you gain insight on how best to manage him, while installing tools you will use from the saddle. Such preparatory groundwork saves time because your horse won't be surprised or inept when you begin riding him.

Horses can't see you when you are astride them, so it is advisable to establish a working relationship on the ground so that the horse recognizes who is doing what to him, and why. Horses need to feel secure, and your leadership helps him feel safe (fig. P1.2). This sets the stage for enjoyable riding. As an added bonus, you get to know your horse personally, and most people find this interaction extremely gratifying. Further, in new environments, like a horse show, using these Ground Rules focuses your horse's attention and calms him.

In the section that follows are some groundwork techniques that only take a few days to teach but reap a lifetime of reliable cooperation. It can help to view these techniques in action as well as read how-to instructions, so links to videos featuring "everyday riders" and a variety of horses have been included for you to scan if you wish to watch demonstrations. Note, all groundwork described is initiated from the left-hand side of the horse, although *everything* is done from both sides. Whatever you do on the left side, you should do again on the right.

Study Guide

Lesson Plans

Why Make a Plan?

At times, in lessons, when I have inquired, "What are your plans for your horse today?" students have looked at me like I have three heads and said, "Ride?" But as the instructor, I then want to know (for example): "Are you going to work on canter departs today?" If the answer is yes, I *then* want to know:

❖ How will you decide when to begin canter work during your ride?

❖ What sequence of exercises will logically prepare your horse?

❖ What are you going to do if he is stiff?

❖ What are you going to do if he is crooked?

❖ What are you going to do if he runs off?

❖ What are you going to do if he won't canter?

❖ What are you going to do if he gets the wrong lead?

❖ How are you going to prepare his mind and body for success?

Study Guide

Lesson Plans

When students don't know the answers to these questions at the outset of their training session, they are just fumbling, the blind leading the blind. Horse training isn't something you can make up as you go. In order to answer these questions with ease, preparation is required. Forming a lesson plan *before your ride* is one method for achieving this.

What a Lesson Plan Is

As you engage in this quest to become partners with your horse, it helps if you are organized and analytical. Creating lesson plans, *daily objectives that guide what your horse needs to learn, how you will teach it, what materials you need and how you will assess learning,* will assist you in becoming a more proficient horseman. Not only will you be prepared to interact with your horse, but the mental process of creating this detailed agenda will help you remember what to do when working with or mounted on your horse. In the process of distilling and organizing the information, you internalize the material, making it your own; what you generate, you know and retain. From this plan, you can create a checklist, audio file, or text message to yourself—whichever format works best for you—so that you have a portable version that fits your style to refresh your memory at the barn.

Why Lesson Plans Help

Taking the time to prepare lesson plans for each session with your horse is highly beneficial. Because they provide structure and purpose for both you and your horse, they maximize the quality of your interaction. Further, engaging intellectually with the material before you set out to do it familiarizes you with what you want to do, may reveal things you don't understand before you set out to do it, and helps you remember what your goals are. Otherwise, you may meander through the material, or forget important objectives altogether. Lesson plans result in productive learning experiences for your horse and yourself, keeping you on track and creating a predictable and consistent environment for your horse. Having a clear sense of what you want to accomplish prevents confusion and allows you to use your time as efficiently as possible.

Study Guide
Lesson Plans

Lesson plans are maps that show both you and your horse the way. They have logical beginning and end points. The act of creating them in a document compels you to be clear on what you want to do, how you want to do it, and how you will know if you achieved it. Being thorough about this will give you clarity about what you know and give you a sense of what you don't. Not only do plans keep you focused, they also keep track of where you left off and where you are headed, especially if you can only get to the barn once or twice a week. Compiling your lesson plans in a file lets you see where you left off with your horse, and come in handy when working with another horse.

Brainstorming for a Lesson Plan

"Pre-writing" is the preparatory process for developing a lesson plan. Select your topic and use the information in this book's subsections as a planning guide. Organize your thoughts by:

❖ *Reading the material, watching videos, doing additional research.*

❖ *Figuring out how much of the material you may be able to accomplish in a time frame.*

❖ *Deciding what supplies you need.*

Lesson Plan Format

A simple format to follow for a lesson plan is to decide on your *topic* and *objective*. For educators, this is referred to as *backward mapping*, in which you set a clear goal, then develop a series of step-by-step instructional methods, the *procedure*, to achieve it. This plan should take into account the nature of the horse you are trying to train. Every horse is different, and you must "meet him where he is." This means that you may need to have modifications in the back of your mind so that you can adapt on the fly, depending on how your horse responds. Be prepared to be flexible. A friend always says, "Horses make the lesson plans." You may go in with a plan but find that your horse is missing a key piece of training that is necessary for you to proceed. At that point you have to stop and fill in the missing piece so that your horse is competent to do what

Study Guide

Lesson Plans

you ask. Consider this possibility ahead of time. As your horse's training progresses, this will be less of an issue. However, you never know when a horse is going to object to something, or really just not get it.

Time management is a significant aspect of lesson plan format and includes managing multiple components:

- *A single training session with a singular objective.*

- *A series of lessons that build toward an overall objective.*

- *Practice time to reinforce learning (but don't drill).*

It is never beneficial to a horse to rush due to a lack of time; therefore, you should organize your horse's training so that he can achieve small victories when your day has a limited time frame. It is necessary to allow sufficient time for your horse to learn in a relaxed manner and to develop physically so that he can do what you want. If it is clear that you will not reach your objective on a given day, be prepared to find a suitable stopping point. Some lessons may require weeks for a horse to master. If you find this to be the case, break this objective down into smaller components.

When planning a new session, allow time to review material from the previous lesson. This gives your horse confidence by starting with a task he can perform. Also, provide time for *intervention* and *extension* activities. Interventions are remedial activities, whereas extensions are excellent for a horse that is performing well. To maintain the horse's interest in any exercise, you must incorporate interesting variations. Note that although you may plan for "X" amount of time, any lesson may take significantly longer or shorter. With practice, you will develop a better "feel" for how long a lesson will take.

Sample Lesson Plan

Your plan doesn't have to be fancy or technical. It just needs to be your portable agenda. Imagine the following scenarios:

- *My horse is reluctant to approach the mounting block.*

Study Guide

Lesson Plans

❖ My horse pushes past the mounting block, wiggles, sidesteps.

❖ My horse walks off before I finish mounting.

Topic: Standing at the Mounting Block

Objective: My horse will approach the mounting block willingly, stand still and stay straight while I mount, and wait for my cue to walk on.

Equipment: Mounting block, halter/bridle, lead shank, dressage whip (to use as an extension of the arm as needed), treats, timer.

Procedure:

Phase 1:

1) Lead the untacked horse to the mounting block.

2) Let him sniff and explore the mounting block; give him a treat.

3) Leave the mounting block and return as many times as it takes until he is unconcerned.

4) While holding the horse, move the mounting block around, stomp on it, and step up on it and jump off.

5) Line the horse up with the mounting block and just stand there (use timer for one minute); treat. (Walk away, return, line up again, and stand for one minute as many times as necessary.) If your horse sidesteps away from the mounting block, step down and direct him back alongside it. You may need to use the butt end of your dressage whip to steer his hindquarters (see chapter 4—p. 77).

6) Stand on the mounting block with the horse in place and face him as if you are going to mount. Pet the horse; act like you are mounting by raising your knee or acting like you are swinging your leg over. Leave the mounting block and repeat as necessary.

Phase 2:

1) Tack the horse up.

Study Guide

Lesson Plans

2) Repeat all the steps in Phase 1.

3) Depending on how the horse is, either stop, or get on and have the horse stand still beside the block for one minute.

4) Dismount. Give treat.

5) Leave the mounting block. Repeat.

6) Do not ride beyond the mounting block lesson. Stop for the day.

Phase 3:

1) Repeat previous day.

2) When the horse stands completely still beside the mounting block for one minute, walk off.

3) Walk a short distance. Dismount.

4) Repeat.

While all of this may seem long and difficult, it quickly becomes automatic as you learn to think this way. The act of committing your thoughts to "paper" is crucial to the learning process. Do the work. Studies show that you remember things better when you write them down.

Try This Lesson Plan Activity: Think, Pair, Share, Compare

"Think Pair Share" is a collaborative learning strategy where individuals work together to address an assigned reading. First, you think individually about an assignment, followed by discussion with a partner. In this vein, you and your "study buddy" will choose a horse training topic and each compose a lesson plan independently. You can write the plan for your own horse or trade and do each other's. Then, put your heads together and compare your plans.

What were the focal points of your lesson? What has your friend done? No two horses are identical, and no two people have identical perspectives. What insights did you draw from the explanation of using

Study Guide

Lesson Plans

lesson plans in this book? What has your friend? Two readers will glean different ideas from the same text, and each of you will pick up on information that the other missed, making the experience of sharing a powerful one.

Chapter

SPACE BUBBLE

01

A "space bubble" is an imaginary boundary that provides a comfortable and safe distance between you and your horse.

1.1 Displacement Behavior. Horses communicate through threatening gestures, utilizing their bodies to move other beings around. •

Space Bubble 1:
Teach Your Horse to Respect Your Space

The first Ground Rule your horse needs to learn is to respect your "space bubble" (figs. 1.1 and 1.2) A space bubble is an imaginary boundary between you and others. To experience a space bubble, stand a few feet from someone. Step closer to each other, then again. You can *feel* the other person encroaching on "your space," making you uncomfortable. Horses use their space bubble to communicate dominance. If the horse being intimidated doesn't move out of the way, the space bubble "suggestion" will often be followed by heels or teeth to cement the point.

Horses can strong-arm humans in the same way, walking too closely, hitting you with their head, bumping you, stepping on your toes. Such crowding of your space is dangerous and therefore unacceptable. You need to establish your "space bubble" and teach your horse to stay in his space, like a dog that has been taught to heel (fig. 1.3 A–D).

Try This:
Use a Lead Shank to Establish Space

Introduce this exercise in the middle of the arena so the horse doesn't feel trapped against a wall or a corner, which can stimulate his urge to flee.

Walk forward leading your horse, and then simply stop. If he keeps going, that's when you "shank him" backward, away from you, using bumps from the lead shank to ask him to take a few steps back out of your space. Keep your energy level low because horses sense intensity and frustration.

1.2 Space Bubble. Your space bubble is an imaginary bubble that surrounds you. It represents a comfortable and safe distance between you and your horse. Establishing a space bubble ensures that your horse respects your leadership. Your horse must maintain his own space in order to avoid stepping on you or bumping into you. This space also acts as a buffer in case he spooks, helping to prevent him from colliding with you. •

1.3 A–D Safe Leading. Your horse should not rush ahead of you **(A)** or act up while being led **(B)**. If he pushes ahead of you, you can use a chain shank against his neck to drive him back beside you **(C)**. He should walk peacefully alongside you **(D)**. When you come to a halt, he must also come to a halt. •

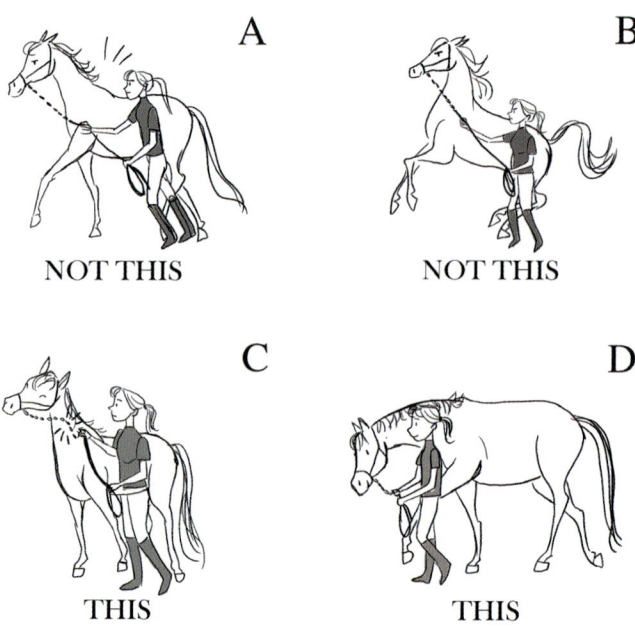

I recommend you use a lead shank with a 30-inch brass "stud" chain (*not* 6 inches) for this exercise (fig. 1.4). Using a chain has advantages: it is more flexible and articulated than a thick cotton lead, and it makes a sound that the horse recognizes (fig. 1.5). When your horse doesn't stop or crowds you while leading, simply flip the chain against the horse's neck, swinging it clockwise in your right hand like a jump rope. The sound and movement will surprise your horse, and he'll likely throw his head up in the air and move backward a couple of steps (some horses react more dramatically). This is exactly the response you seek. If the horse ignores you, keep flipping that chain against his neck and step toward him until he leaves your space.

When the horse backs up, allow slack in the lead and follow him backward. Don't *ever* allow tension in the line. If the lead gets taut, your horse will pull backward against it and could become frightened. Your goal is to get his attention, *not* to frighten him.

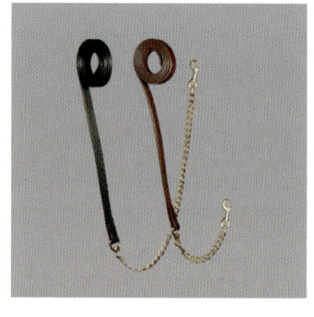

1.4 Chain Length. I recommend using a lead shank with a long chain, 24 to 30 inches, when schooling your horse (left). This is simply for the flexibility and sound the chain makes when you "shank it" along his neck. (It is *not* over the horse's nose for this exercise.) The lead on the right has a chain that is far too short to be effective. •

1.5 Hold Safely. Hold the lead shank in two hands and be sure to hold the leather (or cotton), *not* the chain. Don't wrap the shank tightly around your hand: if the horse suddenly pulls in fright, your hand could be crushed or you could be dragged if you can't get free. If your horse does pull, do not create tension in the shank; that only makes him pull harder. •

1.6 A & B Petting. To reassure or reward your horse, stroke him slowly and gently in the direction of his hair **(A)**. Don't pat him or move too quickly, so he thinks that you're correcting him with a smack **(B)**. •

THIS   NOT THIS

Scan to View Intro to Shanking

Be careful not to stomp your feet as you follow him back, because that also could scare him. The flipping chain isn't punishment. It's just you establishing your space bubble, using a language your horse already understands.

Most horses are accustomed to being told to move or respect space by dominant herd members. You have now attained this status in your horse's mind; therefore, wait a few moments for him to accept your new social hierarchy. Look away from your horse and listen for signs that he is becoming calm. Because a hunting predator would look directly at a horse, looking away can alleviate any stress he may be feeling. Your horse will exhibit signs of relaxation if he opens his mouth and chews, exhales, shakes or lowers his head, or flops his ears. When he is calm, take him a few steps forward and then stop. Your horse should stop right with you and look at you. This is great. Pet him slowly and gently so that he doesn't misinterpret the motion as another correction from the lead shank. Move quickly to shank; slowly to pet (fig. 1.6 A & B).

Shanking is the human version of moving your horse's feet, simulating what occurs naturally in a herd. You make it clear that you are at the top of the pecking order and your horse needs to pay attention to you. Master Horseman Jean-Philippe (JP) Giacomini simplifies, "Dominance is simply defined as 'who gives space to whom?' and 'who controls the other's movements?'"

Perfect Practice Makes Perfect

Prominent Arabian trainer Ray LaCroix once stated, "Horses hate repetition and will cooperate to make it stop." Others say, "Horses like to please." "Horses are either managers or employees and you have to figure out which type you are working with," elaborates USDF Judge Curriculum Manager Sharon Vander Ziel.

1.7 A & B Leading. Your horse should lead politely: walk when you walk, stop when you stop, and stay in his own space **(A)**. It is critical that he walks in a straight line, with his shoulders and hips parallel to you. He should not halt or walk at an angle to you, wiggle around, or enter your space **(B)**.

THIS   NOT THIS

In other words, to teach a horse anything and establish yourself as the leader, repetition is required.

Practice enforcing the space bubble while leading, stopping periodically around the ring. Don't cheat by keeping a little tension on the lead, giving a little tug, or slowing down to hint that a stop is coming. Walk with a loose line and *just stop*. Your horse can do it. If he doesn't stop, shank him, settle, and walk again. Eventually, your horse will obediently walk and stop with you. He should stay at your shoulder, never pushing past or dragging; stopping when you stop; going when you go…*forever*.

You have taught this to the left side; however, you will need to repeat the entire process on the right. *Everything* must be taught to horses at least twice—once for left and once for right (and we should be *patient* as they try to learn the same task on the opposite side or going in a different direction). On the right side of the horse, hold the shank in your left hand. Doing things from the "off" side—the horse's right side—can feel very awkward. It's worth doing, however, because you never know when something will necessitate your horse being cooperative from the non-typical side, and you won't have the opportunity to teach him at that time—for example, you may need to mount from the off side on the trail someday. It is always good practice to take the time to teach everything to your horse from *both sides*.

Space Bubble 2: Turning

Have you ever seen a horse in the pasture "pull" another horse around? No. Horses are more often "push" animals, not pull. Horses use their space bubble to push other horses away, using pinned ears, swinging heads, or heels for emphasis. So, when you want to turn a horse, use *your* space bubble to push him where you want to go instead of pulling on him.

To accomplish this, try leading your horse normally from the left, and turn right. If your horse doesn't respect your space bubble, you will likely run into his head. But your horse needs to recognize that you have a space bubble and he must respect the boundaries of it, no matter where it goes. So, when you turn right, if he doesn't step away, rotate that chain shank like a jump rope against the muscle in his neck until he does (fig. 1.8).

1.8 Turning. When you turn, your horse should turn as well. Because horses respond better to "push" than "pull," turn your horse away from you. He should be able to "feel" your space bubble encroaching on him and move away as a result. When you approach his shoulder from the left, for example, he should cross his left front leg over his right front leg and swing away from you smoothly, rotating on his haunches. There should be no tension on the lead shank. If your horse does not move away when you move your space bubble toward him, use the lead shank to remind him to stay out of your space bubble regardless of where it moves (see p. 35 for a video demonstration).

Scan to View Intro to Turning

The important thing to watch in this exercise is (when you are leading from the left) the horse's left front foot—the one nearest you. At first, he'll step anywhere with it: maybe behind his right front foot, maybe *on* his right front foot, and maybe over his right front foot, crossing left over right. Crossing left over right is what we *want* because it develops the coordination he needs when you are riding. It also lengthens one side of his body, a necessity for turns and circles, and introduces the concept of turning away from the outside rein.

After the horse's left foot crosses over the right, stop shanking immediately—let the lead go slack and wait for him to chew and chill. Don't look at him while he settles. Then pet and praise him. Repeat the exercise. He will eventually learn that when he crosses left over right to turn away from your space bubble, you will stop shanking, and he will then always cross that way when you ask him to thereafter.

★ Caveats

❖ When learning to lead politely, some horses may be confused and seem to be thinking, *Why go at all if we're just going to stop again?* You may need to urge your horse forward until he understands *when* it is okay to move. This reluctance fades after a few sessions, so don't be concerned.

❖ When turning your horse, step into his space decisively so he feels compelled to leave it. Don't be hesitant and wait for him to move; he probably won't. Don't take a step back; he'll likely step toward you. Don't pull his head toward you to pet him. Everything should remain focused on moving "away."

❖ The authors of the book *Horse Speak* (Trafalgar Square Books, 2016), Sharon Wilsie and Gretchen Vogel, demonstrate that all horses understand and respond to common equine gestures. Pushing on the muzzle, for example, is an invitation to play, which sometimes escalates into a rearing romp. However, most horse people make the mistake of pushing the muzzle away with their hand when asking the horse to stop crowding them. We inadvertently invite the horse to play when we *think* we are saying, "Give me space." Instead, we must press what Wilsie terms the "Go Away Button" located on the jaw. Pushing here clearly indicates to the horse that you are not looking for a friendly nip or nudge, but for space. Being aware of Horse Speak allows for more logical and effective interactions with your horse, which will significantly improve your relationship.

❖ Horses often have what I refer to as a "stuck" leg, the leg that seems to want to move last and is firmly planted on the ground. It bears the majority of a horse's weight, and he relies on it for support and balance. He becomes concerned when asked to remove weight from it and is reluctant to move it, even when asked to move out of your space. Imagine standing with your hip cocked; all of your weight is on one leg, making it difficult to move without shifting. To "unstick" this horse, it is necessary to identify which leg this is. I find it is usually the right front leg, but you can tell by tapping a leg above the knee or hock with a whip and watching to see if he moves that leg, or every other leg, first. Alternatively, you can turn the horse and see which leg moves last. Even when it is obvious that a foot *should* move, the horse will move every foot except the stuck one. Resolve this issue on the ground so that your horse can move forward confidently and willingly under saddle; if he won't move a leg *without* a rider, he won't move a leg *with* one. Horses must use all their legs in the activities we pursue together, and it can take some convincing to get them to see that they have support and mobility in *all four* legs and can move them all without losing their balance. The horse will then relax mentally and physically, and will be much more willing to do what you ask.

❖ Some types of equine bodywork practitioners (therapists who target the source of tension or pain and improve flexibility and relaxation) place their hands on a horse's withers and pelvis and gently rock the horse's body from side to side, and forward and back, to diagnose: 1) how willingly he shifts weight, and 2) which way it is easier or harder to shift his weight. You, too, can gain insight about your horse by doing this. You might be surprised at how easily you can move your horse! To avoid alarming him, move slowly, with small movements. This helps your horse learn to feel more secure on his feet as he adjusts to having his weight shifted around.

Study Guide

Rephrasing

Rephrasing is a form of translation. By completely restating something *in your own words* in a new or alternative way, you incorporate the author's meaning into your own thoughts and experiences, with the emphasis on making the statement more clear, understandable, or meaningful to you. Rephrasing is a technique that makes reading an *active* rather than a *passive* experience: if you frequently pause while reading, especially when you come across a particularly beneficial or perplexing idea, you can rephrase that bit and make more sense of it, or derive its relevance or significance.

Moreover, rephrasing is another powerful tool for deducing what you do and don't know based on your ability to articulate or apply the concept. Rephrasing obliges you to engage with the subject matter that you are learning by creating a situation in which you must make it your own. What you generate, you know. The goal is for you to understand, retain, and apply the information presented in this book.

Let's look at an example of rephrasing:

Original sentence: *Effective riding is intentional and systematic.*

Rephrase: *Being able to achieve a goal with your horse takes planning, putting those plans into effect in an organized manner, and evaluating the outcomes to prepare for next steps.*

Study Guide

Rephrasing

Or, if you prefer:

Shorter sentences: *Riding is more effective when it is planned and organized.*

Rephrasing allows you—and me!—to unpack what I really meant by that original sentence.

One can choose to rephrase an entire section, a paragraph, or even a single sentence at a time. Indeed, my students read *everything* aloud in my science classes, from text books to lab directions, and rephrased every word. In this way, their thinking was visible, and I could readily discern what they did and didn't understand. Furthermore, I required students to listen to and rephrase *what their classmates* had just rephrased. This not only sparked a lively discussion among students as they sought clarification from one another, but it also allowed them to observe how others think. As a result of working through the content before attempting to do something with it, class activities went smoothly.

Try it. Rephrase a section, paragraph, or sentence in this book with a study buddy. Take turns reading sentences and rephrasing them. Rephrase each other's rephrases. As you sort through the meanings, the content will become clearer. It's the grappling with the content that makes it stick.

Next, make a list of things to do when you work with your horse or ride so you don't forget everything you meant to do when you get on the horse. Then, go for a ride and try out what you've talked about with your study buddy in order to combine your real-life experience with what you've learned in the book. Even if you don't fully understand or feel confident in the material, give it a shot. When you get on the horse, you will make mistakes, become perplexed, and encounter unexpected reactions—or it may all work out. Questions or misunderstandings will crystallize as a result of trying to use the material because you now have a frame of reference to work from—concrete experience. The resulting "need" will make rereading the book sound different, and ideas you need will jump off the page at you in "aha" moments. Each time you return to riding and to the material, you will see it in a different light and become more clear and skilled.

Your notes

Chapter

TAP TAP

02

Working with your horse on the ground enables you to closely observe his movements and behavior, providing you with valuable insight into what to anticipate when riding. Additionally, horses do not analyze the most efficient way to move their legs and bodies, so teaching them to do so is advantageous. Since horses prefer to move in a manner that is most physically comfortable for them, they appreciate, absorb, and adopt what you show them. This simplifies riding because your horse understands what you want, you know what to expect, and correct movement is easier to ride.

2.1 Tap Tap. To lead your horse down the arena rail "in hand" to the left, extend your left hand (holding the lead) in front of his nose, and with the backward whip in the right hand, tap him gently and rhythmically behind the girth line with the whip handle. Your horse should walk when you walk, and stop when you stop. Do this going both directions (the roles of your hands will switch). •

Scan to View Intro to Tap Tap

The Foundation Exercise of Groundwork

The next step introduces your horse to (or reinforces his understanding of) leg aids by gently tapping him on his barrel with a whip held *backward* in your "tapping hand" (fig. 2.1). Tapping from the ground is preparatory for riding: when mounted, and you often "tap" or squeeze the horse lightly with your heels. By working on this exercise in hand, your horse will know to move forward under saddle.

It is best to work on this exercise in an enclosed area. With the lead shank in your left hand and the whip in your right, move counterclockwise along on the rail. Extend your left arm so that your left hand is in front of the horse's nose, walk forward while rhythmically tapping your horse's barrel with the butt of the whip, behind the girth line. Your horse will move forward at the walk as a reaction to the tap, or he may rush forward or refuse to move. If he rushes forward, shank him back (see p. 34). His front feet should never be ahead of your feet. (Note that even though the shank is in your left hand as you track left, you can use the same motion as described earlier in this book to put him back where you want, parallel to the rail and straight in the body, so there is no angle in his position.) Try again after he relaxes.

If, on the other hand, your horse has turned to concrete, resist the urge to be aggressive with the tapping. Gradually *increase the intensity and frequency of tapping* until he moves forward. Then, stop tapping when he walks a few steps. Once he understands what you want, he'll walk normally and you can return to tapping lightly. Christine Cyr Stokely, an exceptional ranch rider, observes that tapping the horse at a *quicker frequency than the rate at which his front legs are moving* will facilitate a smooth and cooperative transition. (This is also a valuable technique to employ while riding.)

It may be that your horse moves forward but in an irregular, crooked, or tense fashion. Tap and walk until he relaxes and develops a steady tempo. This may take three trips around the ring, as the first trip around, he will be alert and hesitant, the second time around, he may walk fairly normally, and finally the third trip should be "boring" as he puts his head down and simply walks along beside you. Depending on your horse's temperament, and the amount and variety of distractions in an arena, the number of trips may vary, but the goal is tranquility. The key to overcoming opposition or "resistance" in your horse is to associate relaxation with any new requirement. Trainer and founder of the Equus Academy JP Giacomini summarizes, "To fully secure a new movement, the horse must 'Do it, understand it, and like it' (perform in relaxation). Three repetitions usually cements the result."

When walk goes smoothly, try halt. If your horse walks on past you, shank him back, get him straight and calm, and repeat until it becomes routine. Go both directions.

Details

❖ Where you hold the lead shank *matters*; it is the guide. Keep it centered under the horse's nose and push it forward in space in the direction you want the horse to go. Don't let it fall to your side or swing around, because your horse will follow it.

❖ Be sure to go deep into corners so your horse 1) isn't afraid of corners, 2) doesn't get in the habit of cutting corners, 3) begins to experience bending his body through the corners, and 4) unquestioningly goes where he's told. Don't cut corners to shorten your trips. Avoid this temptation by getting close enough to touch the fence line or wall facing you before you turn, or place an object in the corner and walk around it.

❖ If your horse veers in toward you, tap him on the neck or shoulder with the butt of the whip until he returns to the rail. Re-establish your space bubble as needed (see p. 33).

❖ Rhythmic tapping is reassuring. When you use this technique in establishing Ground Rules, and then use it later when in a new environment, your horse will remain calm because it's familiar and focuses him.

Study Guide

Reflection

IN the final "Reflection" section of a lesson plan, you are encouraged to identify areas in which you can improve your practice and evaluate your effectiveness. Immediately after completing a training session with your horse, reflect on the session while it is still fresh in your mind. Ask yourself:

❖ What went well?

❖ What didn't go well?

❖ If I could do this lesson again, what would I do differently?

❖ What will I do tomorrow to fix the problem from today?

❖ What did I learn from the session that I didn't know before?

❖ How can I use the knowledge I gained from this experience in the future?

Sometimes an idea will occur to you later that will enhance your answers to these questions, so feel free to modify your responses when you have had time to think.

Study Guide

Reflection

Horses Are "Latent Learners"

Latent learning is learning that is not detectable during its occurrence but can be observed later. Even if you feel that your horse is not progressing during a lesson, he may just need to "sleep on it," and what you desire will be there the following day. Given that horses do exhibit latent learning, you must consider how you will assess your horse's learning from yesterday to see what stuck, how you will proceed with what did, as well as what you will do to correct what he did not learn. This means you should have a lesson plan for next steps in your back pocket so you can move on if your horse learns this stage quickly.

Be mindful: Going for a hack is good, but once you set standards of behavior and training, you need to stick to them, even on "down days," so the horse doesn't get confused. It doesn't work well for horses to be told, "Some days you do this and some days you don't."

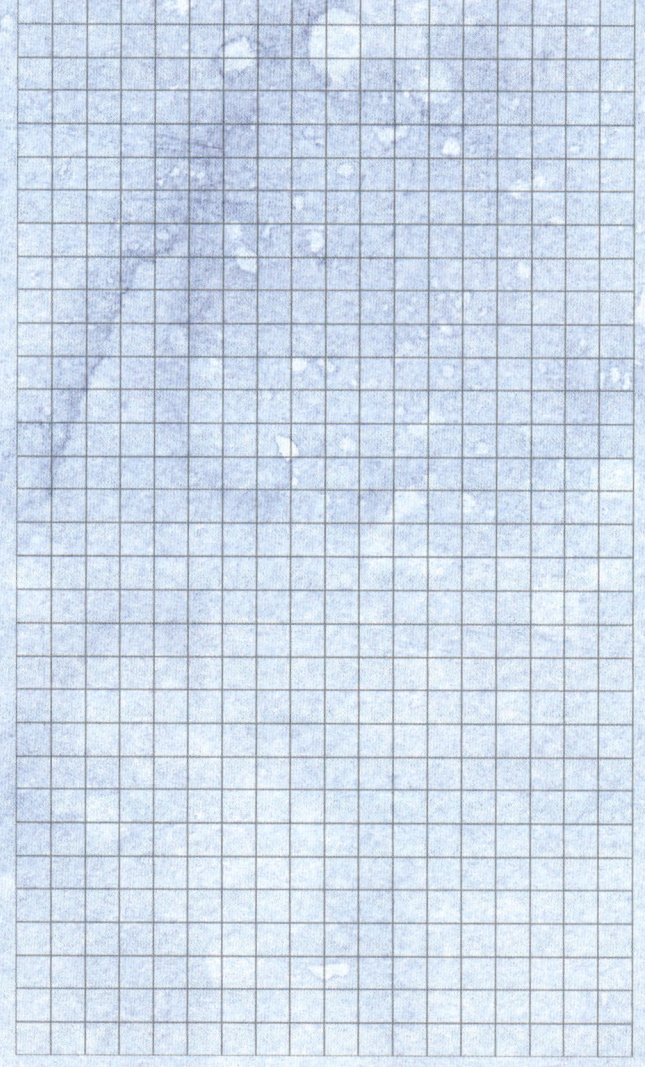

Your notes

Chapter

LONGEING

03

Targeting and developing specific muscle groups, longeing helps prepare horses for riding, improves gaits, and strengthens the bond between you and your horse. Longeing even constitutes a sport in its own right (vaulting).

3.1 Tap Tap on a Circle. The first step in longeing a horse is to do Tap Tap on a circle. Because your horse understands Tap Tap in hand, he should be able to walk calmly in a circle around you. Begin with a small circle at first in order to control him easily. Gradually enlarge the circle by feeding out the length of your longe line. Position yourself *behind* the girth line—when you step ahead of it, the horse will likely come to a halt and turn to face you. Move slowly during this exercise to avoid startling your horse. •

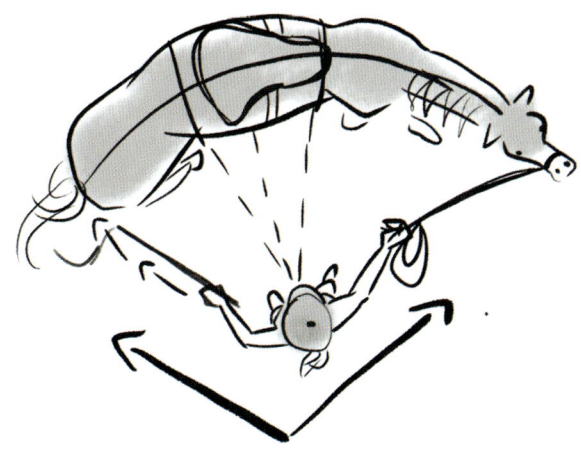

Scan to View Intro to Longeing

Tap Tap on a Circle—AKA Longeing

The next step in the Ground Rules process is to bring your horse into the center of the arena and do Tap Tap on a small circle around you. Feed out your lead shank, keeping your horse on a circle and, *voilà*, you are longeing. When this presents no challenges, use a longe line (and a longer whip if necessary, still holding it backward) and ease him out gradually, one body-width per circle. Do this at walk until your horse is relaxed in the circle. If he comes in toward you, faces you, or makes the circle smaller so that your shank or line is too loose, gently poke him in the ribs or shoulders with the butt of the whip to push him back out onto the circle diameter you want. Saying the word "out" simultaneously helps him learn this verbal command for future use should he "fall in" again (he will). If he turns in too much or turns around, walk to him, use your space bubble to turn his shoulders away from you, and put him back onto the circle line (remember the tips to do this described on p. 36). Turn him until he crosses the front leg nearest you *over* the other front leg; no crossing behind. (If needed, have a friend lead the horse around the circle while you longe him.)

Once the horse is successfully operating at the end of your longe line at the walk, you can proceed to introduce the trot and canter in the same fashion. As the horse is now likely to be out of reach of the whip's handle, reposition it in your grasp to its "normal" orientation, with the handle in your hand.

Circles, or parts of circles, are the basis of most maneuvers. Longeing introduces the circle, bending, turning, and moving the horse forward with a purpose. The horse learns to respond to driving pressure toward the hindquarters, which establishes gait, frame (shape of the horse's topline), and rhythm. The horse learns to maintain a consistent distance from the handler, which develops into his first notion of *connection* (there should be a consistent light tension on the longe line—no "drooping"), and familiarizes him with moving on a curved line. As he learns to keep a steady tempo and develop increasing flexibility, stretching the outside of his body on the curve of the circle, he learns balance. This is important because, if a horse can't go in a steady, round circle on the longe (look at his footprints to assess the quality of the circle), then he's not balanced enough to carry a rider. Don't rush—wait for him to become confident and relaxed before pressing on. Until he can cope effectively with his own body, adding the weight of the rider will only make things more difficult, eroding the confidence and relaxation that contribute to enjoyable riding.

It is important for horses to be longed on different-sized circles in order to learn balance on different curvatures. To *widen* a circle, the horse must *push outward with his inside lateral pair of legs*, which strengthens the horse. When done in both directions, both sides of the horse are developed. Conversely, to *reduce* the diameter of a circle, the horse must *push inward with his outside lateral pair of legs.* As a result, the horse's suppleness improves because the inner pair of legs is forced to flex more, and the horse must also bend more through the body to accommodate to the sharper curve.

It is also beneficial to longe in oval shapes (by walking forward a few feet as you longe) to introduce short sections of moving in a straight line, as well as returning to the curve (stop moving forward and return to where you started to complete the oval), so he knows how to move into and out of a curved line before adding a rider. When your horse is properly muscled, calm, and confident, and it is clear that he knows what to expect when working on a longe circle, he is ready to move on.

Longeing Is Purposeful

Longeing is an essential and beneficial component of your horse's preparation, when done correctly. It allows:

❖ The horse to loosen, stretch, and lift his back without the rider's weight.

❖ You to see how your horse is moving before riding. Is he tense? Balanced? Sound?

❖ The horse to develop confidence to go forward independently (he can't see the rider when being ridden).

❖ You to see how your horse responds to your aids. Is he explosive? Unresponsive?

❖ You and your horse to become familiar with each other in a safe way.

❖ The horse to learn to focus.

❖ The horse to become comfortable with equipment.

❖ You to learn to keep a steady contact with the horse: At first, only allow your horse as far out as you can manage him effectively. If you lose control, your line is too long. Gradually letting him out an inch at a time allows you to learn to maintain connection and control no matter how far away your horse is. This is good preparation for managing reins.

❖ The horse time to relax. (One common indicator is the horse blowing out through the nose. When longeing before riding, this can indicate your horse has loosened up and settled down and is ready to ride.

❖ Your horse to learn walk, trot, canter, whoa, and transitions, both between and *within* gaits, (moving from lengthened strides to shortened strides and back) so that he understands these concepts before you ride.

❖ The horse learns to coordinate himself, moving between a symmetrical gait (trot) and an asymmetrical gait (canter).

❖ The horse to start developing physically so that he becomes fit, balanced, and flexible.

❖ You to teach him verbal commands. (I like to use a "cluck" for "trot" and a "kiss" for canter.) Installing clearly understood ground commands makes riding easier because neither you nor your horse has to guess what to do.

Longeing Solves Problems

Consider what you want to achieve when riding and practice it on the longe line. Longeing enables you to solve problems without being on your horse and to observe his behavior.

For example, if your horse rushes, work on the longe line slowly and relaxedly; if your horse is too slow or doesn't stay in a gait, send him forward with energy. Make it clear to your horse that he must maintain the gait and tempo you requested until you tell him otherwise. Maintain consistent rhythm by saying, "One-two, one-two," out loud when the front hooves hit the ground in trot. Don't change your tempo to match the horse; instead, keep the horse with you. This way, when you mount, you and your horse will already have a sense of the tempo you want. Work on clear transitions. Practice walk/trot, trot/canter, and back again. Don't allow the walk to get faster when transitioning into the trot—make it clean. Be calm, never frantic.

Sample Problem: Using Longeing to Address Stiffness and Hollowness of the Body

Horses' bodies have "stiff" and "hollow" sides, which means they bend more easily in one direction than the other. The hollow side of the body is the side that bends too readily in one direction. It wants to remain bent that way, regardless of the direction the horse is traveling. This significantly impacts how horses travel when circling in different directions: when the hollow side is on the *inside* of the circle, the horse's body bends easily in the direction of travel. This also means that the horse's other (off) side, on the *outside* of the circle, stretches to accommodate this bend.

Because it resists stretching and remains "shortened" or contracted, the hollow side is also known as the "short" side of the horse. This becomes obvious when the horse changes direction on the longe line, placing the hollow side on the outside where it must stretch to accommodate the opposite bend but does not. The horse feels very stiff going in this direction

3.2 Effects of Stiffness. Having a "stiff" and "hollow" side significantly impacts how a horse travels. This illustration shows an exaggerated depiction of a horse that is hollow on the left. This means his left side is "short" and contracted and does not want to stretch and lengthen so that he could bend to the right (the direction he is turning). As a result, he is counterbent and falling in. If you were riding this horse, you would feel the right side of his rib cage pushing against your calf, and you would need to help him learn to push them the other way. ●

because he can't bend to the inside of the circle (fig. 3.2). The inside feels stiff, but it is *really* the outside/hollow side that isn't stretching to accommodate this bend. The trick is to recognize that the body's stiff/unyielding and hollow sides are actually the same side!

As a consequence of this phenomenon, horses "fall/lean in" or "fall/drift out," depending on whether the hollow side is on the inside or outside of the circle. If they are traveling in the direction they are hollow inside, or curved naturally through their body, their neck will overbend at the base/withers causing the outside shoulder to "bulge," "jackknife," "escape," or protrude outside of the circle, causing the horse to drift away from the handler onto a bigger circle. This is often noticeable because the horse pulls on the longe line. When you change directions, the horse's bend does not change, so now the hollow side is facing out, or away, from the handler and the horse is bent in the opposite direction of the circle he's traveling on, with his shoulder still pushing the same way it did, which is now toward the inside. As a result, the horse falls in, reducing the size of the circle (figs. 3.3 A–D).

To visualize this, imagine a banana lying along the edge of a plate, with the stem oriented toward the inside of the plate. The banana's profile corresponds to the plate's curvature. However, if you flip the banana over so that the stem faces out of the plate, the curvature is opposite, or "counterbent" (figs. 3.4 A & B).

One primary objective of riding is to make horses equally elastic and responsive on both sides. Therefore, the hollow side must learn to stretch. Through systematic longeing, your horse's flexibility will improve over time. (And while waiting for his flexibility to improve, you can work on other fundamentals, such as those already mentioned.) Beginning on the longe line, and later when you ride, help your horse learn to keep his:

❖ Ribs curved out.

❖ Neck straight (side-reins can assist with neck stability during longeing).

❖ Outside (of the circle) front leg stepping toward the inside of the circle.

When these three things work well, your horse is more stable, straight, and responsive.

When the horse's ribs bulge in and the inside shoulder falls into the circle, making the horse lean in toward you, "poke them out" by applying a nudge from the whip handle to his barrel. As the horse reacts to the nudge, he will change his bend onto the correct curvature. This nudge simulates your leg aid when riding. If the shoulder is falling in, too, correct this with a nudge on the shoulder, and maybe even cross the whip under the longe line so it's in front of the horse where he can see it. This can have the effect of pushing his shoulder out. Horses "like" these corrections because they show them how to find their balance, making them feel more secure.

It is critical to notice and correct issues such as stiff and hollow sides because horses will continue to do what is easier and more habitual for them if not corrected. Allowing them to proceed in an inflexible manner prevents them from moving optimally for both health and performance. Through practicing, you will develop an experienced eye and begin to notice the pervasiveness of the stiff/hollow side in other horses. And you will begin to feel it when riding. When fixed, this is part of what makes one horse more enjoyable to ride than another.

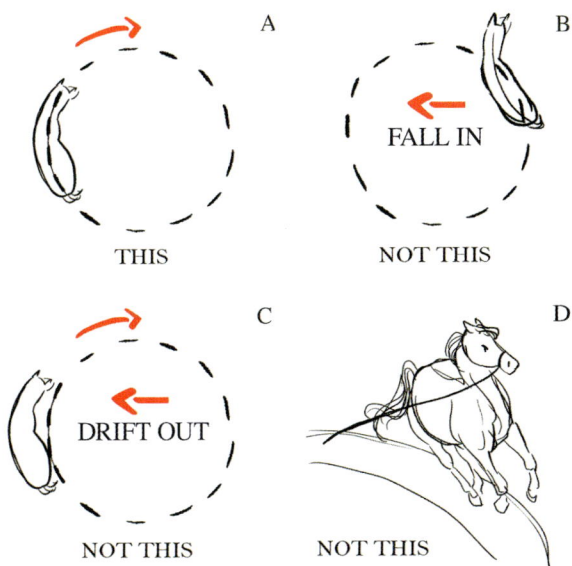

3.3 A–D Drifting Out/Falling In. Due to the fact that horses bend more easily to one side than the other, their bodies tend to bend in the same direction, regardless of whether they are traveling to the left or right. This means that they will bend with the curve of a circle in one direction and *against* the curve in the opposite direction. When they bend *with* the curve, they may stay true to the circle **(A)**, but most tend to drift out and make the longe circle larger **(C)**. When they bend *against* the curve, their inside shoulder falls in, they look outside the circle with their head, and they rush and lean because they are off balance **(B & D)**.

3.4 A & B True Bend vs Counterbend. In "true bend," the horse's entire body conforms to the curvature of the circle he is on, similar to the banana in **(A)**. The horse's entire front end, from the withers to the ears, must maintain the same curvature as the body. When the banana is flipped over, as in **(B)**, it is "counterbent," or bent in the opposite direction of the plate's curve. This is equivalent to a horse bending the opposite of his direction of travel.

Steering the Shoulders

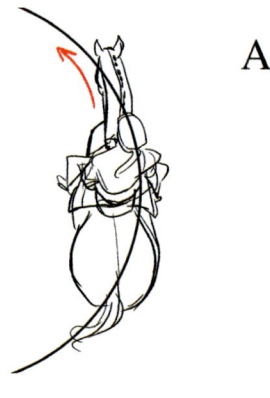

A

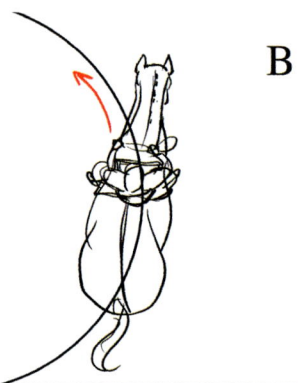

B

3.5 A & B Alignment Poll to Tail. Correct, uniform curvature from poll to tail **(A)**, and a crooked horse with misaligned vertebrae **(B)**. Consequently, the horse becomes unbalanced and is more difficult to ride.

To be properly aligned on a circle, your horse's body must have the same curvature from poll to tail—all the vertebrae in his spine must be lined up in the same degree of bend. Large circles have a shallow bend; small circles require more bend. The ribs must be pushed to the outside of the circle to produce bend. The horse's neck must remain "straight" at the point where the base of the neck meets the shoulder beneath the withers (figs. 3.5 A & B). It is very tempting and easy to bend the neck too far, but this causes the outside shoulder to jut out at a sharp angle. The horse becomes crooked, unbalanced, and evasive. A horse can bend his neck dramatically without moving a leg! Since the legs are what move the horse, steering the shoulders to maneuver the legs to navigate is more effective than merely turning the neck.

You must control the horse's outside (the circle) front leg so that it does not deviate from the line of travel in order to keep the horse's feet from straying off the circle. Right legs tend to step right, and left legs tend to step left, each following their own meandering path. To control the horse, I tell my students that "right legs need to step left and left legs need to step right" to keep the horse upright and on the circle. Because the legs move the body, it is important to "steer the shoulders" rather than focusing on the horse's head. Controlling the legs makes sense. (We introduced the horse to this on p. 36.) It's pointless to steer the head because it just swings around on the neck. You lose control of the legs and body as soon as the neck bends: shoulders "pop out" the opposite way of the neck bend, and the legs follow when they move. When the neck bends to the right, the left shoulder and leg move to the left. So, if you pull the horse to the right to turn, his body will be forced to the left, which is the opposite of what you want. This is why we learn to turn from the *outside* rein (same concept as neck reining). Because pulling the horse in one direction has the opposite effect on the shoulders, the most effective method of steering is by telling him not to go in the direction you don't want to go. Think of the outside aids as "shutting a door," stopping him from going the way you don't want to go, then opening the way you *do* want to go.

3.6 A–D Attaching the Longe Line to the Bridle. Feed the longe line through the the bit ring that will be on the inside of your longe circle **(A)**. *Do not* pass the line through the bit ring from underneath, next to the horse's skin, as it will not slide easily if you need to release tension while longeing **(B)**. Run the line over the poll and hook the snap end to the bit ring on the opposite side **(C)**. Twist the reins and loop them through the throatlatch to prevent them from coming over the horse's head **(D)**.

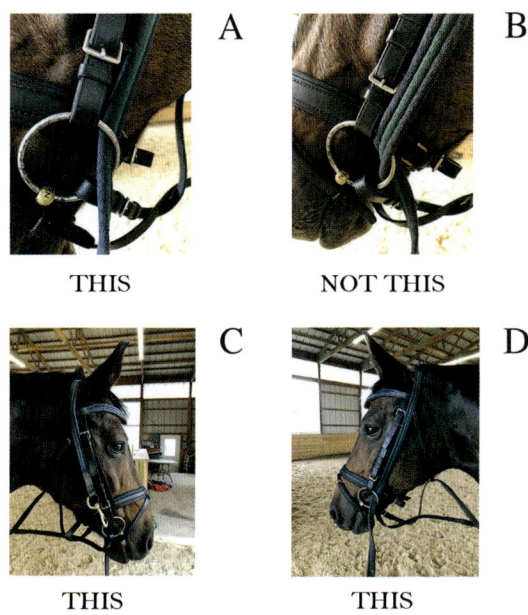

THIS   NOT THIS

THIS   THIS

★ Caveats

There are books and online tutorials devoted to teaching you how to longe safely and correctly. These caveats aren't meant to be a comprehensive discussion; rather, they depict common errors so you don't fall down these particular rabbit holes.

- **Longe lines vary in design**: Some are canvas, others are padded—simple and comfortable for horse and handler is best.

- **Wear gloves**: If your horse pulls and the line burns your hand because you aren't wearing gloves, you will probably let go and your horse will run away with a 30-foot rope scaring him or becoming tangled.

- **Attaching the longe line**: Options include clipping the longe line to a ring on a halter (minimal control), longeing cavesson, or to the bridle in various ways. I prefer the horse wearing a bridle and passing the line clip through the inside bit ring, over the poll, down the other side of the bridle, and snapped to the top of the outside bit ring, connecting both sides of the bit (figs. 3.6 A–D). When changing directions, you must completely remove the longe line and reattach it to the opposite side in the same manner.

- Don't get into a pulling contest with your horse if he starts backing up while longeing him. Always **longe in a confined space** in case your horse gets away.

- Hold the line with **your elbows at your sides and your thumbs up**, just like you would if you were riding. **Maintain small, orderly loops of line that do not drag on the ground.** If you are careless with large loops and step through them, or they get caught on your hand, you may be dragged.

- **Don't let the longe line get twisted**, just like you wouldn't ride with twisted reins.

- The **position of the handler** in relation to the horse is critical. With your shoulders facing the horse, turned slightly in the direction you want him to go, *remain situated behind his shoulders, centered on the ribs, or even behind where the saddle goes.* This encourages the horse to go forward. Horses need to be driven from behind. If you place your body toward the front of the horse, this causes him to stop or face you.

- Keep your **shoulders positioned over your hips**, as if you were sitting on the horse, elbows close to your torso. If you lean forward, you lose stability and the horse can pull you off your feet.

- Turn with the horse. **Stay in one spot** that doesn't change size or shape, so the horse truly longes around you in a **controlled circle** (unless you are practicing an oval shape, as explained on p. 54). You may find yourself crossing your legs or turning backward. Determine what is most effective for you. Do *not* follow the horse passively or you won't have a circle at all; the horse derives no physical benefit from performing the exercise improperly.

- Until you know **how your horse will react to the longe whip,** keep it either vertical against your body or behind you so it doesn't wave around threateningly. Many people are so focused on the longe line that they forget the whip, and it bobs around unnoticed in a limp free hand. You must be able to control it appropriately. I often keep the lash wound around the whip.

- The **whip is used only to provide visual or gentle touch cues**. It is not intended to strike the horse. If you swing the whip and hit the horse, you will get a bigger flight reaction than you are looking for. The same thing can happen if you move the whip too quickly or erratically. Tuck the whip behind you or against your body before you approach the horse so he isn't frightened.

- Horses tend to lean in on a circle, as we have discussed, which creates slack in your line. **Slack is bad** for two reasons: 1) you don't want the horse to step

❖ over a loose, dragging line, and 2) longeing is an introduction to maintaining steady contact. To remove slack, push the horse out (see p 54).

❖ When you first begin working with a horse, he may be unfocused and distracted. He may be unsure about what to do, anxious, or excited. Avoid becoming emotionally involved in his drama. **Maintain a detached and unflappable demeanor** because horses are sensitive to and reflect people's emotions. Don't take whatever he does personally. Show him what you want by being the leader. Remain calm and patient until he comprehends and is able to complete the task with composure. If you are in a hurry, frantic, frustrated, or angry, you will only aggravate the situation. Furthermore, avoid movements that are overly energetic, spastic, or jerky. Excesses of any kind are never good with horses. Move smoothly and methodically.

❖ When horses become **distracted, anxious, or alarmed,** they accelerate, take quick, short, scrambling steps, and "fall in" onto their inside (the circle) shoulder. They may close in on you rapidly. Poke them with the butt of the whip in the shoulder or ribs as we discussed on p. 53.

❖ Your horse may do any number of things you don't want, like whirling, rushing, not going forward, or throwing his head. Work with him patiently and show him what you want. Repeatedly revisiting the space bubble (p. 33) and **methodically repositioning** him pays off over time. Don't try anything new until the exercise you're working on can be done consistently and without incident.

❖ To **stop your horse,** tug gently on the line and say, "Whoa." Repeat until he stops. Practice walk/halt transitions until your horse understands. Never pull the horse toward you. Leave your horse out on the circle and go to him to collect him, winding up the longe line as you go. Otherwise, he'll think he can turn in whenever he wants, and it's not safe to have a horse coming at you, head on.

❖ **Another method to get a reluctant horse to stop** is to gently reel him in onto a smaller circle and turn your shoulders toward the direction he's going. Then, he's immediately *in the same position as if you were leading him*. Take a few steps and come to a complete stop, just as you did with the space bubble training (see p. 33). You may also find that your horse can "read" the energy in your body, or your shift in position as you consider stopping.

❖ To **change direction** safely, stop your horse on the circle without facing you and walk to him, winding up the longe line in neat loops to remove slack as you approach him. Turn his shoulders 180 degrees around his haunches to reposition him in the opposite direction. Reattach the longe line to the new side and longe him in the opposite direction. I feel it is a bad idea to encourage a horse to wheel around to change direction while longeing because he might do it when you're riding. I find it's best to be methodical and consistent.

❖ **Produce tidy circles** by maintaining the horse's feet on a single line of travel, much like a slot car guided by the groove in its race track or a figure skater performing figures. Skating compulsory figures demonstrates the ability to make clean, round circles; the traces left by the skate blades

3.7 Precise Circles. In ice skating, compulsory figures require a skater to make several precise, round circles that are laid directly on top of each other. The tracings made on the ice by the skate's blade must exactly overlay each other and leave no irregular shapes or stray marks. Performing perfect circles develops alignment and core strength, as well as body control, awareness, and symmetry. Your horse must learn a circle's geometry and not resist, pull, drift, or fall in. Accuracy and consistency in the shape of his circles is critical for achieving the symmetry, rhythm, connection, engagement, and suppleness you seek. •

on the ice are precise and do not include any stray marks (fig. 3.7). When longeing, maintaining your position will cause your horse's path to be consistent and circular, like that of the skater. When working on circles, the goal is a narrow circular movement that is consistent in size and shape, so that the horse's tracks are no wider than a foot (figs. 3.8 A & B).

❖ To ensure the **circle is round**, keep the length of the longe line unchanging. You are the center of the circle and the longe line is the radius of the circle. When you keep the radius the same, the circle will be round. Circles must be consistent in shape so that your horse can develop the symmetry, rhythm, connection, engagement, and suppleness he needs (figs. 3.9 A–C).

❖ Working your horse on **different-size circles** introduces him to likely sizes when under saddle and allows him to learn to negotiate differing amounts of bend through his body, making him stronger

A
THIS

B
NOT THIS

3.8 A & B Messy vs Neat Circles. To reap the gymnastic benefits of longeing (or riding), it is essential to sometimes keep your horse on a defined circle so that he can learn to control his body. To ensure that he is truly on a circle, observe his hoofprints. A narrow circular path, one set of hoof prints wide, is ideal **(A)**. A wide and uneven set of tracks indicates that the size of the circle has varied and that it is not round **(B)**. •

and more supple (fig. 3.10). Going both directions develops his body symmetrically. Spiraling in and out gradually teaches your horse to take sideways steps while moving forward. This trains him to cross his legs in preparation for more advanced moves. Spend little time, however, on small circles to avoid putting too much strain on joints.

❖ Because horses differ—some need to be urged forward, while others need to relax—one goal of longeing is to get your horse to **work in a consistent rhythm** that isn't rushed, slow, or erratic. Steady him with gentle tugs on the line. Persist until he understands and maintains the same, swinging rhythm. Don't trot until he can maintain a calm and relaxed walk rhythm. Don't progress to canter until he can trot consistently. Gaits are gaits, *not* speeds. Try "bigger" (more extended) and "smaller" (more collected) versions of each gait with the horse staying in the same tempo.

❖ Use **longeing as a calming ritual** that creates the mindset of the horse you want to ride. Many people longe horses aggressively to wear them out before riding them. This is actually counterproductive because it increases the horse's heart rate and blood pressure, further exciting the body. Instead, longe purposefully, focusing on topics you plan to address in your ride.

❖ **Don't longe too long**. Longeing—in the form we have discussed—is designed to help your horse. You don't want your horse to associate longeing with exhaustion. As he gains fitness, gradually increase the amount of longeing, as may be necessary. A good rule of thumb is to add one circle per day in each direction, as may be needed

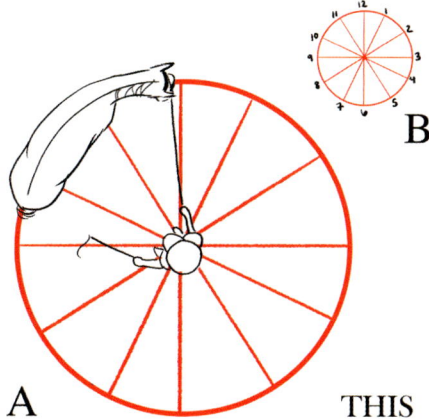

A THIS

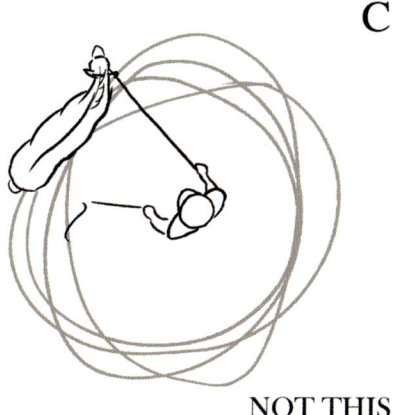

C

NOT THIS

3.9 A–C Accurate vs. Inaccurate Circles. The radius of a circle is the distance from the center of the circle to any point on its circumference. As the person longeing, you are the center of the circle, and should not move. The length of the longe line represents the radius, and it should not change **(A)**. When you keep the same radius all the way around, you create a perfect circle **(B)**. If you move off your spot or change the length of the longe line, the radius changes, and therefore the circumference of the circle changes, creating a different shape **(C)**. When your circle is no longer round, the horse begins to use his body unevenly, losing the gymnastic benefit of bending and stretching. As you become more proficient at maintaining his circle's roundness and his body's alignment over the longe circle's curve, it will become easier for you also to do so while riding. •

3.10 Different Diameter Circles.
Changing the size of the circle facilitates the development of the horse's strength, coordination and flexibility. Use circles of standard dimensions (20m, 15m, 10m) to habituate the horse to the corresponding body curvature. If the same curvature is maintained for every stride, the circle will remain perfectly round. Smaller circles are more challenging, requiring more bending and stretching, so it is advisable to begin with the larger circle. •

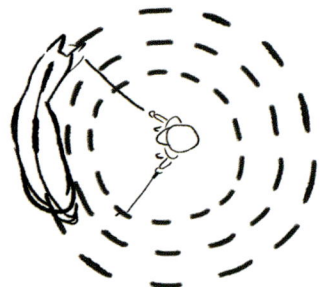

for purposes of conditioning and still within a planned period of time. What you're looking for is your horse loosening up, stretching, relaxing, blowing out his nose, and becoming more focused, *not* sweating and running with his head up.

❖ Be cautious if you must longe in **deep footing**, or in very small circles, so you don't strain joints, or make the horse excessively tired or sore.

❖ If your horse **consistently misbehaves** by bolting, rearing, running backward, or doing anything else that isn't calm and easy to handle, seek the assistance of an experienced horse person.

❖ Don't **canter** until the horse is *very* calm, balanced, upright, and confident trotting in both directions. Confirm walk/trot transitions so both "whoa" and "go" are on command. Reduce the size of the circle as you transition from canter to trot to help your horse transition down during first attempts.

❖ When first asked to canter, many horses lean on their inside shoulder, causing them to pick up the wrong lead. To counteract this, the horse must be properly aligned over the circle's curve in order to transfer his weight to the outside hind leg for a smooth transition. **Request the canter when the inside front leg/outside hind leg swing forward in trot.** This way, the horse can set down the outside hind leg into first beat of the correct lead. An easy approach is to say "*can-*" when the outside front leg is on the ground and emphasize "*-ter*" when the inside front is, and they will naturally get the correct lead. All horses move a little differently: Some move their legs slowly, others quickly. You must change the timing of your transition aid based on your observations.

❖ Give your horse **walk breaks** to catch his breath.

❖ Horses have little conscious body awareness, such as understanding they have four legs, or analyzing how to use those limbs to support their weight optimally during movement. Through deliberate longeing, **you can help the horse discover where his feet are and what each should be doing.** Moving correctly aids in the development of a symmetrical topline and physical strength.

★★ Extensions

❖ To introduce your horse to stepping underneath himself and **engaging the inside hind leg**, longe your horse at a walk using a lead shank, not a longe line. First, position yourself so that the horse's hip is centered between your shoulders, keep your longeing hand on your bellybutton and not stepping off your spot. *Keep your horse walking forward on the small circle with his front legs while crossing his inside hind leg over his outside hind leg.* Tap him on the inside hock with the butt of your whip as the leg lifts off the ground to swing forward. This encourages it to cross in front of the outside hind and step well up under his belly. He must continue walking, and you will feel as if your body is facing his hindquarters. At first, the horse may try to pivot on his front legs and face you or push into you with his shoulders and ribs. With the butt of the whip, gently poke his shoulders or ribs out, and then use Tap Tap (see p. 45) to keep his front legs moving forward on the circle. This can also be done in trot and can be replicated from the saddle. This teaches your horse to balance, shift his weight, and develop strength and coordination in preparation for more advanced work.

Scan to View Longeing Extension

Safety Tips for Side-Reins

Side-reins can serve as a replacement for the rider's arms and hands on the reins, providing stability and assisting the horse in accepting contact and developing a round topline. However, it is important to follow these guidelines when using them:

1. ***Get help from someone who has experience with the proper use of side-reins. Begin with long side-reins so the horse does not feel too restricted, and shorten them gradually, one hole at a time, as he becomes accustomed to them, and until there is a correct amount of contact without forcing the horse into a headset. They should be adjusted in a way to best benefit your horse—some horses need them low and long, while others need them higher and shorter. Experiment with different lengths and heights as you gain experience to see what results you get from each.***

2. ***Don't put side-reins on until you are ready to begin longeing. Attach the outside rein first, then put the inside one on and get the horse moving forward; don't dawdle ("forward is your friend").***

3. ***Never lead a horse with side-reins on, and remove them promptly when finished.***

4. ***Don't allow the horse to back up with side-reins on.***

Longeing with side-reins is preferable to longeing without because it allows the horse to move more correctly and reap the gymnastic benefits of the exercise. ●

3.11 Cavalletti. Using cavalletti while longeing teaches the horse rhythm, balance, suppleness, cadence, adjustability of stride length (via small changes in the distance between cavalletti), body awareness, joint flexion of the hind limbs, lift and reach in the shoulders and forelimbs, roundness, strength, coordination, and sure-footedness. Seek assistance determining the appropriate cavalletti distance and height, as well as when and how to raise and spread them, based on the size, fitness level, and training objectives of your horse. ●

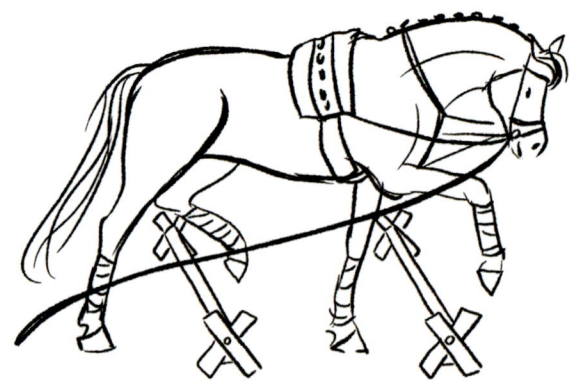

Scan to View
Wiggle the Longe Line
for the Head to Drop

❖ When longeing is going well and the horse is relaxed, **cavalletti** can be introduced (fig. 3.11). Trotting through cavalletti improves the horse's physical condition and muscle tone by loosening the horse's back, increasing his range of motion and improving the rhythm, organization, and swing of the stride. You can adjust the distance between the poles for different gaits, or to encourage a shorter or longer stride. Raising the poles encourages more flexion of the joints.

❖ It is possible to teach your horse to reach down and **stretch his nose to the ground** while on the longe line with a couple weeks of consistent effort. Oscillate the longe line by flicking your wrist to create waves in the line, as you would with gym workout ropes; instead of going up and down, oscillate sideways until your horse lowers his head slightly, then immediately stop wiggling the line. If you stop waving every time he lowers his head, he'll quickly learn that a wavy movement in the line means "Lower your head." Soon, a slight flick of the line will be enough to get him into a "stretchy" walk or trot circle. This is useful for riding because you can wiggle a rein and he will soften.

Study Guide
Thinking About Your Thinking

Introduced in the Introduction (see p. 1), the ideas, especially the "Elements of Thought," shared on *criticalthinking.org* can help you deduce how *clear* you are on concepts covered in these chapters. It is well worth your while to reflect on the questions that follow. Which of them prompt coherent answers that spring to mind immediately? Which do you struggle with? It is more beneficial to write your thoughts down, but at least roll them around in your mind.

It is also a good idea to grapple with this activity twice—once now, but then plan to revisit your answers again in a couple of months to assess to what extent your understanding has grown by observing how much more easily and quickly responses (or new questions) pop to mind. Further, these questions provide a prompt and common language to stimulate rich conversation with a riding "study buddy."

❖ *What is the purpose of each of the following?* (Note: Here I have listed topics from chapters 1 through 3, but this question can be applied to anything.)

- Groundwork.
- Space bubble.
- Turning the horse from the ground.
- Tap Tap.
- Longeing.
- Ribs out.

Study Guide
Thinking About Your Thinking

❖ *What is the problem I need to solve for each of these, or that each exercise helps improve?*

❖ *What are the "big ideas" associated with each of these?*

❖ *What information do I have about each of these?*

❖ *What assumptions do I have about each of these?*

❖ *What is my point of view about each of these?*

❖ *What conclusions/resolutions should there be for each of these?*

❖ *What are the consequences of addressing each of these?*

Let me walk you through an example of answering these prompts while considering the lesson of longeing the horse:

❖ *What is the purpose of longeing?*

- The horse learns a number of "big concepts" through an introductory means.
- The horse develops his body physically to prepare for being ridden.
- The horse develops balance and skills he'll need when ridden.
- The horse warms up: focuses his mind on work; loosens his body.
- The handler is able to see any anomalies in the horse's movement with a view from the ground.

Study Guide
Thinking About Your Thinking

❖ *What are the "big concepts" associated with longeing?*

- The horse learns to go in a circle.
- The horse learns to bend through the body.
- The horse learns to travel in a steady rhythm.
- The horse learns transitions.
- The horse is introduced to the concept of contact.
- The horse learns to stay on a line of travel and remain centered over it.
- The horse learns to stretch the outside of his body.
- The horse learns relaxation.
- The horse learns to keep his head on is his line of travel.
- The horse learns verbal commands.

❖ *What is the problem I need to solve with longeing?* (Note: This question can be applied to each of the "big concepts.")

- My horse doesn't bend well and can't stay on a curved line. He longes in a "D" shape, with a flat (short, stiff) side (see p. 57). He falls in so much that he almost runs over me. He accelerates dramatically when he's going straight.

❖ *What information/data do I have about this?*

- My horse looks outside the longe circle (loses focus).
- My horse rushes.

Study Guide

Thinking About Your Thinking

- I don't have contact with my horse; the longe line droops.
- My horse isn't relaxed.
- My horse is different at the trot and canter than the walk.
- My horse longes differently to the left and the right.
- My horse doesn't leave a neat circle of footprints; the ring footing looks like cows stampeded through.
- I get all tangled up in the longe line.
- I have more success when my horse is closer to me; as our longe circle grows larger, he gets out of control.

❖ What assumptions do I have about this?

- I assumed that I just need to stand there and my horse will go around on his own.
- I assumed my horse would listen to me.
- I assumed my horse would slow down.
- I assumed my horse wouldn't pull me off my feet (I didn't even know I assumed this!).
- I assumed the longe line would stay organized in my hands.
- I assumed my horse would trot and canter on the first try, and respond when asked.
- I assumed that longeing wasn't technical.

❖ What is my point of view about this?

- I have never longed a horse before.
- I thought that longeing's purpose was to run a horse in circles to "take the edge off."

Study Guide
Thinking About Your Thinking

❖ What conclusions/solutions are there for each of these?

- I need to repeatedly flex my horse's head toward the inside.
- I need to work on a smaller circle in a confined space until I have control.
- I need to practice at a walk until he is relaxed and his rhythm is even.
- I need to keep a connection on the line and not introduce, or allow, slack.
- I need to use the butt end of a whip to keep my horse's ribs out.
- I need to make sure my horse is relaxed before moving on to another gait.
- I need to make sure both directions are the same.
- I need to keep the same radius of a circle.
- I should set up cones as guidepoints so I can tell where my horse is on a circle.
- I should count strides on the circle.
- I need to pay attention to before/during/after a transition.
- I should not let my horse throw his head in the air during a transition.

❖ What are the consequences of addressing each of these?

- With practice and help, I will learn how to longe a horse safely and correctly.
- With practice, patience, and correct aids, my horse will learn how to be longed.
- My horse will learn to travel on an accurate circle.
- My horse and I will get a better idea of how to perform an accurate circle.
- My horse will become more fit.
- My horse will get more flexible and learn to bend and stretch.
- My horse will become more relaxed.

Study Guide
Thinking About Your Thinking

Scan to View
The Analysis and
Assessment of
Thinking

- • My horse will learn to go in a steady rhythm at all gaits.
- • My horse will develop balance.
- • My horse will learn how to make smooth transitions.
- • My horse and I will become familiar with a steady contact.
- • My horse and I will begin to understand how to stay on a line of travel.

I encourage you to both visit the website *criticalthinking.org* and consider the book *Critical Thinking: Tools for Taking Charge of Your Learning and Your Life* by Richard Paul and Linda Elder, which has informed these critical thinking guidelines to apply to training and riding. •

* Reproduced from *Critical Thinking: Tools for Taking Charge of Your Learning and Your Life*, Fourth Edition, by Richard Paul and Linda Elder, published by The Foundation for Critical Thinking, reproduced by arrangement with The Rowman & Littlefield Publishing Group.

Your notes

Chapter

MOVING BODY PARTS

04

Learning to manage the parts of your horse's body develops understanding, trust, and cooperation.

Moving Body Parts Independently of the Rest of the Body

Shoulder and hindquarter control are fundamentals of riding. Your horse must learn to respond to your aids so he can isolate and turn his shoulders or hindquarters independently of the rest of his body, on cue. Because they are not born with deliberate body awareness, horses must be explicitly taught these skills; they cannot acquire them on their own. They do not consider where their feet are, how their weight is distributed, or that there are alternative methods of locomotion besides what they've done instinctively and unconsciously since birth. They are, however, able to recognize simpler, more comfortable, and more efficient methods of body usage. After learning the techniques in this chapter, your horse may begin to move more effectively on his own.

Mobility of the Shoulders

With simple Ground Rules, we have taught the horse to cross his front legs, stay out of our space bubble, and that tapping on his barrel or shoulder means to move. We can now combine these skills to perform more complex maneuvers, such as *moving the shoulders* and *moving the hindquarters*. Using the spelling analogy of motivational speaker and dressage coach Jane Savoie, we have taught our horse "alphabetical letters." In this example, the letters are:

- A: Cross your front legs.
- B: Stay out of my space.
- C: "Tap" means "Go."

Next, we combine the "letters" the horse has learned to form words. When we combine the "letters" *cross your front legs* plus *stay out of my space* plus *"Tap" means "Go,"* it spells "Move your shoulders" or "Turn on your haunches" (moving the shoulders around the hindquarters). Eventually, we will be able to combine these "words" to help the horse think in "sentences" and perform more complex patterns that incorporate multiple maneuvers.

To move your horse's shoulders, take the lead shank in your left hand and a dressage or longe whip in your right hand and stand in front of your horse facing him. (It can help to try this against an arena fence line or wall at first.) Turn his head to your left (his right) with your left hand, then tap him lightly on his left shoulder with the butt end of the whip. He should turn away from the whip to your left (his right) and cross his left front leg over his right front leg (fig. 4.1). Continue tapping and turning until he makes a 90- or 180-degree turn. Your horse should pivot on his hind end and shift his weight back onto his haunches. Ideally, his body and neck should be bent in the direction he's going. In order to keep up, you must walk around in front of him, following his shoulders as they turn. Although you will need to cover some ground to stay ahead of your horse's rotation, this should be done slowly and methodically. Only the shoulders should move; no large sideways steps should be taken by the hind legs. It becomes second nature after a few attempts.

Because moving the shoulders introduces the concept of shifting weight back to the hind end, it is the very first step toward collection. Learning to shift the weight back is necessary for ridden maneuvers such as jumping, sliding stops, cutting, negotiating steep hills, and performing pirouettes. The horse's hind legs are quite simply better equipped to "carry" the horse's weight in these scenarios due to their size and musculature.

4.1 Moving the Shoulders. Turning the shoulders around the hindquarters (turn on the haunches), like a pivot, mobilizes the shoulders. The horse bends in the direction he is turning. One foreleg crosses over the other until he is facing the opposite direction. If the horse is going to his right, the left foreleg crosses in front of his right. If the horse is going to his left, the right front crosses over the left front. The hind legs stay where they are. It helps to do this against a wall or a fence as a point of reference so that you can make sure the hind legs do not stray from their proper location. •

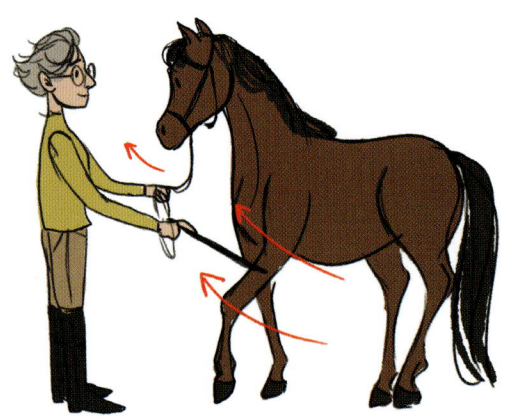

Solving Resistance to Moving the Shoulders

JP Giacomini explains resistance as, "The horse will not perform willingly what he has not experienced, particularly if it is challenging his habitual equilibrium. His resistance comes from his perceived inability to perform the unknown." Because you may be asking your horse to do something he hasn't with this maneuver, your horse may resist moving his shoulders in the following ways:

❖ He may push forward and bump into you, attempting to rush past you instead of turning.

❖ He may stop moving his front end and swing his hindquarters around instead of finishing the turn with his shoulders, so that he begins with a turn on the haunches but ends up doing a turn on the forehand.

❖ The "stuck leg" (see p. 38) may reappear.

❖ He may attempt to back up.

Think of moving the shoulders as a basketball pivot: when a player is stationary, he can move one foot around as long as one foot, the "pivot foot," remains planted on the floor. Otherwise, the player is committing a "traveling violation." Your horse must also move around a stationary pivot point (hindlegs) without "traveling" (figs. 4.2 A & B).

4.2 A & B Resistance to Moving the Shoulders. Your horse should keep his hindquarters planted while swinging his front end around them **(A)**. However, until he learns to shift his weight back to his hindquarters, the hind legs will likely swing around instead **(B)**. To remedy this, move your whip from the shoulder to the hindquarters to prevent it from stepping sideways. Move slowly, one step at a time, giving him time to think. •

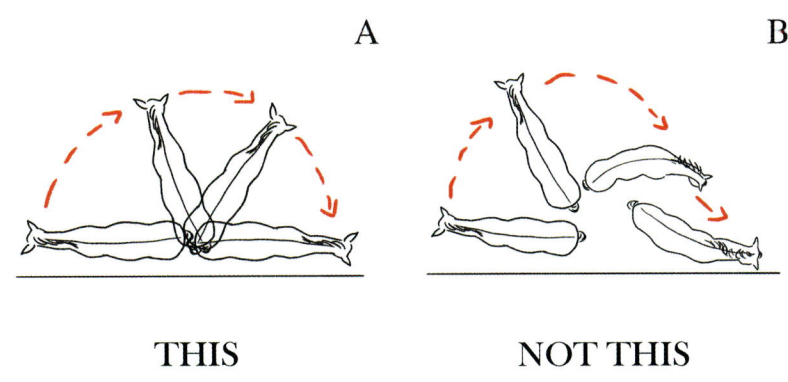

THIS NOT THIS

Scan to View Moving the Shoulders

If he pushes toward you and his hindquarters leave their "pivot point," shank him back and allow him to stand still until he settles. If your horse steps to the side with the *hind* legs, instead of turning just the shoulders, move your whip back from the shoulder you are tapping and tap instead on that side of the hindquarters to prevent them from stepping sideways. Your horse may struggle with understanding and coordination for a few tries, but once he figures out to shift his weight to his hind legs and swing the front end around them, he'll do well and be calm. Take it slow. One step at a time is fine.

Mobility of the Hindquarters

To move the hindquarters, take the lead shank in your left hand and the whip in your right. Stand in front of your horse, facing him. Step to the right of your horse and he'll turn his head to the right. Tap his hindquarters on the right, and he'll swing his hind end away from you, to your left (fig. 4.3). The inside hind leg (the leg on the side you are standing on) should move first and cross over in front of the outside hind leg, up underneath his body. The shoulders should remain fairly still while the hindquarters circle around the forehand. A rule of thumb is that the hindquarters go the *opposite* way of the head: if you move the head right, the hind end will swing to the left. Do this in both directions. (Note: This skill is essential when holding a horse for the farrier: always stand on the same side as the farrier to protect him from the horse's hind end. If an incident occurs, turn the horse's head toward the farrier so that the horse's hind end swings away.)

Moving the hindquarters teaches the horse to use his hind legs independently, reinforces the concept of moving away from pressure, is the precursor to

4.3 Moving the Hindquarters. The hindquarters are mobilized by rotating them in a semicircle around the shoulders while the front legs pivot in a turning walk step (they don't spin or walk forward/backward). The horse moves away from the stimulus of the whip (or your leg when riding), ideally flexing *away* from the direction in which his body is moving, with the inside hind leg (the one "inside" the flexion—the leg you are tapping) crossing in front of the outside hind leg and well up under the abdomen (turn on the forehand). This maneuver is important because the horse learns to move away from "pressure" (whip/leg) and to move his shoulders and hindquarters independently of one another. The sideways stepping also introduces the idea of lateral work.

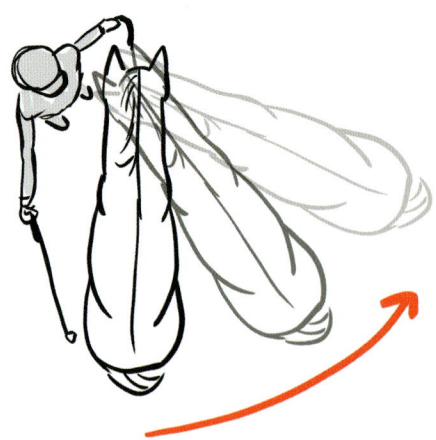

Scan to View Moving the Hindquarters

the turn on the forehand, and contributes to understanding more advanced moves, such as leg-yield. Stepping the hindquarters sideways improves lateral balance, loosens the hindquarters and hip joints, and teaches the horse to step underneath his belly for more stability. It's easier if he learns this from the ground so he's physically capable. Then there's no drama in the saddle, and he offers it because he already understands.

Solving Resistance to Moving the Hindquarters

When asking the inside hind leg to cross over the outside, you want *that* hind leg to move *first*. Chances are extremely high that your horse will move his diagonally situated outside front leg instead, popping that shoulder out and pushing forward into you. Or, he'll move every other leg before he moves the hind leg that you want. Rest your whip on the outside front leg to stop it from moving and let him think about that for a moment. Then ask again by tapping the inside hind leg and quickly counter tap him on the outside front leg if he looks like he will move that instead. In a few minutes, he'll start thinking and just tip that inside hind hoof, drag it a little ways, or move the other hind leg. Praise him for this. Keep cueing and praising, or touching the front leg you don't want to move, until he gets it. Walk him around a little after he does it correctly to relieve mental stress. Before long, your horse will know to begin with his inside hind leg, crossing it over.

To expand this idea, ask your horse to continue stepping around with more than one step, so that he swings his hind end, pivoting around you without

A Conformation Pose   B Halter Pose   C Square Pose

pushing through the outside shoulder. Then, instead of tapping him on the leg, move the whip so that that you are pressing him on his side, just behind the girth where your leg will be, reinforcing that signal. Do this both directions while being calm and persistent. You will start to notice when one of his shoulders is out of control and alignment.

Controlling Leg Placement

Controlling your horse's leg placement is useful for approaching the mounting block, and for competing in certain disciplines or with specific breeds. Once you can control his legs in the manner I describe, you can modify it to suit your needs for other situations, such as standing for x-rays, or taking promotional photographs (figs. 4.4 A–C).

Become familiar with your horse's walk rhythm. Some horses respond quickly to a "Whoa" command, and their legs stop abruptly. Other horses react slowly, and they complete a long, swinging stride before their feet come to rest. This is important to note so you know where his legs typically land when you say "Whoa." This information allows you to plan specifically for your horse's cadence, depending on whether you want him to stop square or with his legs separated.

Halting begins with the hind legs. If you want your horse to spread his hind legs when you stop (flattens the croup), walk faster so that he takes a longer stride. If you want his hind legs to be more square, walk slowly so that the stride is very short going into the halt.

4.4 A–C Posing. When your horse comes to a halt, you should be able to position his legs however you choose. There are various "poses" or ideal positions of the legs for various purposes. The "conformation pose" used for marketing photographs has all four legs visible **(A)**. For breeds that wish to emphasize a flat topline, separating only the hind legs and raising the head creates a "halter pose" **(B)**. Other horse breeds and disciplines may require that the horse stand "square" **(C)**.

4.5 Shoulders Facing. When you stop your horse in a position and face him with your shoulders, he must maintain that "pose" until you turn your shoulders away and permit him to move his feet. Teach him to remain still while your shoulders are facing him, enabling you to walk around his entire body without him moving. •

To begin, lead him forward while keeping an eye on the hind leg on your side. When it lands, say, "Whoa," which allows the other hind leg to finish its swing, land, and freeze. If your horse continues to walk rather than halting on command, shank him back. Repeat this step until your horse stops on cue.

Your horse must learn that once he is stopped, the hind legs must remain in place so that you can position the front legs by moving the shoulders. Turn your shoulders toward him and walk around him a few steps in either direction, reminding him to stand still as you do so (fig. 4.5). He'll eventually realize that when your shoulders are facing him, he's not to move, no matter where you go. Gradually increase the distance you can move around him until you can reach his tail on both sides. (This exercise is also beneficial for clipping and grooming.)

Then, look at how the front legs are positioned. However you want the front legs is up to you, but you have to train them to move where you want them. Whichever leg you want to move, turn the horse's head the opposite way: if you are facing him and want to move his right leg (on your left side), put the lead shank in your right hand and the whip in your left. Turn the horse's head to your right (his left) and ask for just that right front leg to move by tapping his forearm with the whip in your left hand. The leg will move hesitantly at first, either forward or crossing over. He may just wobble a knee. Reward whatever you get until he understands where to put it. Do the opposite for the other leg until both front legs are where you want them, either parallel with each other, "parked out," or staggered for a conformation photo (fig. 4.6). If he pulls the leg back after moving it, put it right back where you had it. Keep putting it back until he leaves it there. When it stays put, just stand still for a minute to

4.6 Conformation Photo. An example of a classic promotional photo, showing all four legs of Envoy, a Hanoverian. •

Scan to View Controlling Leg Placement

let the notion set in and to encourage patience in the horse (he's not to move off until asked). If you do this exercise for a couple of days, the horse will learn to correct his feet on his own and will stop in the position you desire.

Controlling where the horse puts his legs is the first step toward controlling his legs while riding him. He recognizes that *you* control where they go; whoever controls the legs controls the horse.

★ Caveats

❖ A common saying in equestrian circles is, "**You are either training or untraining a horse when you work with him.**" It is important to be consistent. If you are inconsistent, the horse will become confused.

❖ **Be quick about corrections**. The horse needs to understand the relationship between a correction and his behavior. If you wait too long to take a corrective action, the horse may think the original undesirable behavior is okay and that you are actually correcting the *next* thing he did.

The Value of Ground Rules

4.7 Sheila Varian. The Ground Rules section is dedicated to Sheila Varian, horsewoman extraordinaire, from whom I learned these techniques. Sheila was the first woman to "Win the World" in Reined Cow Horse at the Cow Palace in 1961 and is a member of the Cowgirl Hall of Fame. As a breeder, she produced generations of influential Arabian Horses who won World and National Championships in every category. She was a generous teacher and had an amazing way with horses. Thank you, Sheila.

❖ After **making a correction**, be "neutral." Horses usually respond *after* a correction, not during, so you must wait to observe any effect. It is easy to fall into the trap of perpetually trying to prevent the horse from making a mistake by correcting him before he does it again. It is better to let your horse make a mistake so he learns from the correction. It is fine to correct something more than once. Eventually, he'll learn either to do, or not do, something *on his own*. However, if you are getting nowhere over a long period of time, seek assistance. Once you and your horse learn what to do for a particular maneuver, you will develop the feel and skill to proactively and tactfully nip something in the bud.

❖ Watch out for **anthropomorphism**—ascribing human emotions or motives to horse behavior. Horses aren't concocting means to spite you, nor are they doing intentional things to frustrate you. Most animals aren't intellectually capable of deception. They are just trying to figure out what you want. They might not understand or simply might not yet be physically able to do what is asked. Try to stay objective and observant to remedy the actual issue. Break a difficult topic into steps and separately fix the parts that don't work; then try again.

Taking time to do groundwork is immensely valuable. For the handler, answers to questions provide insights to your horse's character and predispositions, such as:

- *Is he cooperative? Attentive? Does he respect you?*
- *Is he aware of what he does with his feet?*
- *Which leg is the first to move? The last? What does this mean?*
- *Can your horse stretch enough to cross his legs easily?*
- *Which is his stiff side? Which is his hollow (easily bendable) side?*
- *Can he shift his weight back to his hind legs? Do his hocks bend?*
- *Does he stop and start when you ask him to?*
- *Does he move downhill? Does he stumble?*
- *Does he rush?*
- *Does he pull on you, or lean in toward you?*
- *Which side does he work better from?*
- *Does he get grouchy? How long is his attention span?*
- *Is he better the next day?*

The answers to these questions provide insight into who your horse is, how he reacts to training and aids, what his physical prowess is or isn't, and how he solves problems. This is extremely useful when riding. You can visualize what he'll do and how he'll do it because you've observed him on the ground. His reactions are predictable. Furthermore, you will have investigated and corrected a variety of problems before mounting the horse, so you should encounter fewer difficulties as a result. This significantly boosts rider confidence.

Groundwork teaches the horse necessary riding skills. It makes ridden work easier because the horse develops his body appropriately in terms of strength, flexibility, and muscle memory. Groundwork also mentally prepares him for being ridden—what you will eventually ask of him will not be an unexpected, random event for him. As a result of careful planning, the horse will produce a more optimal response as his first inclination when asked to perform a task. ●

The Value of Ground Rules

Study Guide

Self-Perception

Frequently, what we believe we see/experience/do does not correspond with reality. Video your horse as you move the shoulders, hindquarters, and control the feet as directed in this chapter. Create a list of what you believe went well and what did not. Then, review your video to determine whether your perception is accurate. Ask yourself the following questions:

❖ *Did what you saw on the video match how the exercise should be done?*

❖ *If not, what was different?*

❖ *What do you think caused these differences and how can you fix them to do the movement more accurately?*

❖ *What caused the horse to react in a certain way? Was it you? Was it more than one thing?*

❖ *What happened right before the horse's response?*

Most events have more than one cause. Training your eye to see these things is as important as learning what to do. This process will begin by identifying the discrepancies between what you *thought* happened and what *actually occurred*. As you observe yourself and others working horses, you will develop a trained eye for distinguishing between what the handler wants and what the horse actually does. The more experience you have, the better your eye will

Study Guide
Self-Perception

become. You will begin to learn what you missed that you need to not miss in the future. Indeed, if you spend enough time with an animal, you can begin to predict what he will do simply by observing the behavior that precedes a behavior. Like driving, you can see something coming and take evasive action because you know to avoid it.

ACTIVITY: Watch Dogs

Have you ever watched a dog walk? Dogs are pacers! A pace occurs when the front and hind legs on the same side of the animal move forward simultaneously; thus, both the left and right legs move at the same time. (This differs from the trot, in which the diagonally opposite legs move forward together.) Once you see a dog pacing, you can't un-see it. You will soon see that every dog paces. Once you have that practiced eye, you will begin to recognize inconsistencies in horse gaits. In this way, your practiced eye takes this knowledge and applies it to a new situation. ●

Part Two

NON-NEGOTIABLES

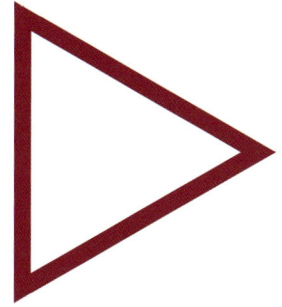

Effective riding is intentional and systematic. In order to achieve the result you desire (the horse traveling on the bit, with an engaged topline, springy gait, and willingness), it is important to have a plan to guide your ride each day. This book provides a mechanism to help you develop that plan before you get on the horse so that you have an organized, purposeful, and satisfying ride. Otherwise, your horse is likely to wander aimlessly around the arena, changing his rhythm, spinal alignment, and direction in a dysfunctional manner without you noticing. Indeed, horses make quite a long list of subtle decisions, of which riders are commonly unaware: how the head is carried, which foot moves first, whether there is appropriate connection with each rein, how long/short each stride is, whether the shoulders are in line with the hips, whether the hind legs are legitimately pushing, and so on. Certainly, horses aren't thinking about what will improve the quality of their performance. That's why *you* need to decide in advance the focus of any given ride.

Riding is a systematic work-in-progress that requires monitoring both yourself and the horse every step of the way. Knowing where to begin and how to recognize and diagnose issues in both yourself and your horse, and discovering how to employ the interconnected network of aids (seat, reins, legs, weight) are necessary to bring forth that fulfilling ride. They can be learned; however, patience and tenacity are required.

That said, the end result you seek begins with establishing a few essential, ever-present rules, or "Non-Negotiables," for your horse. "Non-Negotiable" means that you and your horse must do them every single ride, internalizing and incrementally refining them over time. Non-Negotiables are as basic and necessary as tires on a car; without them the car is going nowhere. If even one tire is flat, a trip is, at least temporarily, ruined.

In riding, six foundational Non-Negotiables that pave the way to the horse developing body awareness, coordination, alignment and flexibility are:

❖ Go (p. 95).

❖ Get Connected (p. 116).

❖ Stay Connected (p. 164).

❖ Transitions (p. 200).

❖ Flexion (p. 228).

❖ Half-Halt (p. 258).

Study Guide
Create Your Own Non-Negotiables

Non-Negotiables are unwavering basic expectations that must be mastered, and that all horses and riders should know. Just as the corporate world embraces the "7 Non-Negotiables of Winning" (from the book of the same name by David Williams) that include respect, belief, loyalty, commitment, trust, courage, and gratitude, and criteria like vision, mission, awareness, and ability to drive change are qualities of a leader, *everything* has its own set of non-negotiables.

Create a list of non-negotiables for something you already know well and may feel you are done learning about, such as driving a car, cooking a favorite meal, or playing a sport. Creating your own set of non-negotiables regarding something you care deeply about will help you comprehend why they are essential to any endeavor.

Your notes

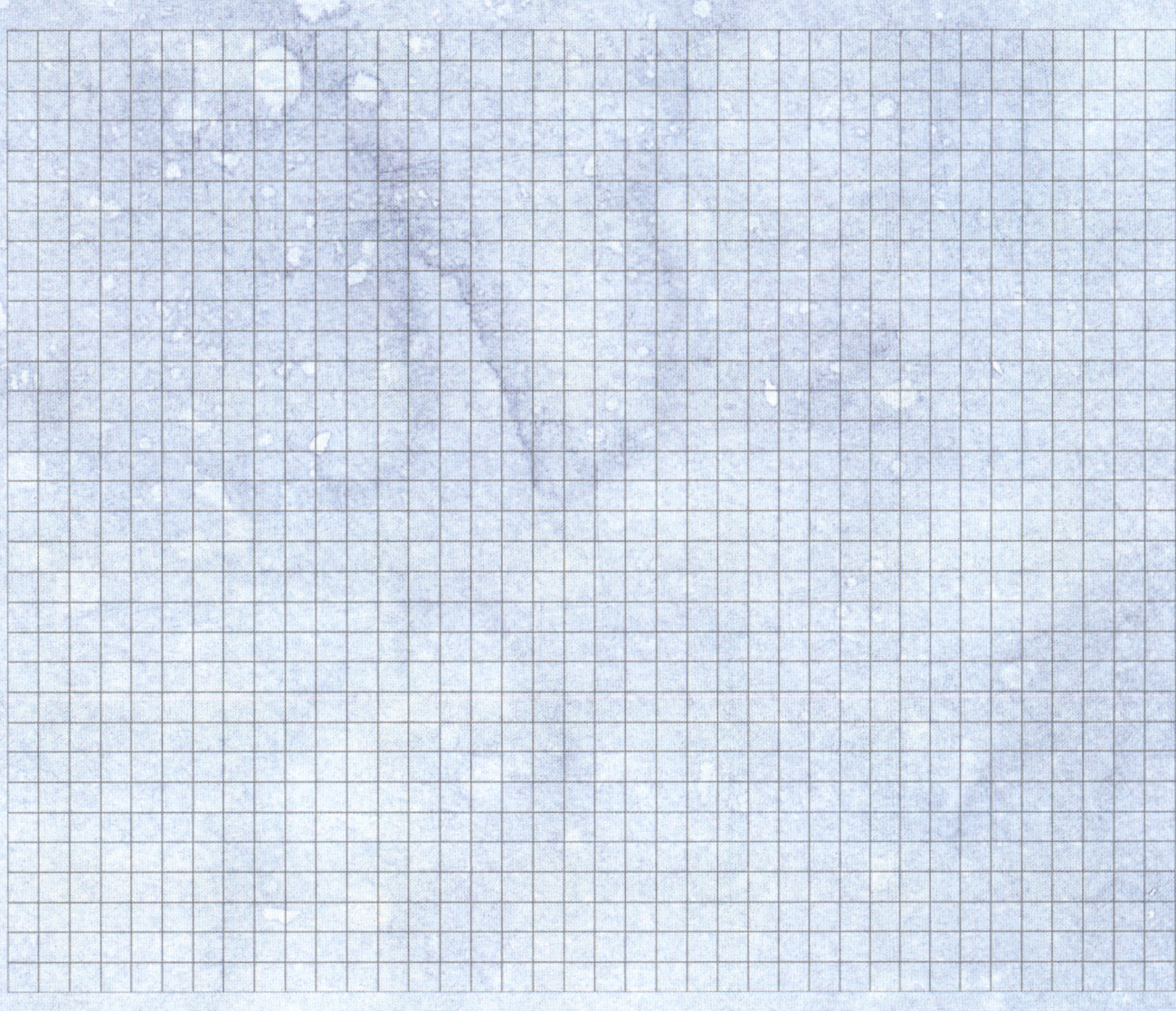

Chapter

GO

05

Riding horses is both exciting and challenging.
There is always something new to learn.

5.1 Nagging, Seat Pumping, Kicking. One of the most difficult habits for a rider to break is the misconception that repeated kicking and seat pumping are required to get a horse to move. Indeed, a rider's body will continue to pump and kick despite her knowledge that she shouldn't! Furthermore, when teaching a horse to move forward from a slight leg squeeze, rider patience is frequently tested. She abandons the first attempt after about five seconds and declares, "This doesn't work." Wait for your horse to start moving. He will! As he gains understanding, he will move more promptly on subsequent attempts. ●

The most basic assumption about riding a horse is to *go*, to move. But there is more to it: The horse needs to learn to move from a cue, and remain moving in a steady fashion of his own volition, in the gait and tempo we dictate, like a car in cruise control, until we tell him otherwise.

To initially set a horse in motion, or move from the halt to the walk, most horses will spontaneously "go" as a result of a slight squeezing of both legs, mimicking "Tap Tap" as described in chapter 2 (p. 45). Leg aids work because they touch and activate the horse's abdominal muscles, which pull the hind legs forward and lift the back.

You want to teach your horse to respond to subtle aids from the outset—quiet signals from the seat, weight, legs, hands, and voice. These are the "natural" aids that communicate with the horse. Whips and spurs are "artificial" aids that should only supplement or refine natural aids.

It isn't necessary to use sharp kicks as are so commonly employed. You *don't* want to teach your horse that harsh or repeated aids, like pumping your seat or kicking, are the cue to go, or you will become tired and frustrated from doing that the rest of your riding life. Indeed, you will likely end up escalating your kicking or pumping as time goes by because your horse may wait to see whether you are finished, or when you finally give that last "hard enough" kick or push (fig. 5.1). In fact, pumping with your seat actually produces the *opposite* effect of what you want: the pressure causes the horse's back to sink, his head to rise, his croup to rise, his front legs move out in front of him and his hind legs move out behind him, so that he becomes shaped like a trapezoid. His lowered back and belly actually prevent his hind legs from moving forward.

Aids Inform the Horse—They Are *Not* the Moving Force

Consider riding aids to be a form of sign language in which gestures convey meaning; a specific bodily movement means "go." Such a signal informs the horse to go; the application of the aid itself does not physically compel the body to move. When a horse understands, he will go.

Because your horse only knows what you teach him, be judicious and show him what he is meant to do when you communicate with him through the use of an aid. Use specific and consistent aids for each response you seek. Apply a gentle aid and see whether you get the desired response. If not, be more aggressive for *one* try then return to the slight aid. Often, horses offer several simultaneous responses when given an aid, so eliminate everything but the response you want. Eventually, your horse will understand that that request is the one and only aid for one action—"one response for one aid."

As riding instructor Sharon Vander Ziel remarks, "People always say that a horse can feel a fly landing on him, but did you ever notice that horses *ignore* flies? They'll ignore you, too!" This shrewd observation reminds us that everything doesn't work perfectly or instantly with horses, so be patient, keep trying, and expect results in small increments. Ask gently. If you don't get a response, ask bigger until you do, then return to the slight aid.

Be Consistent

Many people don't realize they routinely use random aids. For example, many who want to trot urge their horse forward, pumping and kicking, without thinking it through. When I ask students to tell me what they systematically did to ask their horse to trot, they often just stare at me, perplexed. Such inconsistency creates confusion in the horse and puts him in the position of having to guess what you are asking for. When he guesses wrong, he may be blamed for being disobedient.

Be methodical and patient with giving only the cue that you want to use until you get the response that you seek. Remember that alphabet that Jane Savoie told us about (see p. 77): Think of giving aids like spelling a word—if you want your horse to trot, make sure you spell "t-r-o-t" the same way every time; don't spell "k-i-w-i" one time, then spell "c-l-o-w-n" yet another. Giving aids in different combinations, or "spelling different words," compels your horse to guess what you want, and aids should not be unanswerable multiple choice situations.

The minute you turn the corner and decide to be 100 percent clear, precise, and consistent with your horse on everything, you'll find your horse will better respond to your requests. It can help to think of the *kata* in martial arts: a kata refers to a prescribed, detailed pattern of specific, choreographed movements that are repeated under the eye of a master until the movements being executed are perfected. Experts say the purpose of *kata* is to train the muscles. By consistently doing the same motions, your brain will become more comfortable with lacing together combinations and turning and moving a certain way. Eventually, you will be able to habitually duplicate particular movements without conscious effort; it becomes "first nature"—something you "are" rather than something you "do." If you bring the *kata* mentality to using your aids, your horse will never be confused about what you are telling him. It will be *kata* for him, too. The more deliberate you are, the happier you will be in the long run because you will have effectively installed the cue that you want to use. Horses learn from repetition and usually succeed within minutes.

Allow the Horse to Do What You Ask!

It is vitally important for you to *allow* your horse to do what you ask. If you ask him to go forward, you must go forward *with* him. You must be cognizant of, and prepared for, his upcoming movement so that you don't inadvertently restrain the horse by reflexively grabbing and pulling on the reins with your hands for stability. On the other hand, some riders possess the opposite, also detrimental, habit of leaning too far forward in anticipation of the horse's movement. Instead, imagine being pushed on a playground swing: your entire body goes forward with the swing (you wouldn't let yourself fall off the front or the back), and in the same way, your entire body needs to go forward as a unit with the

Understanding Aids Through Analogies

TO train a horse, you must provide him with a means of understanding what you want him to do. This is achieved by teaching the horse a system of communication based on specific combinations of aids, so that he learns to perform what we ask without seeing us (when we are on his back). Using sensory aids to communicate with the horse is similar to how people with hearing and visual impairments, like Helen Keller, use "tactile signing"—they place their hands over the hands of the signer to feel what they're saying through touch and movement. Just as sign language has a specific hand position to signify each letter, unique combinations of aids from the seat, weight, and legs, spell out whatever the horse should do. If you use the same signals every time for the response you seek, your horse will learn to do this. It's a language. In this way It is possible to create a clear line of communication with your horse, a code that both of you understand.

While bit/bridle/hackamore arrangements exert pressure to the horse's mouth, under the chin, corners of the mouth, tongue, bars, palate, bridge of the nose, or poll, affecting the network of cranial nerves that surround the head, here I am only discussing how the rider's hands use the reins and bit to communicate, through touch and movement (like sign language), with the horse's mouth. For example, a rider could touch the outside rein ("outside" the bend) two short times and one longer time in conjunction with the horse's outside front foot setting down. (It can be any leg, depending on which you wish to control.) The first two twitches on the outside of the mouth alert the horse that something is coming, then, the third cue might be longer (part of a "half-halt"—see p. 259) asking him to halt. So, the horse feels "touch, touch, touuuuuch," which means "Whoa." This is similar to Morse Code's "dot, dot, dash." Just as dot, dot, dash is always the letter "U," in Morse Code, in "Horse Code," it's always "Whoa." You can experience this sensation for yourself by hooking the index finger of each hand into the corners of your mouth and twitching your finger.

The inside hand ("inside" the bend) independently asks the horse to remain yielding softly inside so that he doesn't turn his head to look outside when that rein is used for communication. The reason he must turn his head away from the outside rein is to maintain its tautness so that he is able to detect movements in that rein. If the rein you wish to use for communication is dangling, the signal is lost and the circuit is broken.

The bit allows a rider to cue a horse by applying pressure to the horse's mouth and surrounding area, particularly in the corners of the mouth where the rings or shanks of the bit lie. This pressure is used to control the speed, carriage, movement, and direction of the horse. It is not intended to be painful. In response to signals from the bit, along with other aids, the horse changes his shape, speed, or direction, often in an attempt to minimize the pressure he might be feeling. This means that the rider needs to think about what pressure he is going to apply so the horse responds appropriately. Further, because the bit is used in conjunction with other aids, such as the seat and legs, the horse learns to cue off those before the bit needs to come into play. I always say that you want to "save your bit" for other things. Don't use it for everything. A "finished" horse has little need of the bit.

If your horse doesn't respond correctly because he doesn't understand you, don't use harsher aids. More is not better! Your horse will become confused if you do not use a consistent aid for each response you seek. One aid, one response, like Morse Code letters. Jane Savoie addresses this in her *A Happy Horse Study Course*: "For example, if I only spoke English and you spoke to me in Russian, I wouldn't have a clue what you were saying to me. If you spoke slower, I still wouldn't have a clue what you were saying to me. And if you started shouting at me, that wouldn't help me to understand. I still wouldn't understand because I don't speak Russian. This is the trap that we fall into sometimes as riders. We give an aid and the horse doesn't understand, so we start using the aids stronger and stronger and harder and harder in the hopes that the horse will then understand, but you're speaking to your horse in a foreign language and yelling louder at him with your aids isn't going to help you, or help him...If we are fuzzy, muddy or unclear with our aids, or if we have more than one aid that asks the horse to do a couple of different things and we put the poor horse in the position where he has to play multiple choice where he has to ask, 'Do you want me to go sideways, or bend on a circle or do you want a canter depart?' because those aids are very similar and the horse chooses the wrong answer and the rider thinks the horse is being disobedient and punishes the horse."

horse as he steps forward. You are neither behind nor in front of his motion by allowing your upper body to tilt either backward or forward at the pelvis, thus losing your upright balance. Another common riding visualization is thinking of your body as a sail on a boat, blowing forward over the water with the boat as the boat moves. In any case, you must surrender to the forward motion, allow it to happen, and go with your horse. Because your horse may not yet have learned to balance himself, his body may careen around, making you feel insecure and scared. Forwardness and momentum help the horse find coordination and rhythm, which smooth out his gaits. Because we know this is the kind of physical reaction we can expect from a horse that is trying to do what we want, we know the horse isn't misbehaving and can keep our cool during this phase of training or retraining.

The Effect of Balance on the Horse

"Forwardness" in the untrained, poorly trained, or unbalanced horse tends to come with increased speed. Because he's not physically developed enough to manage his body in any other way, he rushes. Since his head and neck are heavy and weigh down his front end, the horse pulls the rider along like a runaway grocery cart descending a ramp. The uneducated horse isn't yet balanced. In horseback riding, there are multiple definitions of "balance":

Whatever type of bit you use, the most important thing to remember is that "holding," or applying pressure for a single long episode, does not work. In reality, it creates discomfort, resistance, and avoidance of the cue. It is far more effective (for any aid) to use a short cue that is repeated until the desired response is obtained. The release between cues serves either as reward for immediate compliance or a respite from the pressure. A horse is likely respond during the release anyway simply because nervous system "reflex arcs" take time to occur. This means that the brain receives a signal, processes it, and sends the message through the body to the appropriate muscle, much like braking with your foot when you see a red light. This requires only a fraction of a second, but it nonetheless requires time. We must also allow the horse sufficient time to respond.

Think of giving aids like dialing a phone: you quickly enter multiple numbers. If you attempted to dial 555-1212 by pressing and holding the first "5" for an extended period of time, you would never move on to dialing the entire number, making the connection, and achieving the desired result. To use a musical example, horses are more responsive to eighth notes than whole notes. Holding or pulling harder never works. The "more is better" idea of making a cue last longer doesn't motivate a horse. It shuts the horse down. Repetition of cues is far more effective. ●

Understanding Aids Through Analogies

5.2 A & B Longitudinal Balance. To be longitudinally balanced, your horse's legs need to stay underneath his body, both in front and rear **(A)**. The front legs should not be out in front of the chest, or "downhill," and the hind legs should not be behind the tail, or "out behind" **(B)**.

THIS   NOT THIS

- Due to the presence and weight of the head and neck attached to the horse's front end, the front legs support a greater percentage of the horse's weight, resulting in a natural "downhill" balance in which the horse pulls himself along with his front legs ("front-wheel drive").

- Through training, the horse learns to redistribute his weight, becoming "horizontally balanced," meaning that the horse's weight is distributed evenly across all four legs ("four-wheel drive"), which removes a considerable amount of pressure and wear and tear from the front legs.

- An "uphill balance" indicates that the horse has progressed to carrying most of his weight on his hind legs, which are more powerful and better suited to supporting body mass, and that his front legs are, thus, more free to move as a result ("rear-wheel drive").

- "Longitudinal balance" refers to the horse's legs being underneath his body, similar to table legs, and not protruding out from underneath the body, neither to the front, nor behind (figs. 5.2 A & B).

- "Lateral balance" means that the horse's legs are squarely underneath his body and not diverting out to the side—left legs don't step left from under the body, right legs don't step right (figs. 5.3 A & B). A horse with lateral imbalance moves similarly to a swimmer performing the breast stroke. Instead, like the freestyle stroke, their limbs should move in a straight line.

Any number of legs can simultaneously deviate longitudinally and laterally from beneath the body at any given time. Riding an unbalanced horse is quite jarring and uncomfortable. Only when all four of the horse's legs are underneath him is he stable, springy, and enjoyable to ride.

Recognizing Balance Issues

It is the responsibility of the rider to determine whether the legs are underneath the horse, and if they aren't, which legs have deviated, where they have gone, and how to correct them. When a horse pulls or resists, he is frequently either laterally or longitudinally out of balance, which makes him feel confused or afraid. JP Giacomini adds, "Most anxiety comes from a chronic loss of balance, and

5.3 A & B Lateral Balance. Your horse must have all four legs underneath him, not stepping out to the left or right sides, to be laterally balanced and stable **(A & B)**. The horse must distribute his weight evenly across all four feet, carrying the same amount of weight on his right side as he does on his left. Otherwise, when viewed from either the front or rear, you can see which legs are carried out to the side of the body, and the horse will lean in one direction or another. ●

A

B

THIS   NOT THIS

chronic anxiety leads to behavior issues. The root cause of resistance is not the horse's character, but a faulty balance that creates an uneven weight distribution. The horse's reaction to an imbalance will be determined through the filter of his character. Rebalancing the horse laterally through forward movement to restore uprightness creates an immediate relaxation and is the first (and often the only) step needed to make the horse safe again."

Riding toward a mirror can help you see which legs are out of line, *adducted* away from the horse's body. You can redirect (*abduct*) them back under the horse's body either by steering the front legs with your reins or legs, or you can move the horse's hind legs laterally back under his body by asking for a leg-yield left or right (see p. 175 for more about the leg-yield). Learn to differentiate between correct and incorrect by feel, so you can tell without looking (and when riding where mirrors are not present). When you show a horse how to be balanced, he then tends to stay that way of his own accord because it feels better.

The Effect of Rider Balance on the Horse

Many people strive for beautiful equitation and looking like "one" with the horse, but appearing "still" or motionless, as is considered desirable, doesn't literally mean being rigid or holding a pose. In fact, such contrived stiffness will *cause* your body to rock back and forth when the horse moves and challenges your balance, like a skyscraper in an earthquake.

A stiff, unbalanced rider will cause imbalance in the horse as he has to additionally negotiate the interfering effects to his own stability. Justifiably, a horse that feels off balance may be reluctant to move, may rush forward, or may become very stiff and brace against the ground as a consequence of his self-preservation instinct. To experience this for yourself, hold hands with someone and have her try to pull you off balance while you resist. You will feel yourself pushing hard against the ground with one leg, as people do in a game of tug-of-war. This is bracing. As soon as you are able to recognize it, you will be amazed at just how much you will see it when watching horses and their riders.

Balance is an urgent priority for horses because loss of balance is linked with a potential fall in their mind, and as a prey animal, falling is a death sentence. Therefore, being off balance is a much bigger deal to a horse than it would seem when, from your perspective, you are merely asking him to "go." Pay attention to where you might be stiff or floppy and remedy that so that you don't impede your horse's balance when he moves. For example, yielding your hands slightly forward when you ask him to go rewards the horse for doing so, enabling him to understand what you want, but pitching the reins to him disrupts his balance. *Reduce* the pressure, but don't remove it entirely so that you retain connection for communication with him.

★ Caveats

❖ Many riders exuberantly **reward** their horses by patting (pounding!) them aggressively and loudly on the neck, leaning dramatically forward and changing the horse's balance unexpectedly. Others draw up hard on the reins as they reach forward to pat. Be kind to your horse and stroke him gently, or give him a scratch. Often a "Good boy!" suffices because horses perceive your uplifted tone. This will feel a lot more like a reward to him than being smacked, jerked, or knocked off balance.

❖ Some riders mean to reward their horse by wandering around on a "**long rein**," but they never truly give the horse the full reins. Instead, they hold their hands high, unconsciously keeping uneven tension on the reins, and causing imbalance.

❖ Taking the time to work on a specific aspect of your riding allows you to observe what the horse gives you in exchange for what you do. Experiment with different approaches and see how your horse reacts. Remove constant heel bumping, seat pumping, leg gripping, and inside shoulder (yours, not your horse's) counterbending. These annoying habits cause stress in your horse, which he shows by raising his head, holding his breath, or having a worried expression on his face. Remove these irritants and observe whether your horse relaxes. This way, you can determine what works best and causes the least stress to your horse. As international clinician Thomas Ritter says, **"Riders help balance, straighten, and supple… or riders can interfere.** There is a reason we talk about *aids* and not *interferences*. Aids are not just commands, they are things we do to help the horse. You can either stay out of the way, get in the way and interfere, or you can help the horse." So, think about what you are actually doing!

❖ Consider the purpose of your actions, the problem you are attempting to solve, the information your horse is providing you, the information you are providing the horse, the assumptions you are making, and the outcomes of your efforts. As you deduce these things, you will become a more astute and deliberate rider, reducing mistakes in the future. It's the **systematic observation of cause and effect** that only you can do. It's not as hard as it may seem since you usually only have two options to choose from: What happens if I give on the left rein? Or on the right? Lean forward? Or back? Lean left? Or right? One motion may make improvement, one will definitely not. Either way, you now know. Note that horses are likely to need very different management going to the left and to the right. It can be like riding two different

"Take the Time It Takes, So It Takes Less Time"

Give your horse, and yourself, the gift of time. Horses don't learn on a deadline. It may take your horse a while to understand what you want and become reliable and anxiety-free about doing it. It may take your horse a while to develop enough physically to be able to respond to you correctly.

Consider doing the splits. Can you do them *today*? Would you be able to do them next week? In three months? What would it take for you to achieve the ability to do them? Bear in mind that your horse can't do things faster than you can, simply by virtue of being a horse. While it is fine to have goals, rushing to achieve anything by a certain date, or because you are impatient, or there is a show conveniently located nearby the next week, is the biggest detriment to learning and can even set your horse back further. *Once you create mental anxiety in your horse, it is very hard to overcome for the long haul.* The ability to hold out now for a better reward in the long run is very satisfying when you achieve your goal in the end. Take time to enjoy the journey. Many things a horse learns evolve over time. Like losing weight, you don't just suddenly drop 100 pounds; little by little, progress occurs almost imperceptibly until, one day, results are noticeable. ●

Counting Strides on a Circle

Riding circles of varying sizes while counting how many strides you take in each quarter of the circle is an extremely useful technique for establishing regular tempo and rhythm. Counting quarters of a circle may be easier than counting the entire circle. Furthermore, counting quarters allows for a more thorough examination of what occurs in various parts of the circle. Take note of which quarters are easy to maintain and which are not. Determine why you're off in the quarters that don't work and make adjustments with your aids to compensate. Typically, the first half of a circle works well. The third and fourth quarter often have a greater number of strides because horses drift out. You will feel a good rhythm and swing set in once you can do the same number of strides per quarter because there are no inaccuracies to disrupt it. This works well at the walk, trot, and canter.

This is a good time to consider whether using inside ("inside" the bend) or outside ("outside" the bend) aids makes the first half of the circle easier. How about the other half of the circle? Generally, you need more outside aids on the first half of the circle (to make the turn happen) and more inside aids on the second half (to prevent the horse from falling in and making a flat side, turning your circle into a "D"), but many horses are the opposite. Furthermore, when you change directions, your horse may be opposite. It's best to ride this exercise in a freshly dragged arena so you can look over your tracks for insights. To make counting strides easier at first, scratch "Xs" into the dirt where the points of your circle are (like horses—one each way! So you will need to analyze each side systematically.

❖ If you must use the whip to reinforce a light leg signal, be mindful of how you do so. It's easy to get into the habit of tapping with the whip first, or using the whip simultaneously. Use your leg; observe the response; add the whip; and repeat as necessary until your horse responds to the leg immediately. It isn't necessary to smack your horse hard; the motion of the whip is intended to touch the horse and direct his attention to a body part he isn't thinking about. **Remember that the whip follows the leg,** which should eventually eliminate the need for the whip.

❖ **Save the use of spurs for later.** If you are skilled, you can use the leg without the spur and then, if necessary, follow up with it for refined communication. However, many riders are unaware of their uncontrolled leg movements and do not realize that if their toes are even slightly turned out, they are inadvertently spurring the horse. Check the hair on your horse's sides after a ride to see if it has been tousled or rubbed off, indicating that your spurs are rubbing him carelessly. When this occurs, spurring and the leg signal occur simultaneously, nullifying the "one-two" sequence required to reinforce, if necessary, the soft leg aid. Spurs are designed to aid the rider in communicating with the horse in a more subtle manner; they primarily cause the horse to respond to smaller cues.

- Constant **gripping and squeezing with the legs** is very common. To get my students to stop doing this, I ask them, "Did your horse take off running as soon as you tightened the girth?" The answer is always no. Well, if the constant grip of the girth or cinch didn't make them go, why would endless squeezing be any different? So, don't do it. In fact, your horse will learn to ignore your leg aids because of the "refractory period" that nerve cells experience: once a nerve has been stimulated to "fire," it becomes *incapable* of functioning again for a moment. Until it recovers, the nerve can't have another impulse. When you keep constant pressure on the horse's side, the nerves are constantly being stimulated and the horse will physiologically tune out, or be incapable of responding. The same thing goes for pulling on the reins constantly and shutting down the horse's mouth for communication. Don't sabotage your aids by disabling them.

- **Horses' reactions are often either too slow or too quick.** Because such fundamental muscle fiber function is genetically determined, this can be difficult to overcome. Some large horses are especially slow to react and will remain so in the future. If your horse is slow, he will need to respect your leg, so lightly tap with your leg, following up with the

12:00, 3:00, 6:00, and 9:00 on a clock). Flat soccer cones also make good markers because you don't have to go around them; your horse can just step on them. They are inexpensive. If you have regular traffic cones, you can set up two at each point and ride between them. (Note: I prefer to use minimal visual assistance for the horse so that the rider is responsible for getting from point to point. When training in a round pen, with poles on the ground, or using large cones, the large visual markers control where the horse goes, removing the rider's responsibilities.) ●

whip. Don't get so desperately kicky that he thinks that's the aid, "Okay, 17 increasingly hard kicks is the signal to go." Insist that one light aid is the only form of communication you will accept. If your horse is quick, focus on relaxation and dictate the tempo with your body and half-halts.

❖ Some horses require a **lengthy warm-up** period before they are ready to respond promptly. Several horses I've ridden simply cannot be motivated until they've walked for a while to "wake up." Plan your time accordingly when dealing with such horses.

❖ **Forward** does not imply "faster," but rather that the horse is "off your leg" and responds instantly. When he responds, don't hang onto the reins, obstructing forward motion. Ride with more leg than hand. Imagine a moving barrier an inch in front of the horse's nose, and he needs to fill that space and touch the barrier, but not by speeding up and moving his legs faster, but by pushing more from the hind leg with a longer stride and reaching. When the horse's legs move quickly, the horse is not relaxed, and the strides are not necessarily long.

❖ Horses that are **hesitant to move or are adamant about rushing** may be suffering from a physical problem. If you don't make progress in a reasonable amount of time, have a veterinarian examine your horse.

❖ When a horse is slow and you have to push him, it may be due to **a problem with a front leg**. If a front leg hurts, he may "point" that leg out in front of the body when standing.

❖ If a horse is rushing downhill, leaning heavily on the reins, and the croup is elevated, he may be attempting to shift **weight off a hind leg** by leaning more on the front end. To help keep weight off his hind legs, he may also step out to the side of his body.

❖ **Horses that pull go too** fast and are said to be "running downhill" or "falling on the forehand." As we have discussed, they are "unbalanced" or "not carrying themselves." This also implies that the horse isn't yet strong or isn't using his hindquarters as the main support for his body. This horse is probably a good candidate for more longeing, until he can balance himself in all three gaits. If you elect to continue riding him at this stage, don't hold the horse to keep him together. Let him go so he can carry himself and figure out how to move with you on him. It is okay if he makes mistakes. If you hold him with tight reins and a stiff body, he'll always expect and depend on you to carry him. This falls in the category of "be careful what you train in, or that's what you will get." Horses don't know any different than what they are told.

* Horses that pull on the reins are said to "**run through**" the bit and horses that leave reins slack and curl their necks so their head is near their chest are said to "**suck back.**" When your horse runs through, repeatedly soften, and if he sucks back, lift the hands a little, and drive the horse forward to create a contact.

* **Don't only work on strengths and ignore weaknesses.** Take care not to spend too much time riding only in your horse's good direction. Ride an equal amount both ways to ensure that the body develops symmetrically. Focusing on strengths may make you feel more confident (or even *over*confident), but dealing with weaknesses is the point of horse training. Working through a weakness can be rewarding, and you may discover that it isn't as difficult as it appears at first glance.

* Your horse may move in an unsteady tempo, slowing and then speeding up without being asked. Try to **establish a steady tempo** in your mind—sing to yourself to establish the pace of a beat—and keep your body in that tempo for your horse to follow. Make sure you don't sing faster or slower to match your horse! Experiment with various tempos to see what works best.

* It doesn't help to practice mistakes repeatedly. **If your horse canters poorly, cantering endlessly won't improve it**. Your horse will only become confirmed in what he *can't* do well because his muscles will develop to support the incorrect movement. Then, insufficiently developed appropriate muscles are overpowered and can't overcome the effects of the incorrect influence.

* The **walk is an excellent gait for you** to learn about your horse and how to perform movements or arena patterns. Because the walk is slow, you have time to concentrate, improve your reaction time, recognize what is going on in your horse's body, and feel, analyze, and react to his evasions, resistances, or stiffnesses. In the walk, there are no bewildering effects of impulsion, power, speed, the timing of a two-beat versus a three-beat gait, or a change in direction to disrupt your concentration and coordination. Furthermore, if you can do something at the walk, you will have the mental composure and preparation to do it at the trot and canter. Situations occur faster and more pronounced at other gaits; whatever the horse did at walk, he'll probably do again in trot and canter—only bigger and faster! When you trot or canter, you will be inundated with data from the horse that you would have missed if you hadn't taken the time to internalize it at the walk. Finally, because a gait is only as good as the gait that preceded it, you shouldn't transition to another gait if the previous gait isn't good. Therefore, the walk *must* be good before moving on to the trot.

★★ **Extensions**

- It would be imprudent not to mention **"Whoa"** as a counterpoint to "Go." Your horse should definitely slow down and stop easily and willingly. Whoa can refer to a halt, a downward transition between gaits (for example, trot to walk), or a transition within gaits (going from a faster, "bigger" trot to a slower, "smaller" trot). It's not necessary to pull aggressively back on both reins to "whoa." Squeezing lightly on the outside rein in conjunction with the horse's outside front hoof touching down is an acceptable way to signal a horse to slow or stop. (Your horse may want to turn his head toward the outside; prevent this by keeping a slight wiggling pressure on the inside rein. Watch the horse's shoulders, and close your hand/fingers on the outside rein when the outside leg swings back (like looking for your posting diagonal). This is when the foot is on the ground. Note that signaling on the rein while that hoof is on the ground causes it to stay on the ground longer, thus causing the horse to slow down.

- **Don't surprise and ambush the horse with a sudden jolt to slow or halt.** To alert the horse that you want him to slow or stop, give two smaller preparatory squeezes on the outside rein across two strides, similar to using a turn signal in a car, then, on the third signal, be firmer and hold longer until he changes to a lower gait, or comes to a halt, as desired. Simultaneously, still your seat (stop moving with the horse). The horse will soon associate your still, or "retarding," seat with the need to slow or stop. Remember, the purpose of an aid is to *inform* the horse, not to actually effect the change—just like a stop sign *informs* you to stop, it doesn't grab your car and hold it still!

- How much retarding seat you use signals either "Slow down" or "Stop." Be clear about which is which. To still your seat, push your hips forward between your elbows, tighten your abdominal muscles and sit up tall, which then "braces" your lower back and your hips stop following your horse's motion. It is good to learn this so that you habitually use **your seat instead of your hands to control the horse**.

- **Don't pull hard on the reins or hold the pressure** for several strides in a row. Squeeze and release in tandem with the outside front hoof touching down, only holding the squeeze for as long as the foot is on the ground. There is no point in holding any longer because you can only affect the foot *while it is on the ground*; keeping the foot on the ground for an extra second slows the horse down. If you do this repeatedly, your horse will learn that you want to slow down or stop.

- If your horse does not respond to a light aid to slow/halt, give a stronger correction (with your body, not your hands) and come to a complete stop so he understands the message. Then, try again softly. If he does what you want, praise him; if not, slow down to halt each time until he understands. It is critical that your horse understands slow down/halt. To avoid him becoming confused, **don't waste any time between correcting your horse and immediately trying again.** You need to respond quickly or he'll forget the storyline. He may even associate your correction with something completely different, so be deliberate.

- If your horse is having trouble deciding when to stop, **riding toward the wall or fence line** provides him with a visual barrier that he understands. Let your arena help you. You will need to be attentive to keeping him going straight, so that he isn't tempted to duck left or right in order to keep going.

- **Stopping is easier on a circle**; use the inside leg to push him sideways while using the outside rein to ask him to stop. Pushing your horse out allows you to use the outside rein more effectively.

- **Your horse needs to learn to stand still and relaxed for a while**, not just halt and move off again. You may *need* to stand for a while if you are waiting politely for another horse to jump a course in the arena, if your instructor is telling you something, if you go on a trail ride and come to an obstacle of some kind, or simply for a safe dismount.

- In order to be able to "**come back to you**," or slow down, your horse needs to be able to go forward so that you have something to come back from. It is a good learning tool for your horse to go forward and come back any time you ask; so practice it. You don't have to shoot forward or come way back; nothing needs to be extreme. Think of your impulsion perhaps on a "1" to "5" scale. Trot "1" is very slow; trot "2" is a little bigger; trot "3" is your "working" trot (the trot that your particular horse finds most natural and balanced, the best trot for him based on his conformation); trot "4" is a little bigger; and trot "5" is the most forward trot possible. Work on being able to change just one level, say, from trot "3" to "2." Managing your horse's impulsion (the push off the engaged hind leg and transmission of an eager and energetic, yet controlled, propulsive thrust generated from the hindquarters into the athletic movement of the horse) up and down within a gait, from your seat, is the beginning of teaching your horse to be responsive. A tip when your horse is a little hotter and quicker is to ride him one notch slower than he "wants" to go, and if he is a little lazier and slower, ride him one notch quicker than he wants to go so he uses his hind legs and back better.

- It is your responsibility to teach your horse **what gait you want and the pace you want within it**, but the horse must continue in that way until you tell him otherwise, like cruise control. Ask him for trot number "3" ("working trot") and then stop signaling him. See how long it takes him to decide to change his tempo. If he slows down, tap him with your legs or whip to get back to your original pace; if he speeds up, squeeze on your outside rein, timed with the outside front foot, and still your seat until you get back to the original tempo. In this way, he'll learn to be consistent and remain in the rhythm/tempo/gait you request.

- Feel which way your hips are pointing: are they straight forward, or is your horse crooked and pushing them in some direction? For example, if your hips are angled to the left, his hindquarters are likely bent right, pushing your right hip forward. This means he's crooked and needs to be straightened. There are a couple of **ways to straighten**: if you want to bring the hips back to the left, squeeze on the left rein and push your left hip forward, and his hindquarters will swing left. (The hindquarters tend to go toward the side of the rein you are using.) If you want to move the shoulders over so they are in front of his hips, open the right rein and bring his shoulders over.

- Verify that the **stirrups are level and even**. Stirrup leathers stretch, so it's advisable to swap sides every month to compensate for pushing harder with one leg. You can purchase stirrup leathers with nylon inserts that prevent stretching. Obviously, maintaining a level seat is ideal.

Study Guide

Applying Intellectual Standards to Riding Terminology

❖ Scan and print the "USDF Glossary of Judging Terms" in Appendix I (p. 282).

❖ Cut the document into strips, one for each definition. Place them in a zip-close bag.

❖ Scan and print the Intellectual Standards in Appendix II (p. 288).

❖ Cut the Standards and their related questions into strips and put them into a different zip-bag. (You may separate the questions or leave them in groupings of three. To adequately address a definition, you may even need to incorporate all three questions.)

❖ Extract one riding term from the USDF Glossary bag and one Standard with its question or questions from the other.

❖ According to the question drawn, elaborate on the riding definition with that Standard. Note: You may need to modify the question slightly so that it makes sense.

EXAMPLE:

USDF Definition

Seat: *The rider's trunk, which includes the pelvis, spine, and rib cage, with supporting musculature. The control of the seat determines the dynamic influence*

Study Guide
Applying Intellectual Standards to Riding Terminology

and balance of the rider and harmony with the horse's movement within each gait and exercise.

Intellectual Standard and Questions

Depth: *What are some of the complexities of this problem? What are some of the challenges we must overcome? What factors make this a difficult problem?*

Modified to: *What are some of the complexities associated with seat control that affect the horse's movement within each gait and exercise? What biomechanical aspects of the rider's pelvis, spine, rib cage, and supporting musculature need to be adjusted in order to improve that person's seat? How does the seat influence the rider's dynamic influence and balance, as well as the rider's harmony with the horse's movements?*

SAMPLE ANSWER:

Ideally, riding a horse is analogous to a "closed system" in biology, in which energy cannot escape. The horse's hind legs create energy and it is up to the rider's "seat" to contain and direct it. However, in reality, riding is more like "entropy," the gradual decline into chaos and disorder. Energy created by the horse leaks out everywhere it can. In the rider, it leaks out anywhere the rider is unstable, through:

- Swinging legs.
- A nodding head.
- A bobbling back.
- Flapping arms.
- Loose reins.

And energy is persistent! If it can't get out through shoulders, it will find its way out the elbows or the wrists or the fingers, and so forth. In the horse, energy leaks out when the horse:

- Becomes crooked.
- "Pops" a shoulder.
- Loses balance.
- Resists.
- Sucks back/runs through.
- Gets hollow.
- Falls in/drifts out.

Study Guide

Applying Intellectual Standards to Riding Terminology

It is the rider's responsibility to maintain the centered stability of her core, allowing the pelvis to move with the horse, so the upper body, head, and extremities remain stable and the horse's energy does not flow through and out of them like smoke from a chimney. The rider must also maintain the horse's alignment, connection, balance, and "throughness" (the connected and willing mental and physical state that enables your aids to influence the horse's entire body) so the energy remains contained in the horse's body between the hind legs (via the bit/reins) and the rider's core. Only in this manner can the rider channel the horse's energy, resulting in forward, elastic, and swinging gaits.

Such rich questions related to the terminology we regularly use as riders provide you with plenty of food for thought and are a tool to help you generate insightful questions whose answers will significantly expand your knowledge. You can delve deeper into a definition by posing additional questions from other standards. ●

Chapter

GET CONNECTED

_06

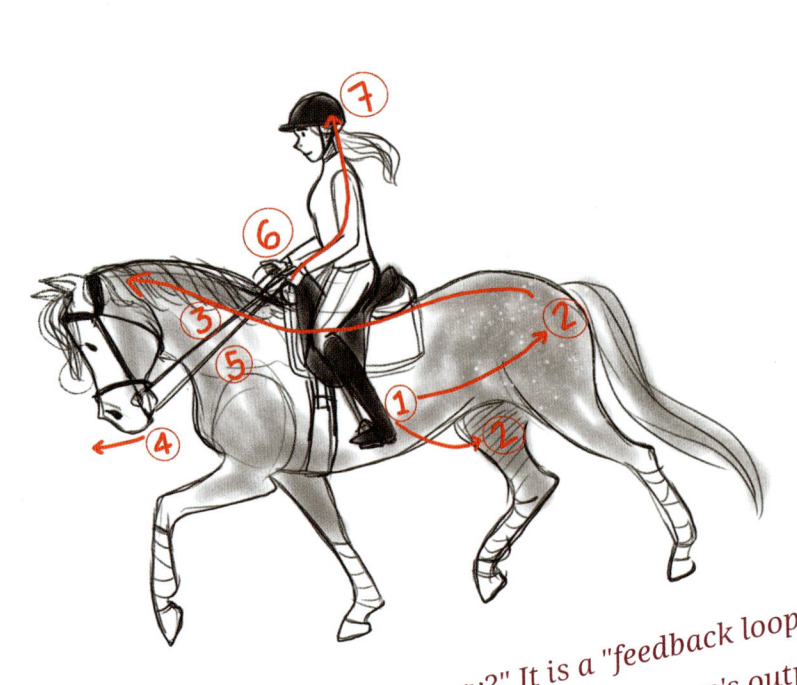

What is the "circle of energy?" It is a "feedback loop"! A feedback loop is a process in which a system's outputs are re-circulated and repurposed as inputs; the feedback provides information to which the rider or horse responds in turn.

The circle/cycle of energy originates with the (1) rider's legs (input to horse), which induce the horse to move his (2) hind legs (output). When the horse's hind legs propel the (3) entire body forward, (4) the bit moves forward in space along with the horse. When the horse moves forward enough in response to the leg stimulus, he will pick up the slack in the (5) reins (as long as they aren't too long) as a result of the bit's forward movement. The (positive) tension on the reins further increases as the horse extends his neck due to the lifting of the spine caused by the hind legs stepping forward under his body. The rider can then feel this connection in the reins with (6) her hands (output of horse is input to rider) and determine (7) from this input whether to send the horse forward with (1 again) the leg or to ease off on the driving aid.

6.1 Connection. Renowned German judge and trainer Christoph Hess describes connection as "energy from behind flowing through the whole body of the horse, into the mouth." In this photograph of Jim Koford riding the Hanoverian Envoy, the connection between Jim and Envoy is unmistakable. The horse's hindquarters propel the horse forward, energizing the horse's body. •

Being "connected" to your horse is the most fundamental form of communication, upon which everything evolves. In its simplest iteration, it just means that a relaxed, forward-moving horse is going into the bridle and taking the rider's hand in a forward-and-downward direction, feeling like a fish drawing on a line. The reins are neither tight nor drooping; they remain "just right" because the rider follows the horse's natural movement. "Connection," or being "on the bit," is tricky to implement because of its complexity and *all the factors that easily derail it*. This chapter delves into various aspects of connection to provide the rider with a more thorough understanding of the concept (fig. 6.1).

In the pages that follow, I attempt to both interpret and provide a pragmatic and systematic way of attaining and using that connection. Revisit this section after you finish the book and see if you gain additional clarity on second glance.

Connection Theory: The Circuit

Connection is important because it allows both you and the horse to feel slight changes in the reins for exchange of information. You can feel if your horse stiffens, changes bend, or backs off. Your horse can feel you asking for flexion, change of direction, and half-halts. The more sensitive and consistent the connection, the smaller the change that can be detected by either party, and the quicker something can be done about it before it becomes an issue. If connection is lost, no such communication can occur.

Connection is hard to understand until you feel it and what it can do for you. It will come and go until you learn to proactively maintain it. Once you learn how to create it and recognize it, the horse will be promptly responsive. It won't take much to direct him to what you want to do, or where you want to go.

Connection between horse and rider is dependent on a "circuit" that unites both bodies into a single unit. A circuit is a circular journey beginning and ending at the same place. In electronics, a circuit is a closed path that allows electricity to flow from one point to another. In riding, the horse's forward energy is analogous to electricity, and the horse's hindquarters serve as the start and end point of this circular path: The horse pushes from behind, giving the rider a connection with the horse through the reins, allowing her to use them to influence the horse as she encourages him to shift

The Importance of Riding Back-to-Front

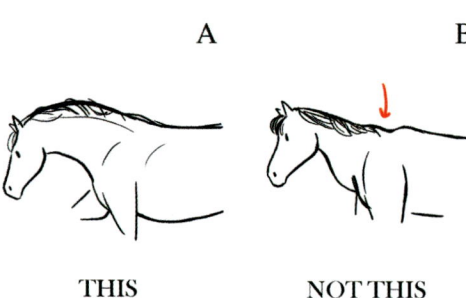
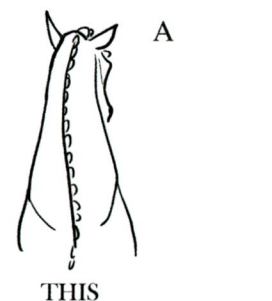

A — THIS B — NOT THIS   A — THIS B — NOT THIS

6.2 A & B Dip In Base of Neck. A horse's muscular development reveals a lot about his training. Using impulsion to connect the horse's hind legs to the rider's contact with the bit, properly trained horses raise the back like a suspension bridge. This produces a topline that is "round," broad at the base of the neck, with soft, loose neck muscles **(A)**. In contrast, front-to-back (pulling) riding causes the horse's muscles to develop improperly. The horse will have an overdeveloped underneck and a depression at the base of the neck just in front of the withers **(B)**. •

6.3 A & B Neck Bulge. The width at the base of the neck (seen from the saddle) is indicative of the horse's back's strength as it extends from the hindquarters to the neck and poll. The muscles in front of the withers should be at least as wide as those closer to the poll **(A)**. The muscles beneath the neck should be loose and supple. Riding "front to back" results in a neck that bulges in the middle, or near the poll, as opposed to being wider at the base **(B)**. •

The phrases "riding a horse front-to-back" (bad) and "riding a horse back-to-front" (good) describe opposing methods of rein contact with the horse. As we have already touched on, front-to-back indicates that the rider is pulling the horse's head and neck back toward her in an effort to artificially shape the horse's front end, with little regard for what is occurring behind the saddle. The restraints outweigh the driving aids. It can also result from the rider pulling on the reins to slow the horse (or simply holding on) rather than using a stilled seat (see p. 110). Front-to-back has a negative impact on the horse's balance, relaxation, and ultimately, physical development and mental state. Since the horse is not permitted to use his body correctly, he will experience discomfort, which will lead to tension, and his muscles will develop improperly. Horses often react to front-to-back riding by either curling the neck to escape the contact or fighting the pressure by lifting the head well above the bit, inverting the neck. This causes an overdeveloped underneck, a dip at the base of the neck just in front of the withers (figs. 6.2 A & B), and a neck that bulges thickly in the middle or up by the poll instead of being wide at the base as it should be (figs. 6.3 A & B). The horse's neck "breaks" at the third vertebrae, as opposed to having a smooth arch from withers to ears. The resultant gaits are uncomfortable because the hind legs are neither up underneath the horse nor flexed at the joints, and shock absorption is lost. There is no "swing" (springy stride).

his weight back onto his hind legs. This causes the joints of the hind end to bend deeply so that there is more spring when they straighten, resulting in more power for the next push forward, completing the circuit and maintaining the connection through the next stride. The horse won't lose energy if this circuit is maintained and the flow isn't broken; thus, the rider won't need to constantly make corrections or re-establish energy.

The horse's hind end propels the entire horse forward, taking the bit in the mouth forward along with him. The horse's momentum, causing the bit to advance, exerts force on the reins and thus the rider's hands. Connection occurs *as a result of this push from the rear*. In this way, the reins act as "data cables," informing the rider about the amount of force (or lack thereof) emanating from the horse's hind end and the horse's willingness to make contact. It's great if the horse takes the reins forward and downward. When the reins are too loose, however, this "data" informs the rider's hands that the horse isn't moving forward enough and needs to be pushed to re-establish that connection.

Issues with connection are rooted in "slackness" in the reins. Either the horse or the rider can introduce slack to the scenario, but it is the horse that must advance the bit/reins, as requested by the rider with the cue for *forward*. However, humans are driven by a primal inclination to secure looseness in the reins by *pulling back on them*, which interferes with the horse's forwardness, suppleness, energy, and good nature. The result is what is referred to as "riding front to back," while the preferred method is "back to front" (where the horse is pushed forward into the bridle, as I've described).

Why does this matter so much? It matters because the powerful hindquarters are the driving

The Importance of Riding Back-to-Front

Riding back-to-front, however, is what establishes that desirable connection we have been discussing. The horse's hindquarters propel him forward so that he takes the bit and contact, and the rider follows. The energy flows from the back to the front, and the entire topline is round with an elevated abdomen.

force behind a horse's forward motion. As the *back* of the horse propels the *front* of the horse forward, the sensation of the bit being carried forward with him is experienced as positive tension on the reins, *created by the horse*. In this way, the power generated behind is transmitted to the rider's hands...*if* the hands are duly prepared to receive it. *Receiving and maintaining this energy is connection.* When connection exists, the channel for communication between horse and rider is open.

However, when the horse is not forward or when your hands and reins are slack, little energy is generated, and the energy that *is* generated is wasted because there is nothing to capture it and use it to produce more. Consider the energy flow in a power plant: coal combustion and nuclear reactions produce heat. This heat boils water to create steam, which is then channeled into a cylinder to spin a turbine, generating electricity. This electricity is stored in a "grid," which consists of substations, transformers, and power lines that connect the electricity producer to the consumer who uses it to turn on the lights or operate an air conditioner. Similarly, the hindquarters ("turbine") of the horse push off the ground and send energy through the horse, where it is caught in the hands and body of the rider (the "substation"), who then channels that energy through aids ("power lines") to whichever maneuver the horse will do. However, if the rider doesn't harness or channel the energy, it dissipates like steam in the wind, and is lost. *Connection* is lost.

How Do You Catch the Circuit Energy?

Olympic dressage rider Jane Savoie provided an effective analogy to help understand how to use the hands to catch the energy generated by the hindquarters of the horse: Think of the reins, or your connection, like a balloon. Your driving aids push the horse forward, like air inflating a balloon. When you feel the horse produce tautness on the reins, "closing your outside hand in a fist puts a knot at the end of it to keep [the balloon] full of air." Keeping the balloon full of air is what keeps the connection; connection is the only thing that enables you to communicate with the horse. To keep this "full balloon feeling," you must keep the horse moving energetically forward so that his momentum maintains the connection. However, the horse shouldn't go faster; he needs to go *bigger*. Think of the rein in your outside hand like a barrier. He goes into the barrier, like he's trotting with his forehead against a wall. Then, you have potential energy to tap into for anything. He needs to stay yielding and soft into your inside hand, and his body comes up as you ask for more effort. This is a wonderful feeling—like cantering up a hill—because the horse is responsive and willing *because he is able*. He's not plowing through the bridle and pulling downhill.

To encourage your horse to remain forward, put your hands *slightly* forward, so he has to push and reach forward "to arrive at them." To encourage him to arrive at your hand, you must exert the same amount of force with your seat and legs as you give with your hands. When your driving aid and your pushing hands aren't equal, slack is introduced: if you drive too much and don't catch it, the energy escapes out the front like air leaking from a balloon; if you hold too much and don't drive enough, the horse slows down, backs off the bridle, and loses energy, like tying a knot in that balloon *before* you inflate it. The latter is *front-to-back riding*, where pulling on the front "chokes off" the energy from the back. The hind legs never have the opportunity to generate impulsion.

Don't be tempted to adjust slack yourself; doing so causes the horse to slow down, lose energy, and lose the ability to communicate. Fiddling with the reins distracts you from focusing on forward, disrupts your position and allows the horse to get away with not taking the bridle forward. Make the horse do it. The more you cover for the horse, the more he will exploit slack. As suggested by Jane Savoie, say to the horse, "Go forward until you meet my hand, and then stay there. My hand is not going away and you need to get used to that." In this way, you keep the balloon filled with air.

The forward press into the hand is as vital and obligatory to riding as treading water is to swimming. To accomplish this, the rider must maintain a firm core while allowing her legs to drape against the horse's side. You must maintain the horse's energy and connection through your seat, legs, and hands. If you allow your position to deteriorate, the energy will dissipate like air from a leaking balloon.

Circuit Breakers

Think of the circuit I've described like the children's game "Pass the Pulse" in which participants stand in a circle and hold hands. One person begins the "pulse" by squeezing the hand of the person on either her left or right side. Once that new person feels the squeeze, she then squeezes the hand of her neighbor and so forth, until the pulse returns to the originator, completing the circuit. When a wire comes loose at any point in an electrical circuit, or when two people quit holding hands in the "Pass the Pulse" game, the circuit is broken and that flow of energy instantly and completely ends. Likewise, if the horse's hind legs don't push, or slack occurs in the reins, the riding circuit is broken and connection as desired is lost.

Contact with the horse's mouth disappears instantly with slack in the reins. He can't feel what your hands are doing, and more importantly, *you* can't feel him. With regard to connection, this is like someone in the children's game who doesn't give a squeeze. No pulse, no energy, no circuit. With the circuit broken, there is no communication between horse and rider. When there is no communication, you won't have functional transitions, straightness, steering, or suppleness—and the horse won't push from behind in order to go forward.

Contact vs. Connection

While the terms contact and connection aren't interchangeable, they *are* interrelated. *Contact* is a sensation in your hands caused by the tactile relationship between the rider's hands and the horse's mouth via the bit and reins. Contact gives horses a sense of support. You should maintain an even contact with the horse's mouth using both reins in a soft manner that does not interfere with his head or neck position and follows the horse's movement.

Contact is touch with a single location. Connection (to join, link, or fasten together) implies that *several* locations are cooperating and moving as one because they are linked. Under the guidance of the rider, the horse learns to initiate, maintain, and respond to connection. Connection and contact are a result of the horse stretching his head and neck forward and down, which generates some degree of traction on the reins, thus forming a link, or "feel," with the rider's hands. To accomplish this, the horse needs to have an active stride so that there is energy to "catch" in the hands. The rider follows this pull on the reins from the horse with proportionate "give"; it can help to visualize the triceps of the arm pushing forward the same amount the horse takes. Move you arms like you are offering a tray of hors d'oeuvres to someone. Conversely—*and this is critical*—the rider does not pull back to create contact; the biceps don't curl like you are using free weights.

Throughout the entirety of a ride, one should endeavor to remain cognizant of *giving*, not taking. It is *very* easy to switch to pulling on the reins without realizing it. The difference between pulling and giving can be a very subtle change in mental imagery. Think of "pushing" the horse's head away from you. You will find that you must be stable in your core in order to push your hands forward (hands

6.4 Following. When the horse reaches his head and neck forward and down, causing some traction on the reins and forming a link, or "feel," with the rider's hands, contact and connection are established. Consider your arms to be springs that give and take with the horse's head, absorbing the motion. Your hands "belong to the horse."

Connection, Shifting Weight, and Balance

Balance is a critical piece of connection. Rien van der Schaft, trainer of the Dutch National Dressage Team, states on his website DressagePro.com, "When you start a horse, you ride it in its natural balance and take a soft contact and ride the horse forward into the bridle so the horse is activated from behind; the energy flows through the body into the hand...Don't try to put them in a frame; as soon as the horse trusts the hand, he'll lay his neck forward in our hands. From that stage on, we can try to get the horse more divided in his weight over four legs, bit by bit, using little turns and lateral movements."

Van der Schaft emphatically notes that the rider "receives the connection" from the horse; she *doesn't* pull on the reins to create the position of his head. Van der Shaft's message is that "you want to focus on the balance of the horse rather than a posture," that riders are "inclined to create a posture" in a horse when, in reality, the posture changes over time as a result of gradual shifting of the balance back to the hindquarters. Van der Schaft warns that "when the rider only elevates the head and neck, the back drops and the horse can't use his body correctly."

Connection enables the rider to affect the balance of the horse over time in order to establish the most effective communication and function. A pretty shape doesn't create a good horse; rather, proper independent of seat). If you find that you are pulling, your body is deriving stability from the reins, or they are too long.

Reins exist as an extension of your arm to be able to reach the bit in order to communicate with the horse. When there is tension on a rein, you have "contact" (touch) with the horse's mouth. Beware: contact can be erratic or consistent, soft or hard, even or uneven, long or short. When you have *too much* contact, you inhibit the horse and encourage him to lean on the reins—if you pull, he pulls. When you don't *have enough* contact because the reins or your arms are limp, the energy from the hindquarters "leaks out"; the circuit is broken. Then, you have to start over by adding leg.

This is where the concept of "recycling" the energy comes in: maintaining a consistent contact—holding the energy steady in your hands and not allowing it to escape—keeps the circuit closed so that the energy you created in the horse by driving him forward isn't lost. This allows you to ride without constantly urging the horse forward, similar to coasting. Do not allow parts of your body to nod, swing or rock, as these movements also allow energy to escape. A rider's body can serve as a conduit for energy to dissipate from the horse, as the flexibility of the torso or head allows for the release of energy, similar to steam from a smokestack or a leak in a hose. To maintain the horse-and-rider circuit, it is necessary to maintain "human self-carriage" and absorb the horse's motion solely through the movement of the pelvis.

Contact vs. Connection

In the April 6, 2021, article entitled "The Difference Between Contact and Connection," TheRefinedRider.com presents the notion that connection is like riding a bicycle:

> **The horse is the same as the bicycle. The horse's rear end is pushing the front end, just like a bicycle's rear wheel pushes the front wheel. With your hands on the handlebars, you feel the front of the bike being pushed freely forward into your hands, just from that simple press on the pedal. The same goes for your horse. You put your leg on to signal the horse to start his engine. Then that energy that's created with the hind end will travel over his back, through his neck and to your hands. It's all connected.**

gymnastic development over time, through being able to move in many ways, creates the pretty shape.

Shifting Weight Back

Why does shifting the weight back matter so much?

❖ By redistributing the weight to the hind legs, they are compelled to bend more, resulting in a spring-like action that propels the horse forward in the subsequent step, thereby preserving the connection. Otherwise the horse will pull himself along from the front legs, putting even more strain on those fragile, over-taxed limbs.

❖ As already discussed, horses naturally carry most of their weight on the front legs. They are designed to graze, so they have that heavy neck and head hanging off the front end of their body. However, most athletic riding efforts, such as jumping or a sliding stop, necessitate a horse transfer this weight to the hind end, freeing up the shoulders. Horses must be taught how to do this on command.

❖ Further, and more importantly, if the horse spends his life putting most of the weight and impact on his comparatively slender front legs, he won't stay sound. The bending joints of the powerful hindquarters are better equipped to support the weight of the horse.

❖ When a horse is carrying his weight on his front end, his hind joints will not be optimally flexed and this stiffness will feel rougher to ride because there is no opportunity for shock absorption through the bending of the joints of the hind legs. The rider gets bounced and it is difficult to move with the horse.

❖ The horse rushes because he's not balanced. It's like being dragged down a steep ramp by a runaway wheelbarrow loaded with bricks. Imbalance is not an enjoyable ride.

Connection Isn't Automatic…or Easy

Why is "getting connected" so difficult? Connection is difficult to teach a horse because it is not his natural default; the process is physically demanding and horses resist. Furthermore, it must be taught in stages that are actually *counter-intuitive.* Ironically, horses must first learn to move their head and neck forward and down before they can learn to shift their weight back and lift their front end for more advanced work. To guide them as a rider, you must comprehend and be capable of doing what is correct.

Learning to prevent slack in the reins is the first step toward becoming connected. Ideally, the horse eliminates the slack in the reins by maintaining his forward energy and posture. Furthermore, you must be mindful of keeping him forward, while not creating slack yourself. Neither should you develop inhibitory tension in your body and reins. The key is that the horse has to learn to maintain connection *intentionally and consistently.* Therefore, the rider has to teach the horse to keep the slack out of the reins of his own accord by first learning to extend his neck down and out in order to *keep the nose advancing forward when the rider eases off on the rein.* The rider simultaneously pushes the horse more forward in order to assist (or remind) the horse with maintaining the connection.

Merely putting his head down, however, isn't enough; he's not "on the bit," he's just "down." He has to "step through" ("Go") and push off the ground with the hind legs with enough forward impulsion/energy to literally push his body, his head, and thus, the bit forward through space "into your hands." This push forward adds (positive) tension to the reins, which is how your hands feel it, initiating and maintaining contact. You want the horse to be taking your hands (bit/reins) forward, much like water skiing, where the boat pulls the person. If the boat slows, the line goes slack and the skier sinks. When the horse loses "forwardness," or loses a steady rhythm to his stride, the reins go slack, the

6.5 A & B Bowed Longe Whip. You can experience the effect of connection with a longe whip: While holding the lash in one hand like a rein, push on the handle grip with the other, as if your seat and legs are driving the hindquarters of the horse forward. Not only will you feel the connection develop in your rein hand holding the lash, the body of the whip will arch up and bow, just like your horse's back will come up **(A)**. However, if you let the lash slide through your fingers, you will feel the connection dissolve and vanish, and the whip will straighten, just like the horse's back will drop when you lose connection with his mouth **(B)**.

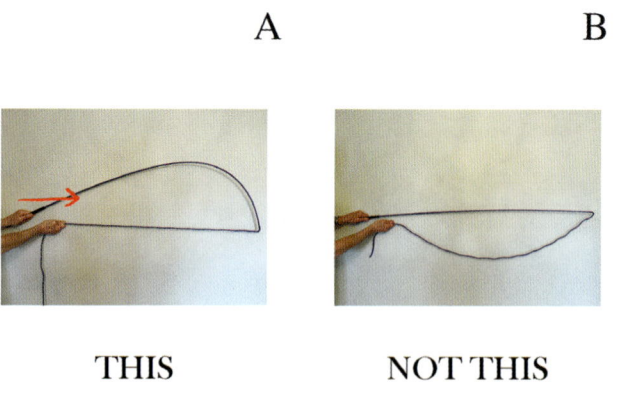

A   B

THIS   NOT THIS

Scan to View Longe Whip Demo of Connection

horse's back sinks, and the rider will feel the loss of positive tension/connection. Therefore, "Go" is a big part of staying connected. When there's not forward momentum, you may discover that you are pulling your hands back to regain the connection, and this further impedes the momentum you need.

In short, contact/connection is a paradox: you give the reins forward so the horse can follow the hands. But the horse has to be going forward energetically in order to produce the energy that you will "catch" through the medium of the reins. The horse has to understand that, like the boat pulling the water skier, keeping the positive tension on the reins is *his* job. Once the horse irrevocably understands that every time you give the rein he reacts by reaching his nose forward, then you can gradually shorten the reins to any length because he takes the bit forward regardless of the rein length or height of his head. Thus, he perpetually "seeks the contact." While it is important for the horse to seek contact by moving forward and downward, it is equally critical for the rider to develop responsive and skillful hands that not only sense and respond to the reins but use them to signal the horse in order to ride him proficiently. It's a two-way street: putting an inexperienced person on a horse that is skilled and knowledgeable in his role *does not guarantee* contact *or* connection.

Harnessing the Energy for Connection

Ultimately, "caught energy," or resulting positive tension on the reins, allows you to communicate with the horse because of the connection created, especially on the outside rein. You can move your fingers/hand/wrist/arm/back (depending on your level of skill, the maneuver you are doing, or the response you would like from the horse) *with* or *against* (a "half-halt"—see p. 259) this contact, in various ways, to tell him different things, such as: turn, straighten the body, stay upright, slow down, take smaller steps, lift the front end, and so on.

This "caught energy" unites the horse's front and back end, while the hindquarters keep pushing, causing the horse's back to arch up. You can experience this "energy" and the resulting arch with a longe whip: While holding the lash steady like a rein in one hand, push on the handle grip with the other. You will feel the resulting positive tension in the hand holding the lash, as if it were a rein. The body of the whip will arch up and bow (figs. 6.5 A & B). This is what your horse's back needs to do so that his whole body participates in movement. This position also means that the long muscle of the back (the *longissimus dorsi*) relaxes and lengthens, and the ride will be much more comfortable and elastic for the rider. The horse will be able to step up under his belly with his hind legs and support the weight of the rider more efficiently.

Let the lash slide through your fingers and you will feel the connection vanish. Without connection, that long back muscle contracts and shortens, the horse's head goes up, causing the back to sink, and the rider is sitting more directly on the spine; the horse can get injured carrying a rider in this way. On the other hand, when the horse is relaxed, the head is down and the hind legs are pushing from behind, the back muscle gets "puffed up," cushioning the spine, and the rider sits on muscle.

Avoid the trap of only riding what is in front of you. It's *not* just about the head and neck being down, or a headset, or a horse looking "round"; it's about having drive and steady rhythm from the hind legs (via the circuit) to bring the back up.

Establishing Contact

Creating contact is similar to painting, where layers of color are added one at a time. An artist starts with a "wash," a featureless background made of diluted paint. As additional paint is added, an identifiable image emerges. Likewise, when training a horse, the first steps toward contact also do not reveal the final picture.

Riders are often overly concerned with what onlookers are thinking and become tempted to desperately pull the horse into a false "frame" (topline, outline, shape) to appear more competent, or to hastily make the horse look "attractive." Manufacturing a bogus frame causes riders to ride "front-to-back," forcefully pulling the front of the horse back toward his body, curling up his neck and causing his back to sink, or become "hollow."

Force without comprehension is detrimental to your horse's psyche. Don't sacrifice your horse just because someone is watching. You are laying the foundation and investing in the future. Instead, remain resolute on riding "back-to-front," pushing the horse forward from the hind legs and following with your hands or, as Rien van der Schaft declares, "Ride the horse's body to his head; don't ride his head to the body." Laying this "wash" can indeed include unattractive, distorted shapes while the horse learns to move from an unstable contact to a consistent one. The stage only lasts a short time. Soon enough, your "finished painting" will be unveiled.

Instant Contact: Widen the Reins

To introduce basic contact, take up the reins and spread your hands like you are reading a print magazine or newspaper until enough tautness occurs that all slack is removed (figs. 6.6 A & B). Widening and narrowing the hands as needed is preferable to frantically lengthening and shortening the reins because spreading the hands *removes slack instantly.* It's far more efficient than trying to frequently adjust the reins when the horse's head moves around. The quickest way to keep up with his movement is to widen (then narrow when he returns to a good position) to the various extents needed until he realizes that he can't avoid the contact and it doesn't hurt. Being quick to adjust to the horse's movement without losing contact is important because it teaches your horse that contact is always present, no matter what he does.

As an added perk, widening the reins creates a "funnel shape" from your arms to the bit, which helps straighten the horse's body/spine by not allowing the neck to divert left or right. If the bit is the narrowest point of the funnel, the horse has to go that direction. If you keep the funnel (nose/bit) in the center of his chest (equidistant from each shoulder), the horse will travel straight. You need to be attentive to make sure his nose *stays* centered on his chest because horses look around or resist carrying themselves in that position. This is the beginning of "alignment" of the body. Therefore, it is useful to realize that widening addresses two issues at once: not only does it help maintain connection, it straightens a crooked horse.

While widening the hands, simultaneously "embrace" the horse with the entire length of your legs. Apply an amount of pressure that feels like you are hugging someone. This driving aid invites the horse to go forward. Your horse may hesitate or take halting steps. The instant he moves, take your legs off as a reward. He will also probably drop his head. As soon as he does that, narrow your hands and follow

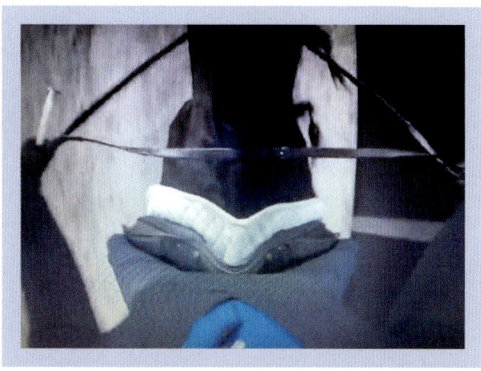

6.6 A & B Widen and Squeeze. To introduce a rudimentary form of contact, take up the reins and spread your hands as if you were reading a print magazine or newspaper **(A)**. Widening the reins is a quick and effective way to eliminate slack and maintain contact without pulling on the reins. As you can see in the from-the-saddle view taken by a GoPro, you may need to spread your hands much farther than you think, sometimes even past your knees **(B)**. Occasionally, the horse will only slacken one rein, in which case you may only need to spread ("open") one rein. To manage slack in the reins, you will make frequent widening and narrowing adjustments, similar to playing an accordion.

Scan to View Intro to Widen and Squeeze

him down; try to maintain contact. Don't give too much so that the reins are loose and contact is lost. Push again with your legs so he moves forward into the bridle. JP Giacomini explains: "The first step in this process is to teach the horse to stretch his neck out as far as it will go in the walk. It is an absolute rule of optimized locomotion for the riding horse. When that occurs, the horse will advance his front legs 'to carry his nose.' His hind legs will match the front legs as a reciprocal reflex and engage under the body."

Don't rush your horse. Avoid the common tendency of drawing your legs back or bending your knees so much that they approach the saddle pad. Visualize more that you are a boa constrictor encircling the horse's rib cage, as opposed to a cobra striking with your heel. Be mindful of what you actually teach the horse! Only train in a manner which derives the result that you seek. If you don't want to spend your riding life kicking yourself into exhaustion and deadening your horse's sides, teach your horse to move off from only that simple squeeze. Be patient. After a few tries he'll understand. Horses don't automatically know that kicking means go, so don't make it your default from the outset.

A further note on the futility of kicking: Kicking causes the rider's seat, leg, back, and hip muscles to contract and tighten. The horse's back is a mirror of the rider's, so if your back is tight, so is your horse's. If the horse's back is tight, it is "blocked" and his hind legs can't move freely, so the horse will be disinclined to move. Kicking your horse is counterproductive.

The Head Drop

Be prepared that "widen and squeeze" might not work on the first try. It may seem like your horse isn't going to respond, but in reality it probably takes about 10 to 20 seconds for him to react. Keep equivalent pressure on both reins while your hands are spread, and on his sides with your legs. As soon as the horse moves or drops his head, even if it's just a smidgen, release both pressures to reward him. If you release both reins and legs as soon as he reciprocates by dropping his head *and* walking forward, the horse will connect his action with your release and learn to repeat the response. Note: When you release the pressure, don't give so much that the reins are loose. Don't *remove* the pressure; just *reduce* it. Learn to soften without throwing the contact away.

To reduce the pressure, narrow your arms a bit or give them forward a centimeter. It is an almost imperceptible difference in the reins, but the horse will feel it and that's the objective. Try imagining that you are holding an egg on a spider web, and you must set it down *very* carefully. To keep his head from simply dropping, only lower his neck as much as you release, and urge him forward exactly that much as well, so that the contact in your hand is generated by *your* legs moving his hind legs to push forward as much as you asked. It's that circuit we talked about: give "X," push "X," and the horse moves the bit forward "X." This way, you can generate how much forward you want, how much connection you want, and how much reach (with the nose) you want.

You will know that you have succeeded in teaching this *rudimentary* understanding of contact when you can lengthen the reins and the horse follows them down, seeking to keep the contact of his own volition. Eventually, you will be able to feel a steady contact and maintain that for the entire ride, with minimal adjustments from you. You will learn to think about contact in degrees, or dosages. You will figure out what amounts to give and take and how to push the horse forward with your leg so that he lifts his back and lengthens his neck. If you squeeze with your legs when you give, to help your horse step up to the bit and come more onto the contact, you will feel the horse surge forward just that little bit, taking a longer stride. This is good because he's reaching up under himself.

Scan to View Seeking the Contact Down

The Key to Connection? Patience

Avoid the temptation to pump your seat, kick, seesaw on the reins, or any number of pathologies your impatient mind will want to contrive in order to get the horse to hurry up and comply. *Just wait.* Don't let up on the reins or leg signals until your horse does what you want, which is walking calmly forward with his head lowered. At first, the horse doesn't have any idea of what you want and will try a variety of other responses (look left or right, lift the head, squirm). Ignore everything but the thing you want, which is for him to drop his head, even if it is only one inch the first time. As soon as the head and neck lower, reduce the pressure. Remember: you are just turning the volume down, not turning it off. It is imperative for you to be exceptionally attentive to even the tiniest response so that you can reward the horse *instantly*. The immediate reduction of pressure lets the horse know that he has done something right. You have just broken the communication barrier; you are both speaking the same language!

Unfortunately, it is common for people to *completely* miss that their horse has lowered his head, even when obvious, and they continue applying pressure, oblivious to the fact the horse has made an attempt to respond. *He* knows he's done something; do you? After a number of these attempts (it might be two, it might be fifty), the horse will catch on and drop his head immediately with your aids. Also, be sure not to release at any other time, or he'll think that *his incorrect response* is what you want!

To get to this point, you will need to determine how much widening and how much positive tension you need on the reins (see "Rein Pressure" section—p. 140) to accomplish your goal. Expect that this will change as your horse learns. He'll progress to where he responds to nearly imperceptible aids because he knows what is expected, but this will only come to pass if you are consistent and release at the appropriate moment *every single time* without fail. Don't confuse the horse by being inconsistent. If you only ask for cooperation sometimes, your horse won't know when to respond and when not. Keep in mind that you ultimately want to give as little signal as possible so that your horse doesn't think that harsh cues are what are required. Train in the cues you want to ride; don't set yourself up for having to work hard.

The majority of horses walk off right away, but some linger, or are perplexed or stubborn. The motionless horse won't stand there for six months, but if you are convinced he has irrevocably turned into a "concrete pony" after a few minutes, you can tap lightly with the whip at the same time. This is why you *widen* **and** *squeeze*. After a few hesitant tries, your horse will tentatively begin to understand both of these requirements. Repeat a few times until his confidence builds and you both are sure that you are getting what you want, and in a relaxed manner.

It is advisable to stop the lesson in contact and connection as soon as you are feeling reasonably confident that you and the horse understand. It is better to do a few attempts that are really good and quit. Here's why:

- The horse might respond just a little differently each time and if you don't notice and respond, he'll be confused.

- The more times you do something, the more variability can creep in.

- Horses are "latent learners," which means they process information while they "sleep on it," and the skill you need is expressed much better the next day rather than at the actual time of learning. This is thought to be the result of the horse's brain needing time to construct new neural pathways. Also, if your horse tends to be one of these "concrete ponies," don't be surprised if he starts out the second day (and the third, and the fourth...) with the same behavior. You will notice that he resists for shorter and shorter periods of time until, one day, it's just gone, and he moves forward and into the contact freely and immediately.

The Kinesthetic Conundrum: Being Sure You Know What Contact and Connection Feel Like

You already know that you are not supposed to pull back on the reins, nor should you force and hold your horse's head in a position. You already know that he is supposed to move forward into the contact. But how can you know whether you are doing it correctly, whether your horse is doing it correctly, or whether either of you are doing anything at all? What does what you want *feel* like? The inherent problem is that this fundamental of riding communication falls under the purview of *kinesthetic learning*, which means that *you learn something through physically doing it.* With no other tangible input beyond your awareness of the position and movements of your body and your horse's body through sensation, *you* have to deduce what feels "right" from what doesn't.

While it helps to ride a "schoolmaster" (an experienced and well-trained horse) who is confirmed in contact and connection in order to *experience the feel you are seeking*, success on your own horse can remain elusive due to lack of coordination, conceptual misunderstandings, unconscious riding habits, insensitivity, or insecurities, all piled on top of having to overcome any dysfunctional patterns you may have already unwittingly established with him, but that are comfortable and familiar for you both. In addition, a schoolmaster's assistance is limited because every horse feels different and no horse provides a "free ride." Since horses are input/output creatures, if your input has shortcomings, you may not obtain the desired output. But, at least you will gain a useful inkling of the path ahead.

Furthermore, riding a schoolmaster can be perplexing because it may not feel like you anticipated. One of the biggest surprises is that the horse is not as "light" as the rider might imagine. One hears a lot about "lightness in the hand," but lightness, or "softness," doesn't necessarily mean that connection should be like gossamer.

What Is "Soft"?

One of the most important facets in any interaction with your horse is "softness." People confuse the word "light" with "soft." They are not synonymous!

"Soft" means the horse is *willingly responsive, doing what you ask with no resistance or negative tension.* Soft is what we are after. "Light" means that you don't have to use a lot of pressure to get a response, but it does not necessarily imply willingness. Some horses learn to *avoid* a rider by never taking a contact with the bit, so that the reins always feel light. The horse is simply shutting you out to defend himself from unsteady or insensitive hands by holding an artificial posture. This pose fools people because the horse looks pretty and feels "light" in the hand, but there is no actual communication or control.

When your horse is yielding to your aids, he is not resisting. On a rein, it may feel as if you are pulling an apple or watermelon on a string. There may be some "heaviness," but there is no opposition. He yields easily to your request. When a horse is "light," it may feel more like a marshmallow. When a horse resists, his head/neck will feel more like a watermelon skewered onto a rigid pole, or a dog on a leash chasing a squirrel while you hang on in vain. The horse may even attempt to wrench the reins from your grasp, dislodging your seat from the saddle.

The mental state of the horse contributes to softness in the body. When your horse understands what is expected of him, he becomes less anxious and more eager to perform. He only displays resistance when he is confused.

The goal is for a horse to be steady and straight on the outside rein and softly yielding on the inside rein, willingly performing any maneuver that you ask, at any time. The simplest iteration of this is to go either straight or in a circle in any gait, while being flexed in one direction or the other. The horse should yield his jaw/poll, following the slightest touch of the inside rein, responding without resistance, exactly as much as you signal the rein. The outside rein keeps the horse straight through the body, preventing the horse overbending the neck to the inside, and is used for half-halts and communication. The inside rein keeps the horse soft, reminding him not to look to the outside when the outside rein is used.

Really, riding is nothing but this! If you can maintain a soft horse, anything you do is merely a test to see if you can maintain the horse's softness and straightness while performing various tasks. If he remains willing, harmonious, and unconfused, you're golden. JP Giacomini notes that, "All training must lead to the progressive yielding of the aids; yielding the aids implies that the horse understands the rider's demands and is willing to perform them happily without constant physical support of the rider."

Softness Comes from Correct Contact

To be willing and soft, the horse must have faith in the hands holding the reins. To earn this trust, the rider must demonstrate unwavering steadiness and predictability to the horse. This places the "burden of proof" squarely on the rider. The following exercise demonstrates what steady contact feels like to *both* horse and rider so that the kinesthetic learning barrier can be overcome.

The rider learns:

❖ What a solid connection feels like.

❖ What consistent feels like.

❖ What amount of positive tension the horse likes on the reins.

❖ How her shoulders and arms should move with the horse.

❖ How to *give/push forward* to prevent slack in the reins.

❖ How not to pull to remove slack in the reins.

❖ How to recognize the insidious nature of slackness in the reins.

6.7 A & B Shorten and Widen Your Reins. Adjust until you feel an unmistakable contact, even if your arms are straight **(A)**. Widen enough so you don't touch the horse's neck **(B)**. Follow the horse's every movement in this position until you are certain you understand how it feels to maintain a consistent tension without pulling. There should be no introduction of slack, but if you feel slack, widen more. (Note that if you have to widen too much, however, your reins are too long.) When you learn how to maintain contact without introducing slack, or pulling to eliminate it, the horse will learn to trust your hand and he will relax. This teaches you to carry your own arms.

The horse learns:

❖ What unwavering connection feels like.

❖ What amount of positive tension he likes on the reins.

❖ That release (reduction of pressure) is a reward.

❖ How to push with the hind legs.

❖ That the rider/bit will not bump his mouth.

❖ How to relax into the outside rein.

❖ How to be soft on the inside rein.

❖ How to be willing to respond on both reins.

❖ That it is his job to take the bit forward, preventing slack in the reins.

❖ That aids have specific meanings.

It is worthwhile to make this effort to fully comprehend and, perhaps, rethink your understanding of the function of reins. Furthermore, you may also need to change your horse's understanding of the bit and reins in order to overcome his negative responses to avoid them.

Feeling Steady Contact

When you try the exercise I am about to describe, where you shorten and widen the reins, holding them toward the bit, you will encounter an *unmistakable* connection/tautness *that persists*

6.8 Ideal Arm Position. Your arms should hang vertically from your shoulders with your elbows bent in a relaxed manner. Your hands should be held so that, when viewed from the side, your forearm, hand, and the horse's mouth form a straight line. This position maintains the upper arm's functionality with the torso, enabling them to work in tandem with the seat and upper body to provide you with more influence because the torso is more stable than the arms alone. When your arms are away from your body, they are weak compared to the strength of the horse's neck, and it is more challenging to keep them from flailing around, resulting in intermittent contact with the horse's mouth. •

(figs. 6.7 A & B). It will feel quite firm and will move your arms forward from the shoulder. This position will undoubtedly feel awkward, but that is fine for the temporary purposes of learning how to feel the contact.

Remember the balloon analogy from Jane Savoie (see p. 122)? To keep the "full balloon feeling," you must keep the horse moving energetically forward so that his momentum maintains the connection. The trick is to keep the positive tension in the reins *exactly the same no matter what*. You must focus on pushing your hands forward toward the horse's ears, and *use the horse going more forward to prevent slack* in the reins. It is imperative that you *not* pull your hands back, push them down, stiffen your arms, nor lay them on the horse's neck. (I tell my students that they can't ever touch horse hair.) It may take 15 to 20 minutes before you fully grasp, and can intentionally repeat, the sensation. Be patient; the feel and coordination slowly dawns on you. The short distance between your hands and the bit makes connection easier to identify and feel. Remember, this is just a very short-term mechanism for you to identify a sensation. It's not how you will ride; eventually, you will settle back into a correct position, with the humerus of your arm hanging straight down and your elbow bent (fig. 6.8).

The Hands Belong to the Horse (aka, So How Do You Do This?)

Begin by extending your arms forward from the shoulder to shorten and widen the reins. Hold the reins as close to the bit as possible until you detect a persistent, unmistakable contact/tautness. The firmness of this contact will be

6.9 Pantograph. Follow your horse's head wherever it goes even if he sticks his nose in the air and waves his head all around. Consider yourself a pantograph: a pantograph is a mechanical device used for copying drawings in which the movement of one pen **(A)** in tracing an image produces identical movements in a second pen **(B)**. Similarly, your hand **(B)** (particularly the outside one) moves along the same path as the horse's head **(A)**, tracing the air until he accepts the contact and relaxes. Your hand does whatever your horse's head does (even if he draws a star!) until the horse accepts and trusts the hand. Eventually, he will drop his head and stay steady in the contact.

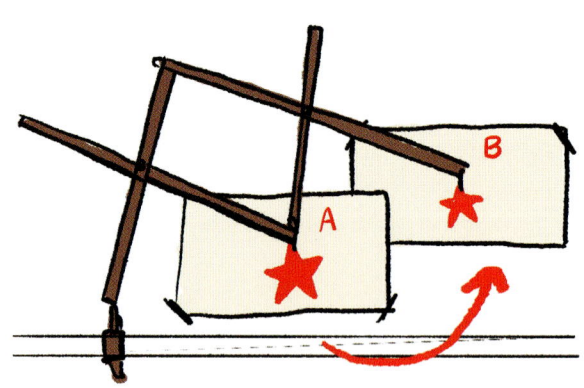

Scan to View Following the Horse's Mouth

apparent. This position may feel contrived; however, this is acceptable for the temporary duration of this activity.

Once you have established this contact, allow your arms to move in accordance with your horse's head, regardless of his actions. Think of yourself as a *pantograph*: a mechanical device used for copying drawings where the movement of one pen, in marking an image, produces identical movement in a second pen (connected to it), resulting in a second identical image (fig. 6.9). The horse's head is like "Pen Number One," tracing an imaginary path in the air as he moves his head around. Your hands are "Pen Number Two," tracing the identical path, just distanced by the reins. This method of softly and steadily following your horse's mouth will lead to your horse accepting that *the contact is constant.* This is because the bit remains steady as long as the head and hands are synchronized (see fig. 6.5). Refrain from interfering or attempting to inhibit the horse's actions. It is crucial that you learn to move in unison with him, as this will enable your hands to become independent of your seat. *Move* with your horse's head, following *everything* he does (see more about this on p. 124). Do not interfere or try to prevent him from doing anything. It doesn't matter what he does. What does matter is that:

❖ You find, understand, and maintain that connection.

❖ You learn to prevent slack without pulling backward.

❖ The horse understands the hands follow him unfailingly, and they *never* hurt or pull on him.

Scan to View Head Bob and Following

Through this process, the horse discovers that maintaining contact on the reins does not cause him any discomfort or hinder his movement, leading him to develop trust in the rider's hands.

The Following Hand and the Head Bob

It is imperative that you maintain the tautness and length of your reins. This proves tricky because, in addition to random movements, horses rhythmically bob their heads up and down with the walk—one bob for each front leg as it steps forward—as well as the canter; the neck is in constant motion. To keep the bit motionless in his mouth, you must move your arms in a synchronized, rhythmic manner that matches the timing of his gait. *Your elbows should move forward every time a front leg moves forward.*

This is analogous to the "relative motion" principle in physics, which considers the motion of one object in relation to another moving object: The horse's head (including the mouth holding the bit all as one object) bobs up and down. When you move your arms (the other moving object) in relation to the motion source (the head-mouth-bit), the two objects move at the same speed and remain still with respect to each other. (Think of how when two cars traveling side by side at 50 miles per hour, the passengers appear motionless to each other.) Developing a fluid sensitivity in your hands to move precisely with your horse is essential to contact.

When a rider's arms aren't coordinated with the head bob, the rein pressure will alternate between too loose and too tight, opposing the motion of the horse's head, and the bit will bump his mouth with every stride! Furthermore, "floppy" reins allow the bit to move unanchored in the horse's mouth, like a rock shaken in a gallon jug. Consequently, horses ridden with dangling reins often raise their heads in a defensive posture, relying on gravity to act on the bit and pull it downward in a way that is somewhat still. Clearly, it is much kinder to keep steady contact so the bit remains reasonably immobile in the mouth and the horse learns to trust the rider's hands.

A horse unconsciously uses his bobbing head as a lever to help pull himself along in his natural downhill balance. As your horse learns to shift his weight back and become more "uphill" longitudinally, coming back to you instead of you accommodating him, this tendency fades. just as your horse must learn to reach forward into the contact, you must learn to have sympathetic arms and hands that aren't bouncing around or stiff and rigid. Learning to keep time with your horse's head bob improves your sensitivity. Soon, you will have tactful, subtle, pro-active hands.

Rein Pressure

What is an appropriate amount of rein tension and pressure in this exercise? Different horses seek different amounts of tension and put different amounts of pressure into their contact. The ideal rein pressure for one horse might be "5" but another horse may pull quite a bit harder and *wants* to be a "10." Another horse may be anxious with "5" and you need to keep it at "3." It's okay for the horse to suggest the pressure, as long as it's not ridiculous, evasive, or him leaning on you to carry his head.

Think of the ideal rein pressure for your horse as "X," just where there is no slack in the reins. "X" plus any amount of pull is *too much* pressure; "X" minus anything is *too little* pressure—but may serve as a momentary reward (see discussion of "release" on p. 131). "Zero" represents no contact. Because your horse moves his head around, you must move with him in order to maintain that tension of "X." As you know, you should *not* pull back to the equivalent of "'X' plus '1'" (much less "'X' plus '200'") no matter what he does! Nor can you drop the contact—instant zero. Follow him wherever he goes, even if he sticks his nose in the air. Widening your hands is the mechanism that allows you to maintain contact without exerting excessive force. In this way, without forcing a head-neck frame, we ensure that a good connection is made by the horse, *not* by the rider. A following and kind hand creates a situation in which the horse will trust the contact and continue to reach out for connection.

Widening and Shortening Benefits: Horse Critical Thinking

This exercise is for you. *You* need to find out what consistent contact feels like so that you can *recognize and claim it at other rein lengths*. You need to understand what it feels like for the *horse* to make the contact so that you stop incessantly adjusting and shortening the reins, pulling them back to you to create a contact that the horse won't like or trust. Practice this as long as it takes for you to be sure you know what secure, unchanging contact feels like. Your horse will like it.

Recognize what your body is doing and what it is not doing. For example, your core needs to be firm and your arms soft, not vice versa. Your legs need to be soft, not gripping. Store all of these discoveries because it is the feeling you will need to employ every time you ride.

❖ Even if the reins are *very* short, that is fine for this purpose.

❖ Your hands may be quite close to the bit.

❖ You may have to reach significantly forward, temporarily modifying your position (straightening your arms).

❖ It doesn't matter, for this exercise, where your horse's head goes. It's actually better if it moves.

❖ Think of reaching forward, then more forward, but the reins are so short they won't droop.

❖ You may find that your legs or core become tired because, while you are learning to use your hands independent of your seat, your body must then learn to support itself instead of leaning on the hands.

Placing your hands near the bit as required in this exercise has several advantages:

❖ With short reins, there is less length of rein to dilute the feel.

❖ With extremely short reins, *no opportunity for slack exists*, enabling the rider to release the rigidity in the shoulders, elbows, and wrists that would otherwise be instinctively struggling to compensate for slack by unconsciously pulling back toward the rider's body. This release is an important sensation to discover. To some, this epiphany feels like relinquishing control and several students have compared it to "giving Jesus the wheel." Surrender to the motion. It changes everything.

❖ Instead of the reins slacking and tightening with the motion of the horse (which tugs on the horse's mouth with every stride), the rider learns to keep a steady connection, following the motion with only "give" or "not give." There is no more need to take back because, now, there is no slack to compensate for. Pushing your hands toward the horse's ears to *prevent* slack formation is a subtle, but *very different* feel than taking back to accommodate slack when the horse's head moves back toward you. As you push forward, you can widen—sort of like doing the breaststroke. And, however much you need to widen tells you how much you need to shorten the reins. I tell my students to pretend that they are swordsman, always pushing the sword (rein) forward toward the opponent. One would never be inclined to draw a sword back, opening yourself up for attack. As you thrust forward, ask the horse to move forward with the leg, so that he keeps the bit going forward in advance of you. In this way, both the horse and you learns to prevent slack by going forward, onto the bit.

❖ Because of the way length of rein works in physics, the object (you) that is farthest from the pivot point (the bit) must move faster and larger (like the person at the end of the line in the "Crack the Whip" game). As the rider's hand moves farther away from the bit, the length of the reins compels inexperienced riders to make movements that are large and insensitive. When the reins are shorter, all movements are smaller and easier to control. As you become accustomed to the correct feel, you can eventually manage longer reins in the same manner.

After a while in this contrived position, your horse will relax and become more still, drop his head if he carried it high, and probably push his nose forward and move in a more swinging manner. Wait for *however long it takes* for this to happen. When you achieve this and you are confident in your understanding of this connection, gradually lengthen the reins and find the same feeling at various new lengths until you are able to maintain this contact at the length at which you normally sit. When this settles in, it is obvious! The horse is round, relaxed and soft; just want you wanted.

Expect, however, that your horse may repeatedly revert to his previous behavior. Horses rarely "stay" where we would like them; you don't finally accomplish a training goal and one resolution is all that is needed forevermore. Horses need ceaseless reminding. What is critical is that *the instant that you lose feel or your horse becomes uncooperative and resistant, you return to the short rein position and begin anew.* This is worthwhile because your horse will eventually become much more cooperative. He may revert to old resistances at the beginning of the next ride, but he'll probably soften sooner. He may do it again at the start of the third ride, and so on, but it might only take him seconds to realize that evasion is pointless, and it'll be over and forgotten before you know it. This is what I call "horse critical thinking." When you let the horse figure out for himself that you're going to outlast his antics and he might as well not bother, he'll correct himself on his own, freeing you up to think about other things. Eventually, the "reminding" just becomes more subtle, proactive, and less frequent.

If you persist in pulling on the reins, however, problems with contact will *never* go away. You will never have the ride you seek because the "operating system" will have encountered a condition it cannot resolve. Use your warm-up every day to establish the contact and connection so the rest of your ride is functional and trusting.

Don't Give Up

Since your horse is learning during this exercise, too, it is important that you don't give up (tired, impatient) and just "let go" of the contact before your horse drops his head, or the horse will become confused. It is critical that he learns that he can't get away from the hands, but that this is okay because the hands are benign. When your horse is moving his head all over or trying to look to the left or right, this is a prime teachable moment for him. During this stage, you must keep your hands wide and his nose centered directly ahead so that he learns resistance is futile. You only relax a little by pushing your hands forward even more when he drops his head or becomes still. Avoid dropping the reins completely, as this will necessitate a restart. And this is unnecessary because the horse can detect even the slightest amount of give. Lowering and stilling his head is crucial for him, as it indicates that he is acknowledging the consistent contact and is confident that he does not need to avoid it. The release informs him that this is what you desire. However, if you let go at any other time, you tell him that whatever else he just did was what you wanted, and that will be incorrect. A release is one of the only rewards you can give to a horse, so use it wisely.

At the outset, horses only drop their head/relax/get still in tiny, random increments, so don't miss them! As we have already discussed, if you miss rewarding for what you want, he won't learn. When he does drop his head, he will also likely surge forward, pushing more effectively with his hind legs and rolling his shoulders in a bigger stride. Welcome this and do not pull back to slow him or fall back out of balance. You have worked hard to get him to push the bit forward in space with his hind legs, so tell him this is the right thing to do by going forward with him. In fact, you will probably be able to feel your shoulders rolling in tandem with his shoulders if you are following well with a good connection.

Whenever you do give, squeeze with your legs as much as you gave to send the horse forward after the bit so that the initial connection you felt remains the same. This is the crux of the matter.

This is a short-term training method that will only last a few days. It only serves to guide both of you toward dependable, confident contact. Soon, you'll only need to pick up the reins, and your horse will know what to do, allowing you to sit normally, hold the reins normally, and enjoy a soft, happy horse. Remember that training does not have to resemble riding. It just needs to work so that your goal is met.

Moving On from Here

Once this exercise makes sense to both you and your horse, you can move on to a more sophisticated approach. When you are confident that you can understand and maintain this forward connection on the reins at a normal length, keep your outside rein steady, but loosen a bit on the inside rein and let your horse "settle" on the outside rein. I often put my outside thumb on the saddle to be sure that rein is not moving. Then, while asking the horse to move more energetically forward with your legs, you can gently "wiggle" the inside rein and see if the horse drops his head or softly responds to the inside along with you. The goal is for him to be soft, yielding/giving willingly and easily to the inside without resisting and pulling the other way. (Note that the "stiff" and "hollow" sides we talked about in the longeing section may impact how much rein your horse needs on either side. Be sure to take this into consideration.)

When you "give" the inside hand, use the inside leg simultaneously and the horse should surge forward into the connection. It feels great and is unmistakable. The flexion inside maintains that connection on the outside so that you can use the outside rein to half-halt as necessary (see p. 259). If slack is introduced in either rein, communication is gone, so you must start over again—as many times as necessary—until you both remain in consistent connection.

You should ride this stage a few feet off the fence or wall, and remain going in a straight line. This way, you can tell if your efforts are what is keeping the horse straight, as opposed to him just following a visual guide. If he veers off the line, use your legs to put him back. His body should remain straight off your steady outside rein. The horse should be soft and compliant on the inside rein.

It is possible you will meet resistance. The horse may be stiff, lift his head or turn it to the outside, or present a number of other issues. You might find that he becomes more resistant as you try using the inside rein to ask him to yield softly. Be resolute about his body staying straight while he flexes his poll to the inside. Eventually, he will do this, and the instant he becomes soft and drops his head, even an inch, give the reins and push him forward with your legs. Repeat this process until it becomes "how you ride." With repetition and practice, you will be able to make very subtle changes with your seat and fingers that no one will see; because you took the time to work through this, you will have created a communication tool with your horse that becomes refined over time.

Note that one direction will be considerably more challenging than the other (because of that stiff and hollow issue). If you are having difficulty, try going the opposite direction to see if it is easier for your horse. After mastering the exercise in one direction, teach it in the other.

Overcoming any "resistance reactions" to get the horse to a peaceful, trusting mindset is why we are doing this exercise in the first place. He must learn and trust that the hands will follow him, that the bit will be still in his mouth, that slack will not punish him, and that the reins provide language he can learn to understand.

Tactful Hands

There are several things to be mindful of in order for your horse to learn to trust your hands and the rein pressure:

❖ As noted on p. 129, you may need to start out with extremely short reins—as if your hands are reaching forward to hold the bit rings—until you find that feel of consistent and unequivocal contact (the length where you *never* get slack). This shortness of the reins isn't for pulling—it's so the horse can't wiggle away from your feel and create any slack. Gradually let the reins out as the horse understands and responds, and as you learn what consistent contact feels like. Once you get the feel, you will become capable of proactively pre-empting evasions because you understand what you seek.

❖ Whenever you aren't "assisting" your horse in keeping the contact, be sure to return to following his motion. Some horses pull and head bob more vigorously than others. Try to be a "pressure mirror" and reflect the contact he creates. On a rein pressure "scale" of "1" to "10," for example, if your horse pulls at "3," you follow with "3" of your own. Don't add extra! If your horse is pulling and leaning on you more than is appropriate,

6.10 A & B Cup and String. The old-fashioned cup-and-string phone is a way for two people to communicate with some distance between them. The key is to keep the string taut between the two cups, and they must be connected by a straight line **(A)**. When you speak into one cup, the sound waves produced by your voice are transmitted inside the cup, vibrating the bottom. These vibrations travel down the string, across the string, and into the bottom of the other cup, where your partner can hear you. Your reins provide the same means of communication as the string between the cups. If they have a droop in them (loss of contact), no communication is possible **(B)**.

A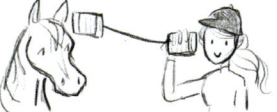

B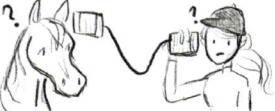

THIS   NOT THIS

don't get into a pulling contest with him. As the saying goes, "It takes two to pull," so keep a light connection and use your leg to ask for more "Go." Don't get drawn into his game.

❖ Practice appropriate rein pressure and tension with a human assistant holding a set of reins and acting like a horse with erratic contact for you. Your helper can give you valuable verbal feedback on your pressure, consistency, and rapidity of response.

❖ Because horses can make dramatic moves with their body, people get scared, overreact, and pull with "'X' plus '2000.'" People also tend to pull when they need to regain their own balance, using the reins (alas, the horse's mouth) for stability. Humans are naturally hand-oriented, and our first inclination of self-preservation is to grab onto something. Balance is as important to the rider as the horse, but we shouldn't use our hands to achieve it! The reins aren't a handrail for you to clutch for stability, nor are they straps to hold you on the horse. This is a phenomenon that needs to be overcome in order to ride with the tact and finesse that lead to the horse trusting and knowing that you won't hurt his mouth so that he's willing to take the bit and move forward.

❖ Reins aren't intended to be the braking system. Reins aren't present to force the horse into a position. They are more akin to a kid's cup-and-string phone—a line of communication between rider and horse (figs. 6.9 A & B). As long as the string between the cups is straight and has some tautness, it works, and you can hear each other.

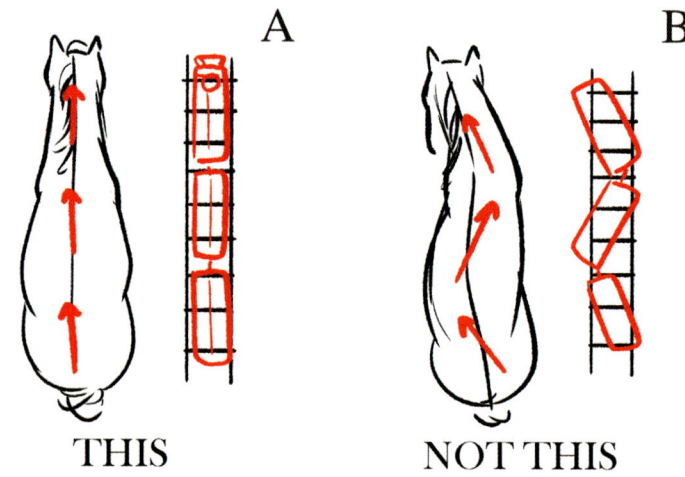

6.11 A & B Train on Tracks. A straight horse has his body aligned over the path he is traveling, similar to a train on tracks **(A)**. If your horse's body develops a zigzag shape, he is "crooked" **(B)**. When a horse is crooked, he may lose his ability to move forward, or become "stuck," similar to how a derailed train is no longer able to operate. Any time the reins become slack, the loss of contact opens the door for one or more segments of a horse's body to derail. ●

❖ In order to have your hands independent of your body so that you can manipulate the reins to maintain this dynamic and empathetic linkage, you must have a secure seat. If you don't have a secure seat, every time something happens you grab to preserve your own balance. This creates three problems: you throw off your horse's balance, you can't give the aid you were trying to give, and you confuse your horse.

❖ Remember widening your hands to create that funnel shape from your arms (see p. 130)? This allows you to help the horse's spine stay lined up from nose to tail, like a monorail on its track. If his body gets shaped like a zigzag with his nose going one way, his neck going another, his shoulders jack-knifed, his ribs falling in, and his hips out of line with the rest of him, he loses the ability to go forward, or becomes "stuck," just like a derailed train is crinkled off its tracks and can no longer operate (figs. 6.11 A & B). Any time the reins become too loose, the loss of contact opens the door for one or more segments of a horse's body to go where it shouldn't, and your "caught energy" (see the circuit on p. 123) escapes there. Simply widen the reins again to restore contact and straightness.

❖ Horses "like" fair and steady contact; they feel reassured by it. They like to have you be their leader and know you are there for them. As from back to front connection becomes "the way we do this," the horse's anxiety settles down, he loosens mentally and physically, his gaits become steadier, and he "drops" into the hands of the rider. Your horse's stress level is reduced because he understands what is expected of him, and that gives him confidence.

Connection Takes Practice and Time

Practice until a reliable contact becomes second nature and is deeply ingrained and automatic for both you and the horse. Eventually, you will need only subtle adjustments to re-establish it throughout the ride, or to proactively prevent loss of connection. As your horse develops the confidence to take the bit forward, it will be easier to maintain the contact. Being attentive to contact is a very simple concept; however, for some reason, remembering to keep contact is abandoned almost immediately by most riders! I have to remind students to reestablish it dozens of times during a single lesson. Without an instructor there to help you, it is up to you to focus on retaining the concept during every moment of every ride.

Testing Connection

Inviting the horse to stretch forward and downward on the circle while maintaining contact (the same "stretchy" circle you encouraged on the longe line—see p. 66), verifies the authenticity of your connection. Gradually move your hands forward and downward and allow the reins to slide through your fingers slowly, while continuing to ride your horse rhythmically forward. The contact should remain steady since the horse will reach forward to "follow your hands" and seek the bit because the horse now understands to do so. When your horse *doesn't* maintain the contact during this test, this reveals that you aren't yet properly connected. Common errors include head tossing, dropping the head down but not forward, speeding up, loss of steering, and stumbling.

While there is much to learn to master this challenging movement ("the stretchy circle"), it is introduced here so that you have a means of evaluating the legitimacy of your contact. It is not necessary for the horse to lower his head below his knees. Since your horse is learning during this exercise, too, it is important that, as explained on p. 143, you don't give up (because you are tired or impatient) and just "let go" of the contact before your horse drops his head. Remember: only when he drops his head or "gets still" do you "give" a *little bit* by pushing your hands forward even more. Don't throw the reins down so that you have to start all over again! A tiny give is enough for the horse to feel it.

At the outset, horses only drop their head/relax/get still in tiny, random increments, so don't miss them! As we have already discussed, if you miss rewarding for what you want, he won't learn. When he does drop his head, he will also likely surge forward, pushing more effectively with his hind legs and rolling his shoulders in a bigger stride. Welcome this and do not pull back to slow him or fall back out of balance. You have worked hard to get him to push the bit forward in space with his hind legs, so tell him this is the right thing to do by going forward with him. In fact, you will probably be able to feel your shoulders rolling in tandem with his shoulders if you are following well with a good connection.

Whenever you do give, squeeze with your legs as much as you gave to send the horse forward after the bit so that the initial connection you felt remains the same. This is the crux of the matter.

This exercise is only a short-term training technique, and the process should only last a few days. It serves only to *orient* both you and your horse to reliable, confident contact. Before long, you will only need to pick up the reins and your horse will know what to do, and you will be able to sit normally, hold the reins normally, and have a soft, happy horse.

The Role of the Rider in Contact/Connection

❖ You must understand what correct contact/connection is, and how to find it, keep it, and use it. In order to react instantly in the saddle and maintain communication with the horse, you must comprehend that you and the horse are intertwined, as well as the full spectrum of causes and effects of what you or the horse might do. You must possess a toolbox of strategies to deal with situations as they arise.

❖ You must *not* find other ways to unconsciously pull back once you lengthen your reins! Shoving your hands down toward your knees and cocking your wrists or little fingers down and back are stealthy examples of actions performed to remove slack that you may not even be aware of. They cause your arms to lock from the shoulders to the wrists and break the straight line you want from the bit to the elbow.

❖ I suggest to my students that they imagine that I have cut a section out of a basketball and secured the remaining part of the ball over the horse's withers. The rider must keep her hands over the imaginary basketball. This not only gives the rider a "place" to put her hands, it stops her from letting them sag, forgotten, or be tempted to push them down against the withers in an attempt to shorten the reins to find contact.

❖ It is essential to emphasize the significance of the rider's position while mounted. The more you perceive that you are seated with all your joints "open" (versus "bent" or "closed"), the easier it is to separate your hands from your body and position them effectively. Slouching with a rounded back, pushing too far forward with your legs, or collapsing in the waist make it very difficult to manage the contact. Your hands become trapped and ineffective in your lap. You need to have your torso upright, your hips and hands forward, and your toes at or behind the girth. Do not allow your thighs to become parallel to the ground, by drawing up your knees and closing your hip joints. Keep your femurs *perpendicular* to the ground. This does not mean that you should push hard on the stirrups, however. Tap your toes periodically—as if keeping time to music—to keep your weight out of the irons. The stirrups dangle from the saddle, and when you push on them, you pull the saddle down and apply pressure to the horse's back.

❖ Focus on the up-and-down motion of the horse and avoid succumbing to the back-and-forth motion. The back-and-forth motion of the horse rocks your body and moves you about in the saddle. It is best to remain stationary in the saddle while maintaining positive torso tension. As I've heard other riding instructors say, "The waist is not a joint." Think of yourself as a component of the saddle and move along with it from the pelvis.

- Holding the fingers open even slightly allows the reins to slip, so keep your fingers closed. When the reins are held firmly between the thumbs and index fingers at the top of the hand, your ring and pinky fingers can "play" with the bit as needed without the reins slipping.

- Some people realize they tend to pull or balance on the reins, so they try to be kinder to the horse and protect him by letting the reins be long and loose. However, this often only makes matters worse because you have to wade through the slack before you can "find the horse," which usually results in the horse getting yanked in the mouth. It is much kinder to keep a steady connection so the bit remains still in the horse's mouth than to use exaggerated movements to occasionally communicate.

- Riding in a "perfect" position is not always possible. Remember that your own conformation and balance, as well as your horse's conformation and balance, stage of training, and acceptance of contact, all play a role in your ability to carry your hands and arms in ideal positioning. Riders with long arms can bend their arms more than riders with short arms. The length of the rider's torso also has an effect on this because a long torso elevates the shoulders; consider the difference between someone with a long torso and short arms and someone with a short torso and long arms. Horses with long necks will carry their heads differently than those with short necks, and advanced horses have higher, more consistent head carriage than green horses. All of these factors (and others!) influence rein length, stability, and the degree of "following" required by the rider's hands and arms.

- Avoid making riding an emotionally charged experience. When your horse displays resistance, "misbehavior," or fear, he is not "doing it *to you*." When a horse responds negatively to establishing contact, he is most likely not understanding, confused, or physically uncomfortable. Do not become frustrated or angry. Instead, maintain a level head and clearly and consistently redefine to him what you want him to do. Remain emotionally responsible and do not place blame for your failures on the horse.

- Don't be concerned about how messy and unattractive this activity might appear to others. As I've already mentioned, "training" can look very different from "riding."

The Role of the Horse in Contact/Connection

Once you feel confident that you understand and can unerringly find that steady, following connection, and you no longer fall victim to slack, you are ready to address the role the horse plays in this dialogue. The main thing is the horse needs to be *responsive* to you. Being willingly responsive—that softness we talked about—is the goal, but horses often resist. Two common resistances to the bridle are "running through" and "sucking back."

A "run through" occurs when a horse attempts to avoid the bit by moving away from it, forward and upward, while "bracing." The horse pushes against the bridle to protect himself from hands that he assumes will not be steady may "saw" at, pull on, or bump the horse's mouth. Imagine playing tug of war. When pulling on the rope, you exert force with one of your legs against the ground, tense up, and prepare your body to resist the pull of the opposing team. This is how the horse responds when he is accustomed to riders pulling on him: he braces himself. Horses can brace anywhere in the body, but the most common braced position consists of the neck and head being raised while the back is lowered, which presses the horse's front legs into the ground. Horses cannot move correctly in this position, and as a result, cannot perform well, if at all.

Since the exercises in this chapter are designed to alter the rider's feel, create forgiving hands, and improve the rider's awareness and timing in order to eliminate confusion, anxiety, and tension in the horse, it should remove the horse's need to brace. But a rider who is aware of bracing and is able to identify it when it occurs is better equipped to intervene before the situation escalates. Knowing what to and what *not* to do helps:

❖ **DO** hold the outside rein steady while jiggling, opening, or lifting the inside rein (depending on which works best for your horse) to encourage a slight flexion at the poll. The steady hand gives the horse something to rely on, and more importantly, straightens the horse's body, after which the inside rein is used to "break the front end loose." Since the poll is only a small portion of a massive muscle that spans the entire length of the horse's body, if you can loosen it through flexion, the rest of the muscle/body will also become more flexible. This also helps shift more of the horse's weight to his hindquarters, making it more difficult for him to push against the ground with his front legs.

6.12 The Correct Connect™ Aaron Vale Rein. This training aid provides riders with a simple way to keep their rein length constant until they are able to manage it with regular reins. The design also enables riders to "give" without losing connection.

Grand Prix show jumper Aaron Vale collaborated with Correct Connect™ to create the Aaron Vale Rein, which features padded hand grips. I find these reins offer riders a straightforward method for maintaining rein length. Because of the uniquely padded, large hand stops, the rein length cannot change without the rider noticing, and it is easy to find and maintain a correction hand position. The reins are soft, comfortable, and adjustable (the grips can be placed precisely where the horse and rider have the best connection). The design also allows you to "give" without losing contact, keeping the connection stable.

These reins can be game changers for riders who want softer, more stable hands and a consistent length of rein. The experience is enlightening—you quickly realize what you thought you were doing but weren't (fig. 6.12)!

Scan to View Aaron Vale Reins and Contact

A Handy Riding Aid for Maintaining Contact

- **DO** release as soon as he gives the correct response. Timing is crucial. If you hold for too long, the horse will believe that his response was incorrect, and he will seek alternative exits, which is precisely what you don't want. When the horse yields to you, you must act immediately.

- **DON'T** pull, pump with your seat, or kick when the horse braces and resists. Some people yell or curse. Clearly, these approaches only serve to heighten the horse's anxiety.

- **DON'T** overtrain! If you obtain a desirable response, quit on a good note. Remember, horses learn better overnight, so let them sleep on it. They'll do better tomorrow.

- **DON'T** try to prevent a mistake. If your horse performs poorly, go back to the very beginning and build him back up, using this exercise, until he is comfortable. Confident horses are more successful and happier riding partners.

"Sucking back," on the other hand, is when the horse tries to avoid the same thing in a different way by going "behind the vertical" or "behind the bit." He drops the contact, creating slack in the reins to remove the pressure he feels from the rider's hands. He is avoiding contact with the bit. Think of how, when driving your car behind another vehicle, you maintain a safe distance to avoid coming in contact with it. You never want to get close enough to touch the other car and cause damage. This is how the horse who sucks back responds to the bit. He "poses" by curling his neck and tucking his chin toward his chest. The bit in his mouth just hangs in the air, and he does not connect with it…or with you.

Sucking back is bad because a horse's head and hind legs work like they are tied together: When your horse's nose is out and he is going forward, then his hind legs are tracking up underneath him. When his head is behind the vertical, his legs are trailing out behind him, so there is no driving push to create connection through the bridle. And no connection means no communication.

Pain (teeth, body soreness, lameness), ill-fitting tack, unyielding hands, insensitive riding habits, misunderstanding of "light," incompatible bits (too thick, too thin, too severe, pinching rings), and use of mechanical devices can all lead to sucking back. Perhaps the most common cause is front-to-back riding, which is caused by riders using only the reins to make contact, rather than using "go" and the forward impulse like we've discussed in this book.

Sucking back is a symptom of bigger training issues (a lack of trust, contact, communication) that affect the horse's overall way of going. Don't worry about how your horse looks or feels while you are addressing this issue. When your horse is going well, the frame sorts itself out. One of my own instructors always says, "Round is free." It is.

The exercises you just learned are intended to improve the horse that is not going forward into the contact, as well as helping you establish a soft feel. In addition, sucking back can be solved by:

❖ Getting the horse forward from leg and seat.

❖ Doing lots of transitions.

❖ Using light aids and following through so the horse knows even when it is "light" you still mean it.

❖ Using leg-yield (see p. 175) to create more contact on the outside rein.

❖ Riding outside the arena to provide a fresh, stimulating environment.

❖ Practicing forward on the longe line until the horse knows he must "go" until you say, "Whoa."

❖ "Stilling your seat" instead of pulling on the reins to transition down (see p. 110). Put energy into a downward transition, rather than "stopping" it.

❖ Thinking of riding up a flight of stairs to lighten the horse's front end and engage the hind end more.

❖ Doing circles where you invite the horse to stretch forward and downward with his nose.

❖ Doing short lessons. Sucking back is an avoidance of work, so the horses who do it frequently will not be fit and will tire quickly. Keep it short so the horse doesn't revert to sucking back when he gets tired.

❖ Using positive reinforcement and encouragement.

❖ Incorporating ground poles to organize the horse's legs, encourage impulsion, and keep work interesting.

❖ Riding up hills to build strength and forward "push" from the hind end. When the horse is strong, work with contact is easier.

❖ Testing periodically to see how your contact is: "give" and see if your horse reaches toward the bit.

Using What You Have Learned

Once you're more confident and skillful at maintaining consistent soft contact that results in a willing horse, experiment with different gaits, arena patterns, and movements. Ideally, every one of them should ride exactly the same. It is likely they won't at first, but this problem-solving aspect of riding is what makes it interesting!

★ Caveats

❖ Think about that monorail train ideal (see p. 146). It does not matter whether a horse deviates a body part by .01 percent or 100 percent—**any deviation ("popping" a shoulder, stepping out from under the body, overbending the neck) destroys connection and therefore communication.** A rider will notice a 100 percent deviation more readily than a .01 percent deviation, but both are equally damaging. It is the subtle deviations that will perplex you.

- Don't be surprised if your horse exhibits different issues with connection going the other way and may even feel like a different horse. As we have talked about with the "hollow" and "stiff" side, **horses typically work differently in each direction**. Symmetry is a long-term goal. Plan on reminding him in both directions again the following day. A skill takes several days to become reliably ingrained, but each day becomes easier, more relaxed, and takes less time. "Everything gets better in three days," is my mantra, and it's usually true.

- In order to escape contact, some horses will jerk their heads down unexpectedly, **"diving" or "rooting" on the reins**. This behavior is one sign the horse may have been subjected to excessive restraint at one point, or that you are currently applying too much pressure and he is attempting to gain some relief. This is not the correct "forward and down" movement that we test for and should not be interpreted as success. This is the horse telling you that you have—or someone else has—pulled too much.

- **Horses also like to stretch their heads down to relieve muscle tension in their hind legs**. (For a human, this is equivalent to bending forward to stretch out the lower back.) Don't be fooled by this reason your horse reaches forward. If he isn't honestly reaching for the bit and into your hands, be firm in your core and limit the length of rein you let out. Early in training, however, it is a good indication that he is using his hindquarters. Until he becomes fit, his hind end will tire, causing him to want to stretch. It is essential during this work to provide him with breaks to walk and relax.

- Be aware that **stumbling** may occur when your horse is learning to stretch forward and down. Because your horse is going on the forehand, he may rush the tempo of his strides or the length of them may be uneven (his front legs may take longer strides than those of the hind legs that aren't tracking up underneath him, or his hind legs may take longer strides than his front legs), causing him to be off balance and trip. Furthermore, he may be tense in the body or not yet skilled at negotiating the rider's extra weight. Such factors can cause stumbling, so be cautious. Don't allow the horse to go too fast or too low for too long.

- In order for the reins to work effectively, be sure to keep your hands oriented with your **thumbs up** as if you are reading a book, so that your arms can remain soft and elastic. Allowing your hands to face palm down ("piano hands") causes your wrists to twist and your arms to become rigid. Turning your palms down also causes your elbows to separate from your body, reducing your stability.

- When widening the reins and creating the funnel (see p. 130), many people widen farther with their non-dominant hand, but their writing hand droops—for example, the left hand might be opened a foot and the other hand is a mere inch from the withers, limp and ineffectual. **Discrepant aids are unclear to the horse.**

- **Steering** can initially throw a wrench in the works of maintaining connection. Early in this

6.13 A & B Driving Hold. "Flipping your hands" to hold the reins as if you were driving a horse and carriage improves your ability to feel the contact. Instead of holding the reins so they enter your hand between the ring and little fingers (the bottom), hold them so they enter your hand between your thumb and index finger (the top). It may feel strange at first, but this position significantly amplifies the sensation of contact and is much easier to maintain. It's easier to give from the shoulder and follow the motion of the horse's head bob. Think about moving your arms as if you were passing a tray to someone. Try to replicate the same feel while riding with the reins held traditionally. •

A   B

practice, ride on straight or gently curving lines to avoid disrupting contact. Prioritize maintaining contact when your horse moves his head around. Refrain from pulling the inside rein. When you pull left, the horse's shoulder goes right, and vice versa. Instead, steer with your seat and thighs, pointing your hips or belly button in the desired direction. Turning from the saddle directs the horse's legs, which move the horse.

❖ The rail serves as a barrier, keeping the horse upright and preventing him from escaping the arena's confines. If you always ride along the fence or wall, you cannot determine whether you are in control. **Riding away from the fence line or wall tests your aids and your connection.**

❖ **Mirrors and videos come in handy.** Riding rarely feels like it looks. "If it feels good, it probably isn't," one of my trainers always said. While "feeling good" is the goal, chances are that a dysfunctional idiosyncrasy will "feel good" in the early stages, when the horse and rider don't know what "good" is. What one imagines to be good is frequently not, and this can lead to self-deception.

★★ Extensions

❖ "Flipping your hands" to how driving reins are held **improves the ability to discern contact:** Instead of holding the reins with the portion closest to

6.14 A & B Droopy Reins. Maintain enough tension on the reins to prevent slack, so the reins always look like straight lines and aren't sagging **(A)**. Do this by moving your hands in unison with the horse's head bob. Droopy reins result in a loss of connection and permit the horse to go wherever he wants to, which feels like a car sliding on ice, while you become a helpless passenger, scrambling to shorten the reins. Since the horse can no longer feel you, he becomes unsure and more likely to take hasty, crooked steps **(B)**.

the bit coming into your hand between your ring and little fingers (bottom of your hands), place the portion closest to the bit between your thumb and index finger (top of your hands) so that your thumb points toward the bit (figs. 6.13 A & B). It may initially feel awkward, but it is well worth experimenting with! The contact's sensation is significantly more pronounced. Once you have experienced this, you can attempt to replicate it with the reins held traditionally.

❖ Even if your horse **accepts contact**, he won't necessarily offer it at the beginning of a ride. Each ride should begin with a **warm-up phase** focused on loosening/suppling his body, relaxing, and moving forward rhythmically to establish the connection. Other work can begin *once your horse is stable in the contact.*

❖ Don't expect your horse to stay connected all by himself. Riders who appear to maintain **constant contact** are proactively monitoring the horse with slight widenings of the reins, pushing for more "forward," and half-halts (I really dig into the latter in chapter 10—see p. 259).

❖ Don't restrict your horse's head and neck by "holding him together." **Allow him to make mistakes in the contact** until he can carry himself forward on his own, pushing from the hind legs. As mentioned, holding him in a position will result in his body assuming the wrong shape and he'll pull himself along with the front legs. Remember: Front-to-back = bad!

❖ When **introducing widening the reins and squeezing for forward**, it can be useful to have someone longe your horse so that you can focus on getting him to comply without having to worry about steering. "Fake longeing," or having a person stand in the center of your circle without a longe line but calling out gaits and other instructions can be beneficial. The horse automatically follows the instructions of the person in the center of the circle because he understands what to do when longeing (see Ground Rules—p. 19). The longeing cues reinforce what the rider is asking, making the lesson easier, at first.

❖ Try **holding a belt, a lead rope, or a single rein with both hands,** one on each end. Imagine the bit is located in its center. Pull with one hand and follow that pull with the other. Feel what your left hand is doing with your right hand, and vice versa. With one hand, release the tension on the "rein," and feel the complete loss of contact. Try to feel one hand with the other while riding your horse, too. Consider the bit and reins as a single loop, similar to a necklace, and not as two separate reins working independently.

❖ To get an idea of what it should feel like when you give a little and your horse takes the reins forward, fasten a bungee cord or piece of elastic to something it won't pull free of. Pull lightly to stretch it. When you give, your arms will be pulled forward. Follow that elastic pull slowly forward so it doesn't become suddenly loose; learn to stop just before it becomes limp. The control you use to **maintain the connection with the bungee cord without over-releasing** is a good simulation for staying connected to your horse while following him forward and down.

❖ With the vigilant assistance of an experienced companion on the ground leading your horse, close your eyes so you can feel how your horse's head bobs at the walk. This allows you **to feel the timing to follow the rhythm accurately with your arms**. It is imperative you learn this feel so that he's not restricted in the walk and canter. Bend and straighten your elbows gently in sync with the horse's body movements—blend in with his motion so that he has freedom to swing his head and neck into the movement. Give through both elbows to move the hands and bit with the horse, making the reins appear still (figs. 6.14 A & B). Horses who have previously been ridden with very restrictive reins stiffen their neck and have virtually no head bob. If you have one of these horses, it may be difficult for you to have a clear sense of contact with him until he learns to trust the hands, relax, and move his neck normally. You'll need to be very sensitive and feel for a bob that's no more evident than feeling a pulse in your wrist, but you can find it. Encourage a bigger walk with more push from behind and the head bob will gradually return.

❖ Following the bit has also been compared to winding a spinning fishing reel spool: **your hands push forward counterclockwise.** The diameter of the wind is small, and one rotation of the handle takes about the same amount of time and space as one head bob, so a rhythm is inherent. This type of visualization keeps your hands from moving excessively. Note that the head bob rhythm at the canter uses *clockwise* circles.

6.15 A & B Two Whips. Riding with two whips is a powerful visual tool for revealing what your hands are actually doing while you ride. Hold one whip in each hand, both held parallel to the ground and parallel to each other, handles pointing toward the horse's head, one on each side of the horse's neck. Hold them at least in the middle of the shaft, where they will balance level. Depending on how long they are, be sure that the handles reach at least halfway up the horse's neck **(A)**. If they wobble around, point at each other, cross over the neck, or point up or down, it shows you how unsteady your hands are—and you need to do something about it **(B)**! •

A

THIS

B

NOT THIS

Scan to View Use of Two Whips to Demonstrate Hand Stability

❖ People often struggle with **where to place their hands**, yet it is important to learn as soon as possible to keep them stable. Tie a polo wrap loosely around the base of the horse's neck, positioned just in front of the saddle. Utilize this as a visual reminder to *keep your hands ahead of the polo*. This will keep you thinking to *push* your connected reins forward, and to widen to remove slack, rather than pull back. Envision yourself rolling a rolling pin up the horse's neck toward his ears. Your hands belong to the horse, not you: Your body is doing *your* thing; your hands and arms are doing *the horse's* thing (unless you need to restrict your movement for an aid or correction).

❖ **Riding with two whips is an effective test to determine whether your hands are truly steady** and "thumbs up." Hold them parallel to the ground and parallel to each other, with the handles pointing toward the horse's head, one on each side of the neck. Hold them in the shaft's center, where they will balance level. As you ride, keep them parallel (figs. 6.15 A & B).

❖ To help **determine the "right" amount of pressure or tension to apply to the reins**, have someone take you for a drive. Cup your hand outside the car window to catch the wind. At slower speeds, like 30 miles per hour, wind pressure on your hand is minimal. The faster you go, the greater the pressure. I like the feel of right around 40 to 45 miles per hour and try to keep that as my consistent contact on the reins when things are "neutral." There is a discernible increase in pressure at 55 miles per hour, and that's about what I likely use for giving signals with the reins to horses in the early stages of learning about connection; in more educated horses, I like to stay around 40 miles per hour. There is quite

Improve Connection with "Ribs Out"

You will feel a better connection develop on the outside (outside the bend) when you "push the horse's ribs out" while riding on a circle and softening on the inside rein by wiggling or squeezing it until the horse "gives" (fig. 6.16). Get in your mind early on that you can't push your horse's ribs out enough. You can push them out much farther than you think. And when your horse resists or exerts too much pressure on the inside rein, wiggle it and push the ribs out farther until he softens. It is preferable that he learns to stop resisting you on the inside rein as soon as possible. Keep your horse traveling on the line of the circle (see p. 62), and don't let him step off it, either to the outside or inside, when you push the ribs out with your inside leg (figs. 6.17 A & B). Connection is lost as soon as he moves any part of his body off the exact circle line. When successful, you will notice the swing in his stride as his back rises and becomes more free and relaxed. He'll be supple, willing, soft, and comfortable to ride, with the same curvature in his body from ears to tail.

 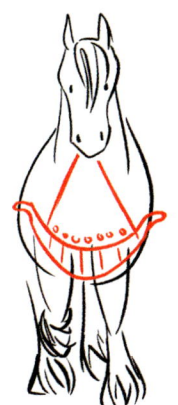 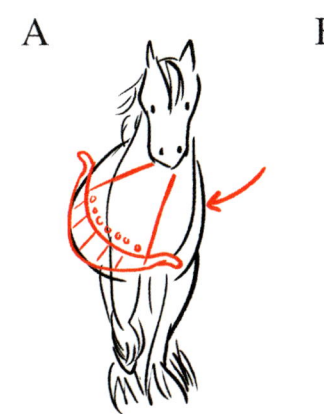

6.16 Moving Away from Inside Leg. It's crucial to learn to detect whether your horse's ribs are pressing against your calf, especially if it's on the inside of a bend. Your inside leg should be able to hang free of the horse. As soon as you feel the inside ribs on your leg, "push them away," back to the outside of the curve. The horse must not lean on you ("fall in") or push his ribs in the wrong direction as a form of resistance. The horse flexes and moves onto the outside rein as a result of pushing the ribs out.

6.17 A & B Ribs Out. The spine of the horse does not actually "bend" into a curve when viewed from the front. Instead, horses' ribs sway to and fro from the vertebrae, similar to the viking ship ride at an amusement park, or a swing on a swingset. When the ribs swing out in one direction, the horse appears curved. The swing is important because that clears the way for a hind leg to step forward, under the horse. The abdomen swings to the right to clear the way for the left hind leg and vice versa. In the horse on the left, the "viking ship ride" is centered **(A)**, and the horse on the right is stepping forward with his left hind leg, so his abdomen swings to the right to make way for it **(B)**. This creates flexion to the left, so the left is the "inside" of the horse. You can feel this swing when you ride. It is *good* when the ribs sway away from your inside leg and bad when they push back against it. If you feel the ribs pushing against an inside leg, push them back the other way.

6.18 Equicube. The Equicube, designed by Linda Grandia, is a useful tool that is held in front of the rider while mounted. The accessory, a weighted rubber apparatus held in both hands just high enough so that it doesn't touch the horse, places your hands in the correct position and orientation. The Equicube's weight is designed to quiet the hands and encourage core muscle engagement to assist with proper use of the seat. Most riders notice an immediate improvement in their balance and stability in the saddle.

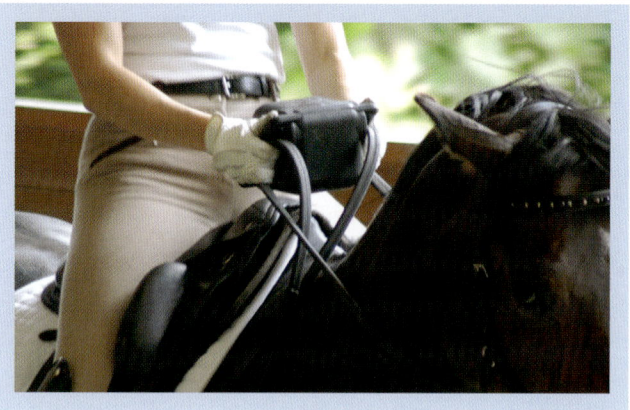

a bit of pressure on your hand when driving at 70 miles per hour, and that's about what a very strong aid might feel like, or what it might feel like if the horse is pulling on you too much. You surely don't want an absence of pressure on the reins, like when the car stops and no wind is filling your hand at all. Every horse and person is different, but this approximation is something tangible you can make sense of. And remember: It's not necessarily about how "light" or "heavy" the horse is; it's about how the connection from back to front works.

❖ As your horse becomes accustomed to you following with your hands, he will notice if you *stop* following with your outside hand. **This introduces part of a very important aid I've already mentioned: the half-halt,** which serves to get your horse's attention in order to notify him that he should get ready to do something (find out a lot more about the half-halt in chapter 10—p. 259).

❖ **The horse must push evenly with both hind legs.** Often, one hind leg pushes harder than the other, or one stride length is longer (or shorter) than the other. If you feel an uneven contact in the reins—one either drooping or pulling more—the hind legs probably aren't being used evenly. Whichever side droops, add pressure with that leg and push. His back may also feel uneven beneath you. Use your leg on the side he has dropped to energize that hind leg. If you are unsure whether this is occurring, have someone observe you riding and confirm whether the hind legs are moving uniformly.

❖ If you want to fine-tune your riding and augment the "widen and squeeze" technique (see p. 130), **press down on your outside stirrup when the horse's**

outside front leg is on the ground (many aids are used when the outside front leg is on the ground so it is good to be familiar with this timing). This coordination should be familiar to you from posting to the trot. Your weight shift will cause your horse to bend toward the outside to get under your weight, and the pressure in the stirrup will encourage his outside front leg to linger on the ground for a second longer, shifting the weight there and causing the horse to lower his head. You may need to repeat this "step" (like pumping a barber chair or piano pedal) for a few strides to get the desired effect. Experiment with different pressure levels to see how light you can be with the weight shift and still get a response. (you can learn more about the technique of "stirrup stepping" at *artisticdressage.com*.)

❖ When riding, your hands should be steady. Humans, being hand-oriented, tend to move their hands all over the place, making it difficult for many riders to find "the place" for them. Further, riders struggle with the concept of "riding from the seat" and often have a hard time believing that the horse can be controlled in this manner. The **Equicube** (*equicube.net*) helps with these issues, placing your hands in the correct orientation and encouraging core muscle engagement (fig. 6.18). Because the Equicube is heavy (don't rest it on your horse's withers) and has movement-restricting handles, your body is forced to figure out how to support the Cube with your core and you learn to ride with your seat. You can tell when this happens because the Cube feels suddenly much lighter and your arms relax. (It is a good idea to have an experienced person longe you and your horse while you figure this out.)

Connection in Closing

Being connected is a "feel." If you can, take lessons on a horse that's confirmed in contact, so you learn what you are feeling for. Asking an experienced rider to tune up your horse before you get on is another way to access this feeling. Focus more on *what your horse feels like* than how he looks.

I was fortunate enough to ride one of the stallions at the Spanish Riding School in Vienna, Austria. I wanted to know what riding one felt like, but when I got on, it was *so much more* than that! The sensations made crystal clear to me what the rider's *standards and expectations of his horse* were. The horse offered zero resistance of any kind. In fact, "offered" is a good word to explain how he was poised and ready, instantaneous and correct. He was balanced on his hindquarters and yielding in the shoulders. He went forward readily, responded promptly to the lightest of aids; he turned, bent, half-halted at any time, in any location; he was symmetrical in both directions, his transitions were impeccable and his tempo and rhythm didn't vary. I understood immediately what was possible to expect from other horses, and that it was *up to me*. (I imagine the experience in reverse can be similar for a horse when a really good rider gets on him and shows him what's possible in a fair and correct way. This is why having a more correct, more experienced rider than you get on your horse can be beneficial.) It is my hope that this book gives you some useful tools and small achievable steps to help you be that really good rider and your horse be that amazing stallion from the Spanish Riding School.

Study Guide
Clarity/State, Elaborate, Illustrate, and Exemplify (SEIE)

SEIE is another activity gleaned from Dr. Richard Paul (*criticalthinking.org*). He presents "intellectual standards" that include:

❖ *Clarity*
❖ *Accuracy*
❖ *Precision*
❖ *Depth*
❖ *Breadth*
❖ *Relevance*
❖ *Significance*
❖ *Logicalness*

*The following text within this sidebar is reproduced from *Critical Thinking: Tools for Taking Charge* by Richard Paul and Linda Elder, published by The Foundation for Critical Thinking © Dr. Richard Paul & Linda Elder, 2000, and reproduced by arrangement with The Rowman & Littlefield Publishing Group.

These standards are criteria that assess the quality of the thinking being done (see Appendix II, p. 288), but this SEIE activity singles out *clarity*. As stated by Dr. Paul, "Clarity is a gateway standard. If a statement is unclear, we can't determine whether it is accurate or relevant. In fact, we don't know anything about it because we don't know yet what it is saying." To make a statement more clear, one can *tell more about it* (elaborate), *illustrate it* (give an analogy to describe it), and *exemplify it* (give an example.) By the time you finish doing these three tasks, you are considerably clearer about what you can and can't articulate about a topic.

For example:

Statement: *Effective riding is intentional and systematic.*

Study Guide

Clarity/State, Elaborate, Illustrate, and Exemplify (SEIE)

Elaboration (give more detail): *Being able to achieve a goal with your horse takes planning, putting those plans into effect in an organized manner, and evaluating the outcomes to prepare for next steps.*

Or, as the late Portuguese classical dressage master Miguel de Lancastre e Tavora advised: "The work must always be progressive, gradual, logical, and systematic in order to develop the horse's physical abilities."

Illustration (give an analogy): *Intentional and systematic riding is <u>like</u> putting a child through school. There are different and progressive goals for each grade level in which the students are taught, assessed, and graduated based on their development. Depending on their aptitude, success, and shortcomings, students move into different careers.*

Exemplify (give an example): *For example, I tried a new lesson with my horse, "stopping into each foot" in turn (see p. 7). Then I tried stopping into each foot with each rein in both the walk and the trot. I discovered that the horse didn't stop well into the front legs, but did stop well in the hind legs. It worked better in the walk than at the trot. I learned that I could go ahead and use stopping into the hind legs, but I needed to work on fixing the resistances in the front legs and improving willingness and responsiveness in the trot.*

Now you try, based on what we've experienced in this chapter:

Statement: *Being "connected" to your horse is the most fundamental form of communication, upon which everything gradually evolves.*

Elaboration (give more detail): ....
....

Illustration (give an analogy): ....
....

Exemplify (give an example): ....
....

Try SEIE for each of the Non-Negotiables, as well as any other areas you want to delve more deeply into.

Chapter

STAY CONNECTED

07

The horse must be ridden forward with sufficient energy to stay connected. Connection is a dynamic feel that informs the rider of how much push is coming from behind to unite the front and back of the horse. But, because no two horses are alike with regard to energy and preference, the contact a horse makes in the bridle as a component of that connection is as individual as he is. Furthermore, the nature of the connection evolves over time as a horse develops and the rider becomes more discriminating—it's not a one-and-done outcome.

7.1 When I had the chance to ride a stallion from the Spanish Riding School (see p. 161), I learned what it can be like to keep that desired connection through an entire ride. Maintaining contact and connection, and reestablishing it when it is lost, is what we will work on in this chapter. •

Now that you have established contact with your horse, you both have a sense of its existence. At first, it will likely be elusive and intermittent. *Everything* disrupts connection: changing direction, gait, a comment, a neigh, wind. *Any* distraction and *poof*—gone. Since contact and connection are indispensable to communicating with your horse, maintaining and utilizing them are top priority (fig. 7.1). Your next goal is to learn to:

❖ Ascertain when you have contact and connection and when you don't.

❖ Maintain and improve connection when you have it, and reestablish it when it has been lost.

❖ Use connection.

Contact and Connection: Now You Have It, Now You Don't

Since horses move, contact is *never* static. In addition to motion generated by the gaits, your horse may move randomly at any point. When you do not adjust promptly (with the rein widening and leg squeezing you learned in chapter 6—see p. 000), you will lose contact. Horses can also drop contact in just one rein (figs. 7.2 A & B). Ultimately, you want continuous, equal contact on both reins. With consistent training, the horse will eventually realize that he needs to "carry himself" (self-carriage) and maintain a consistent connection from back to front.

Knowing when you have or don't have contact/connection is a skill that requires dexterity and experience. Once felt for the first time, your job isn't done! Unfortunately, it's not something you simply establish at the beginning of a ride, like turning the ignition in a car, and then you're good for the rest of the ride. On the plus side, having to re-establish contact/connection repeatedly gives you plenty of opportunities to practice finding it. As you become familiar with the sensation, you will begin to notice when it is about to drop and take proactive measures to avoid that. Through practice, you will learn to detect when the horse backs off the bit, gets strong, raises or turns his head, begins to move downhill, stiffens his neck, sinks his back, or looks at distractions. Quickly recognizing that you've lost 10 percent of your contact/connection is far easier to recover from (by pushing the horse forward and straightening

7.2 A & B Horse Drops One Rein. During a ride, some horses frequently "drop the contact." Sometimes, the horse will drop contact with only one rein **(A)**. To correct the problem, place the horse's nose in the center of his chest by widening only the loosened rein, while keeping a steady connection on the other rein **(B)**. To reestablish the lost connection, push the horse forward into the rein with "slack" using your leg on the same side. The objective is to maintain an even, consistent contact on both reins and connection equally through both sides of the body. •

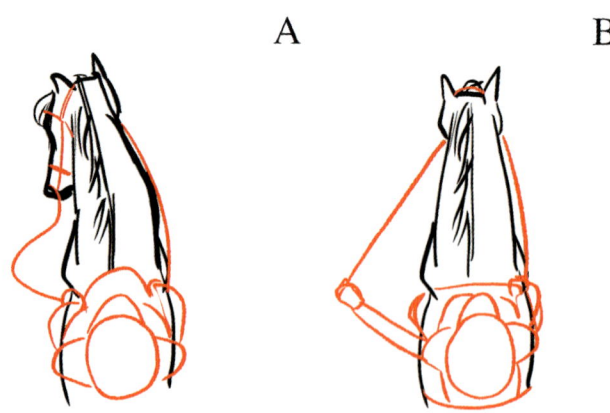

him with a widening rein) than not noticing until it's too late and having to start over. Maintaining contact becomes second nature—for some riders, out of convenience! It's far easier to keep it than to have to reconnect every few seconds.

Maintaining Connection: It's Not Just Reins!

Reins should not be regarded as the sole means of communication. As we've touched on, other factors contribute to contact and that circuit of connection, including your body, thoughts, horse, and surroundings. Each of these elements has its own subset of components to manage. Connection is jeopardized when any of these aspects are neglected.

The Role of the Rider

❖ Avoid tilting or tucking your **head**. Its weight shifts your alignment, throwing both you and your horse off balance. Look between the horse's ears.

❖ Maintain an upright **torso** that advances with the horse, like the pole on a carousel horse. Do not lean back, forward, or sideways. Remain centered. Be neither rigid nor floppy. Ride with Your Mind founder Mary Wanless suggests forcefully saying, "*Psshhttt*," as you ride. This utterance creates positive tension in your abdomen, which strengthens your core stability.

❖ Be mindful that your **body** does not behave like a chimney, allowing energy to escape like smoke, resulting in a loss of connection. Remember that the energy produced by the horse's hind legs "wants to escape" via your head bobbing, upper body rocking, legs swinging, and so on, and when you correct one area, the energy will likely attempt to escape through another. If it does not escape through you, it will exit the horse through his "popped shoulder" or other deviation from the line of travel and contact you are trying to establish and keep. Maintaining energy in the system by exercising vigilance is critical.

* Be mindful of your **arms**. Don't keep them rigid while your torso rocks; don't let them flail with excessive movement; and don't let them dangle, limp and forgotten.

* Maintain a straight **back** and bent **elbows**. Use your lower back in conjunction with your arms. When your arms separate from your body, they are no match for the horse's head and neck, and he is able to pull them, and you, forward. Because your torso is stronger than your arms, you can leverage the weight of the horse's head and neck to your advantage by keeping your arms at your sides. This is the position you ultimately wish to attain, anyway. Once you are no longer pulling on the reins, throwing them away, using excessive inside rein, or being out of sync with your horse, it is time to "graduate" to this more refined position, riding from your core.

* It is time to **keep your arms steady** so that your hands through the reins function as a giving "barrier" in front of the horse, as if he is pressing his forehead against a padded wall. He continues to move forward because you push his body with your seat and back, analogous to compressing a folding door: as you push on the panels, they stack when they reach the end of their track—the doorframe. His body arches upward like the panels stack and the energy from the completed circuit makes it feel like he is "between your seat and hand" or "coming back to you."

* The outside **hand** needs to be steady. The inside hand asks the horse to flex the poll when he resists, stiffens, or inverts, and releases when he yields. As clinician and co-creator of Artistic Dressage Thomas Ritter advises, "You don't want a passive or dead hand; but you don't want it to be too busy—hands must be as intense as necessary, but they must yield as soon as they achieve their effect so the horse can relax in the new posture. If the rider's hand becomes stuck, it provokes opposition—even in an obedient horse—the moment the horse is no longer able to yield more, and this moment arrives very quickly."

* Keep your **pelvis** level. Don't lean to one side or tilt it forward or back. Mary Wanless suggests visualizing your pelvis as a bowl filled with water and avoiding any movement that could cause the water to spill. To move just your pelvis with the horse's motion, practice the dance move "twerking." This motion enables your torso to remain upright and still on the horse. Twerk forward and up, lifting the pelvis toward your chin; don't arch your back. Best Ride Lessons instructor Denise Sobering reminds us that "the waist is not a joint," and you shouldn't bend there and bob your chest up and down with the motion of the horse.

* The neck doesn't move the horse. Rather than "steering" with the reins, it makes more sense to **control the horse's legs by influencing his**

shoulders and hindquarters. When in the saddle, your legs have a number of responsibilities: your knees position the shoulders, your thighs push the rib cage over (see p. 188), and your lower legs direct the horse's hind legs. Maintaining proper alignment of the shoulders, ribs, and hips balances the horse by keeping his legs underneath him. (This is why we worked on moving the shoulders and hind end on the ground earlier—see p. 77.)

❖ You **can guide the horse with your pelvis**, turning him with pelvic rotation, weight placement, and thigh and knee pressure. By rotating your pelvis like a math compass used to create circles, you can push the horse's shoulders around a turn—shift your outside hip forward while using your inside thigh to maintain the arc of his body and your outside leg to prevent drifting onto a bigger turn (fig. 7.3). Turning your pelvis more or less makes the curve tighter or wider.

❖ Any muscle tightness in the rider's body causes a **corresponding tightness** in the horse's body. If the rider's hips are stiff, the horse's hips will become stiff. The horse's poll and jaw will brace if the rider's wrists are stiff. Allow your horse to breathe with "breathing legs." Remember, *you feel as stiff to your horse as your horse feels to you.* Muscles with lower levels of negative tension facilitate the transmission of information, while muscles with higher levels of negative tension are less receptive to incoming signals and less likely to convey information. Stiffness prevents connection.

❖ Keep all your **joints** loose and "open" so that they can absorb the horse's motion, allowing you to move in unison with him. "Open" means that the joints are not overly flexed. When hip and knee joints are overly flexed, your torso leans forward and your knees are drawn up. This insecure position hinders connection. Good posture in the saddle is a key ingredient to maintaining connection.

The Role of the Reins

❖ Think of reins as data cables that transmit and receive information between the horse and rider; the horse's mouth and rider's hands are the ports. Reins inform the rider about the horse's straightness, balance, adjustability, and relaxation. On the basis of the rider's observations, reins can be used to improve the horse's actions by widening, softening, flexing, yielding, and supporting. Managing these factors improves connection. The quality of contact and connection evolves over time based on the horse's developmental needs.

❖ **Reins are a two-way street.** They aren't just for the rider to give the horse instructions. They enable the horse to communicate with the rider about where he is stiff, heavy on one, soft, or supple. According to Thomas Ritter, there is both a "quantity" and a "quality" to contact: the quantity is the amount of weight you feel in your hand, and the quality is its consistency, meaning whether it feels hard, soft, or something else.

❖ As established in chapter 6, rein **length** should remain constant, the tautness steady. Riding forward to a shorter rein with a forgiving arm is preferable because shorter reins are easier to manage.

❖ Keep your **fingers closed** on the reins to preserve consistent length. Some riders believe an open

7.3 Compass. To turn your horse, use your pelvis like a math compass: the pointed tip rests on the paper, and the top of the compass is rotated to create a circle. Your inside leg and hip function as the point around which the horse arcs, while your outside hip pushes forward to rotate the pelvis like the top of the compass to create the curved path you wish your horse to travel. Make sure your shoulders remain in line with your pelvis and they do not counterbend in the other direction. •

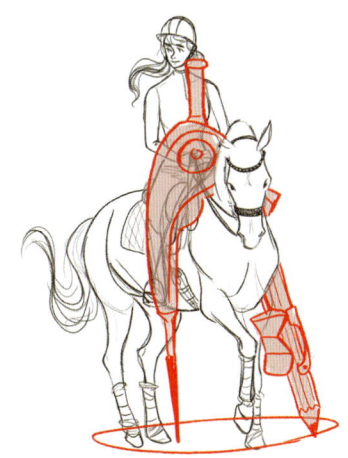

hand is more considerate, but straight fingers are ineffective for communication. I instruct my students to imagine their gloves are sewn onto the reins so they cannot slip. If you need to reestablish connection, widen (see p. 130).

❖ Many riders put their hands down by their knees, straightening their elbows. Typically, this occurs when the reins are too long and the rider attempts to apply tension to them. This is incorrect and unyieldingly rigid. In the end, the reins must be "**just right**." Keep your arms soft and yielding, and position your hands close to and in front of the withers (see p. 160). This keeps the line from the bit to the elbow straight and makes it easier to reward the horse. After being rewarded, horses try noticeably harder. It is best to stroke the neck as a reward with the inside hand because you don't want to lose the contact on the outside rein.

❖ Each horse has unique contact and connection. The rider must feel this. **There is no set rein length or pressure for any horse.** Your horse may require one length or pressure in one direction and another in the other. Many horses require a longer outside rein when traveling to the right. As you gain experience, you will discover how to maintain contact with the reins at any length and different levels of pressure or tension. Depending on the task at hand or the horse's level of development, you will also need to ride your horse with his neck at different heights (reaching forward versus collected, for example).

❖ The reins can be used to test the **poll's mobility**. (This means that your horse's head is easily movable, but *not* from a bend in the neck; instead, it nods freely just behind the ears.) If you meet resistance in the poll when you gently draw on a rein, he has stiff muscles in that area. Resistance in the poll hinders forward movement and disrupts connection. Your signal cannot pass through it to access the hind legs. (Rein aids go first through the poll—the "gateway to the spine," which must be unlocked.) When related muscles are loose, your communications can pass through; in addition, the horse's hind legs are able to step under his body and the connection is strong.

❖ **"Drifting out," "falling in," and "counterbending"** all disrupt connection. Your horse needs to remain flexed to the inside without drifting out on the path of travel. The outside rein prevents drift by counteracting bend at the base of the neck; the inside rein prevents the horse from counterbending when the outside rein is applied. The reins help your pelvis say "don't go that way; don't look that way" so you maintain connection while steering.

❖ Don't forget: reins should reward! A little release tells the horse he has performed well.

The Role of the Horse

❖ When the horse is **unbalanced** it is impossible to maintain contact/connection. The first step is to position the horse's nose in the center of his chest, his shoulders in line with his hips, and his legs both laterally and longitudinally underneath him. If the horse leans on the forehand, sucks back, steps out from under the body with a leg, speeds up, slows down, or bulges a shoulder, the contact fluctuates between too much and too little.

❖ Any muscle groups that are **stiff** must be loosened so the horse can move forward. When a horse is stiff, he feels resistant and unresponsive. Massage and other bodywork can help loosen stiff muscles, reducing the amount of effort required when riding.

❖ Uneven contact can indicate that the horse is **crooked** and leaning more heavily on one rein than the other. A common crookedness is "diagonal sprawl," in which the hindquarters track to the inside and the horse leans on the opposite (outside) shoulder. You must push that shoulder back under the horse and move the shoulders in front of the hips. Performing a leg-yield in the opposite direction, which I teach you beginning on p. 182, is an effective solution.

- The horse must react appropriately to your aids, but the **timing** of them is essential. Aids cannot be administered haphazardly. You *must* provide an aid when the horse is biomechanically capable of complying. For example, you can control one of his legs by *keeping it on the ground* for a fraction of a second longer if you want to slow, stop, or prevent drift. Or, you can access a leg *while it is in flight* and capable of greater movement—for example, if you want it to cross over another leg. If you ask at any other time, it's impossible for the horse to comply.

- Typically, horses reach forward and comply with an aid **when the rider yields**, rather than in response to the aid pressure or correction. Therefore, you must "give" and observe the results. Then, either provide a reward or try again. You must be aware of the aid's intensity and duration. If a small (less intense, shorter) aid does not elicit a response, try a larger one...until a small aid *does* elicit a response. Remember: It is preferable to employ a short aid rather than a long hold. "Holding" an aid causes the horse to stiffen and pull back.

- Not surprisingly, the horse's **conformation** affects his ability to connect, so you have to take what his build is like into account. Neck shape can tell you a little about whether contact/connection will be easy or hard. Short, thick necks lack flexibility, are heavy, and weigh down the horse's front end. On the other hand, long, slender necks can weave around, suck back and curl up to evade connection, or "break" in the middle of the neck. Horses with low-set necks tend to pull down. Horses with high-set necks often raise their head, push out the underneck, and drop the back. This causes the hind legs to trail "out behind" so the hocks don't bend and the horse is rough to ride. Horses who are thick through the body and short-coupled have a hard time bending through the spine and have limited mobility. Horses who are long wiggle out of your grasp. Thick, stiff horses need a lot more suppling. Slender, wiggly horses need more stabilizing. Obviously, every part of the horse anatomy can be analyzed, but this gives you an idea!

- Horses have a propensity to lose connection during **transitions**. This causes a cascade of issues, including loss of balance, frame, rhythm, and alignment. Therefore, focusing on maintaining connection and making a good transition before/during/after is incredibly useful for enhancing connection.

- Don't let the horse think a **down transition or a halt** is collapsing into quitting. Think "work harder, more uphill" (imagine riding up a flight of stairs) and "don't lean on me." If he loses energy as you begin to transition down, continue forward, maintaining the connection. Then ask him to take shorter strides and think, "Almost walk." If he collapses, go forward again. Through this exercise, the horse will learn to anticipate the possibility of an immediate upward transition and will keep energy to be ready. This gives you good connection. (A useful exercise is to ride five steps trot, walk one step; ride four steps trot, walk one step; ride three steps trot and so on. Then go back up from one to six. Lilo Fore, a master clinician and international dressage judge, suggests that a down transition should be conceptualized as "riding an up transition into a lower gait." This method will lead to a transition that is more precise, energetic, and uphill.)

- To maintain connection during an **up transition**, the horse must respond promptly with his body by moving forward while avoiding breaking connection by lifting his head. If you imagine riding the horse's hind end into the bridle—like it is the Energizer Bunny walking against a wall—you'll keep a good connection with your body.

- Don't be frustrated or disappointed if you worked hard to connect your horse and it only lasts one or two strides. Don't get upset if you lose it, and don't expect your horse to do it once and then stay that way forever. Riding is a game that requires skill, patience, and repetition. You'll eventually learn to maintain the contact and connection by anticipating when and how your horse might abandon or lose it and **staying one step ahead**. That success can be incredibly satisfying, and it quickly becomes second nature.

The Role of Thought

To maintain contact/connection, you must think analytically about what the horse is telling you. Accept that things in the horse's body will change all the time, and it is your job to guide these changes to help the horse keep his balance, energy, and alignment. You cannot become frustrated; this is the nature of riding. It is what it is.

As Thomas Ritter clarifies, "A light rein contact is the result of balance; an even rein contact is the result of straightness; a steady contact is the result of the hind legs pushing steadily; and suppleness plays a role in all three demands." Evaluating the status of these and deciding what to do about each is the thinking rider's role.

- If you don't like the contact, adjust the **balance**. Too heavy? Lift neck, weight back. Too light? Push forward. Uneven? Straighten the horse, or encourage the lagging hind leg forward so both hind legs push under the horse's body evenly.

- Unsteady **tempo**? More impulsion. If you are posting at the trot, *you* set the pace—*don't* follow his.

- **Counting strides** on circles until the horse maintains the same number of strides per quarter circle and sustains a steady tempo improves balance, straightness, and contact significantly (see p. 106).

- It is difficult to establish and maintain a connection when **traveling in a straight line**. Going straight allows horses to rush, drop their back, and lose alignment, so use circles, serpentines, figure eights (changing bend), squares, diamonds, and lateral movements such as leg-yield (see p. 175) to supple the horse while also creating a bend to connect to the outside rein.

Always ride on a predetermined route, such as a pattern, circle, square, or other shape, so that your horse has a **deliberate path** to follow. If you wander aimlessly, the horse loses balance because he doesn't know where to put his legs. Dressage tests, reining patterns, and arena exercises are great places to get ideas.

❖ Use the **arena** itself to help with connection. Set up markers to ensure your circles and serpentines are precise and consistent; use the rail for lateral work.

❖ Use the **warm-up** to establish contact/connection. This is where you figure out what is disrupting it and how to fix it.

Improving Connection

In addition to all the preceding material, **lateral work** (moving forward and sideways) improves connection. Lateral work, including "leg-yield," "shoulder-in," "renvers," "travers," "half-pass," and "spiraling in or out" (leg-yield on a circle with concentrically smaller or larger circles) create bend through the horse's body that help you maintain a good connection. (Note: in this book I only provide specific instruction in how to do leg-yield, but I recommend seeking out a solid reference with descriptions of other fundamental lateral work if you are not already familiar with incorporating it in your riding.) When the horse bends as he moves forward and sideways, it creates a connection on the outside rein. In addition, lateral work strengthens, coordinates, balances, and aligns a horse. Practice lateral work until the horse is relaxed while doing it.

Leg-Yield

The act of encouraging your horse to step laterally (sideways) with your leg is known as a "leg-yield." The leg-yield is useful for addressing a variety of issues that a horse may exhibit, such as unevenness in the reins, lack of contact in the outside rein, rushing, moving downhill, bulging a shoulder, or being stiff. During a leg-yield, the horse moves forward and laterally away from an inside ("inside" the flexion) leg aid, with his head turned *away* from the direction he is traveling. He moves straight forward with his outside pair of legs, and he moves sideways by crossing his inside front and hind legs in front of and over the outside legs. This alternation of *straight* and *sideways* crossing steps takes him on a gradually diagonal path in the most basic version of the exercise. It is critical in this movement that the horse's whole body remains "straight," meaning that his shoulders, hips, and neck stay aligned with each. Neither the shoulders nor the hips should angle, or lead, toward the destination.

Purpose of the Leg-Yield

Usually when you ride a maneuver with a horse, it is done for a specific reason, seeking a particular outcome. As such, many riding exercises are designed to be diagnostic and therapeutic, rather than simply "fun tricks" to ride. They are *diagnostic* in that they reveal which aspects of the movement the horse is unable to perform, either because he does not understand it or because his body lacks the required flexibility to perform it. They are *therapeutic* because the horse develops both mentally and physically during training and practice, which is the ultimate aim of performing the maneuver. The leg-yield serves many purposes. It:

❖ Introduces **moving away from the rider's leg**, or "yielding."

❖ Teaches the horse that the rider's **leg can mean more than just "go."**

❖ Helps an anxious horse learn to **accept the leg** and not run away from it (it's harder to go fast going sideways).

❖ Encourges a response to **weight cues** from the rider.

❖ **Places the horse on the outside rein**, assisting the rider in discovering and maintaining that contact.

❖ Helps establish a **secure contact and connection.**

❖ Teaches the rider to exert more **sophisticated and complex control** over the horse's body.

❖ Compels the rider to **utilize each aid and limb independently** and at various times.

❖ Teaches the rider **when and why to use specific aids.**

❖ Helps the rider recognize the necessity of **a straightness and poll flexion.**

❖ Teaches the rider to keep the horse's **shoulders and hips in line.**

- **Repositions a bulging shoulder** beneath the withers, causing the horse to be more upright.

- Helps **straighten** a crooked horse throughout the whole body.

- Helps the horse become more symmetrical, or **equally flexible** in both directions.

- **Stretches** the short side of the body.

- Encourages the inside hind leg **to step underneath** the horse.

- Teaches the horse to reach and **cross his legs.**

- Teaches the rider **the timing of the aids** required to identify and control both a grounded foot and a leg in flight.

- **Organizes the footfalls** of the horse.

- Enhances **transitions** because lateral movement causes the joints of the hind leg to bend more deeply, thereby increasing spring.

- **Supples** the hindquarters.

- **Improves a horse's gait** by lengthening stride through lateral movement and adding expression.

- **Slows a rushing horse** (see p. 183).

- Helps the rider learn **how to initiate a lateral** maneuver, and how to exit from it.

- **Prepares the horse** to learn other lateral work.

- Provides a good **warm-up exercise**, loosening and stretching the muscles and relaxing the horse.

Preparation for the Leg-Yield

It is essential to maintain the horse's straightness during a leg-yield. If you can identify whether the horse's body becomes crooked or deviates from the line of travel in one direction or the other, you will have a better chance of success with the leg-yield. You'll be even more successful if you understand how the horse's body moves and when to give him cues. Mastering the following four preparatory exercises makes it much easier to execute the leg-yield:

- Begin by teaching your horse to walk in a straight line, a few feet *away* from the fence line or wall, with his head flexed to the left or right (you will practice flexing to both sides, so it doesn't matter what you start with). It is good to practice moving in a straight line several feet off the track for a number of reasons. First, it allows you to learn to detect when your horse strays off the line in either direction so that you can correct it. In addition, the fence line or wall helps keep your horse straight for you as you learn to do this on your own. Choose an object to keep centered between his ears, and ride directly toward it, keeping his legs underneath him and in line with each other. This is called a "balancing line." Maintain his alignment with your seat and legs. It's helpful to draw a line in the dirt and ride with it between your horse's front legs. Having someone on the ground watching the legs from the front and back and alerting you when they deviate is also beneficial. When you have achieved success flexed in one direction, switch to the other. Your horse should be soft and submissive in this flexion, not rigid or fussy. As you learned in chapter 6, you should not pull or hold; the horse merely looks slightly in one direction in response to a light rein and leg aid, readily yielding his poll and jaw upon request.

❖ The second skill you must acquire is the ability to feel the horse's rib cage sway as he walks in a straight line. If you pay close attention, you will feel the horse's belly sway back and forth, pushing first on one of your legs and then the other. Remember the viking ship ride (see p. 159)? The rib cage swings to the left to make way for the right hind to advance, and vice versa. When you feel the horse's barrel pressing against your calf, push it back toward the other side, alternately applying pressure to the horse with each leg in turn, in a rhythmic manner. When you do this, that push will give the leg that is in flight more space to come forward, resulting in a longer stride for your horse. You will know you have succeeded when you feel your horse surge forward.

❖ Your horse needs to be able to turn, straighten, and stop obediently when the outside front leg is on the ground, so that it remains there longer. He needs to understand that a gentle signal on the outside rein means "don't go that way" or "don't step sideways out from underneath your body with that leg." Outside legs must travel straight ahead in leg-yield. Riding a square with neat corners (with neither his outside legs stepping out on the turn, nor his rib cage swinging in after the corner) is a good exercise for controlling where the legs are placed and ensuring the turn, straighten, and stop skills are solidified.

❖ Through riding circles and changes of direction, a horse learns to yield away from the rider's leg in manner that makes sense to him. Practicing figure eights and serpentines will increase flexibility through your horse's body and accustom him to respond to and move away from your legs so that he is ready, willing, and able to do so when you ask him for the leg-yield (see p. 220).

Any time your leg-yield fails you should return to one of these basic exercises to practice the components that aren't working. Fixing leg-yield by going back to the fundamentals is more effective than attempting to force it by leg-yielding more or leg-yielding more forcefully. Determining which aspect of a movement isn't working and separating it out to correct *that* before returning to the maneuver is an important, basic training tool that applies to *all* aspects of riding.

Introducing the Leg-Yield

When the effects of the four preparatory exercises are combined, a leg-yield is produced. Here's how:

❖ To begin, walk parallel to the long side of the arena, but some distance from it (along the quarter line, for example), by turning early from the short side. This gives your room to leg-yield a few steps *toward* the fence line or wall. Horses usually gravitate toward the wall, which will make the movement easier, at first. Be sure to be moving forward well before you ask for leg-yield. *Forward is always first.*

❖ When you are tracking left and enter a leg-yield to the right, toward the fence line or wall, *do not change the flexion.* This means that, if you are going around the arena to the left, your horse will be flexed to the left, and you keep the left flexion as you leg-yield the horse to the right.

❖ After you turn down the quarter line and are ready to begin the leg-yield, step into your outside (right) stirrup, using your weight to guide the horse in the direction you desire as he reacts by stepping underneath your weight. Use the outside rein when the horse's outside front leg is on the ground in order to keep it there a second longer to stop it from possibly veering sideways and to give the inside pair of legs more flight time to cross over in front of the grounded outside pair. The outside rein also serves to keep the horse's neck and body straight. Push with your inside (left) leg when the horse's left leg is in the air.

❖ Don't hold either your inside "push" or your outside "step"; instead, but do them in an alternating rhythm. Think, "Step right, push left; step right, push left," and your horse should go forward and sideways (to the right). If you don't get a response the first time, you might have to use your legs a little more dramatically, or even lean your weight to the right, but you can work to use the smallest aids possible to get the desired response once he understands.

❖ If your horse is unfamiliar with leg-yielding, at first, he may not understand what to do, but they catch on very quickly. It usually only takes one or two tries for the horse to associate the push with your inside leg and the weight shift to the outside stirrup with moving toward the rail. Once the horse understands, you won't need to shift your weight so exaggeratedly. And when he responds willingly at the walk, you can try leg-yield at the trot, which is the gait primarily used for the movement.

★ Caveats

❖ If your horse becomes askew, leave the leg-yield and go forward a few steps until you are straight again. **Alternating straight with leg-yield is often referred to as the "staircase" exercise**.

❖ Don't let the horse be lazy and just fall toward or drift to the wall. Make sure you are leg-yielding with **quality and correctness.**

- Hold your outside leg slightly behind the girth to **stop the horse's hindquarters from taking the lead** and to keep him going forward. **Prevent the outside shoulder from taking the lead** with the outside rein.

- Avoid leaning in either direction. **Stay upright and centered in the saddle**. Do not lean forward or sway in response to external forces created by the horse's movement.

- In all gaits, concentrate on **maintaining the horse's rhythm and tempo**.

- If the horse is not moving sufficiently forward, the diagonal you create will be **too steep**, too sharply sideways to the wall, and too advanced for your horse. The horse loses impulsion, energy, and rhythm when this happens. Stop the leg-yield and ride forward to restore these qualities, then repeat.

- If your **horse rushes, leans, or takes an excessively large, fast, or sideways first step, immediately do a circle in the direction of flexion, away from the leg-yield**. Repeat the circling correction each time until the horse waits on your aids to begin the movement. He should be resistance-free, attentive, and soft upon entering a leg-yield, or any maneuver.

- If your **horse becomes tense and hollow**, abandon the leg-yield and ride forward until relaxation, connection, and throughness are restored. Then, try again.

- Avoid excessive leg-yielding. Don't do it **too far nor too frequently**. Gradually increase the amount so that your horse develops both mental and physical fitness.

- If you discover that the horse is walking diagonally toward the fence line or wall with his shoulders in front and his hind legs trailing, this indicates that the horse's front end has yielded away from your inside leg more quickly than his hind end has. Do not pull on the inside rein to attempt to make the horse parallel to the long side again. This will only worsen the situation. **Use the outside rein to straighten him instead. This places the outside shoulder back under the horse and allows the inside hind leg to "catch up" and step underneath the body properly**. It seems counterintuitive, but using the outside rein causes the horse's hindquarters to swing to the outside (feels like he "fishtails") and straightens the horse in this scenario. Remember, the shoulders move in the *opposite* direction of the rein you use.

★★ Extensions

Leg-yielding toward the straight, long side is only one possible application of the technique.

You can also:

- **Leg-yield in and out on a circle**, spiraling out to enlarge, or in to decrease, the diameter. This exercise helps the horse learn to bend correctly and come onto the outside rein. Be sure to keep his shoulders and hips in line; neither should angle toward the inside or outside of the circle.

- **Leg-yield into a corner.** This pushes the horse deep into the corner so he doesn't lean like a motorcycle in a turn, cutting the corner off.

- Change flexion on the rail and then **leg-yield *away* from rail toward the quarter line**.

- Leg-yield a few steps away from the rail, **change flexion**, leg-yield back to the rail, repeat.

- **Try the "staircase" leg-yield I mentioned before**: leg-yield a few steps, ride straight a few steps, then leg-yield a few steps again in the same direction. This emphasizes the rider's control of the horse with the outside aids and teaches the horse that leg-yield is not just aimless drifting until a wall or fence line is reached.

- Leg-yield more steeply **sideways**.

- Leg-yield across on the **diagonal**.

- Leg-yield a few steps, **circle in the direction of the flexion, return to leg-yield**, then circle again.

- **Change gaits during a leg-yield**, both up and down. For example, begin on a smaller circle, leg-yield out to a larger circle and make an upward transition upon reaching the larger circle, or start on a larger circle, leg-yield onto a smaller circle, and do a downward transition upon reaching the smaller circle. As the rib cage swings out of the way of the inside hind leg, forwardness is unblocked and the horse's hind leg joints are flexed more, making him inclined to spring into the desired gait as they straighten. Stepping slightly to the side encourages the horse to lift the withers rather than fall forward, preventing him from charging or rushing forward.

- **Practice while out on the trail or hacking**. You can practice a few steps of leg-yield on the trail, or longer distances down a fence line, in a fresh environment, keeping the movement interesting for the horse. Leg-yield is a great way of keeping your horse's attention if he is excited by being outside.

- **Leg-yield nose to rail or tail to rail.** The fence line or wall blocks the horse from going forward or contains the hindquarters, depending on which you do, making it easier for the rider to practice coordinating the aids. Leg-yielding in these two ways also makes it evident when the horse is going sideways (see more in the sidebar}.

Two Fundamental Leg-Yield Exercises

Scan to View
Nose-to-Rail Leg-Yield

7.4 A & B Nose-to-Rail Leg-Yield (Front and Rear View). The nose-to-rail exercises prevents the horse from pushing forward through your connection. If he is leg-yielding to the right, he is flexed left, away from his direction of travel. His inside ("inside" the flexion) legs cross in front of his outside legs. This maneuver will help your horse become more connected and responsive to the outside rein, making it easier for you to identify what contact and connection should feel like and how it should feel when it works. Consequently, you will gain greater control over the horse's body.

Nose to Rail

Two simple ways to start a nose-to-rail leg-yield are:

1. *Ride a short diagonal across the arena straight forward toward the long side, then maintain that angle (approximately 35 to 45 degrees) as you ride down the fence line or wall, flexed away from the direction of travel. (Note: if you ride too long of a diagonal, there will be no wall left to leg-yield down!)*

2. *As you come out of a corner onto the long side, change your flexion to the outside, and proceed at the same angle named above down the fence line.*

Either way, your "inside" (direction of flexion) will be next to the fence line or wall, and since you are going down the rail away from the direction of flexion, the inside of the arena is the "outside" of the horse (figs. 7.4 A & B). This is important to be aware of because you may want to "fix" something on the "outside" of the horse (like contact in the outside rein), and you need to realize that is the "inside" of the arena!

Drive the horse down the rail with the previously described rhythmic leg pushes and steps (see p. 178). Because of the help from the fence line or wall, you should really feel the horse coming onto contact on the outside rein as his inside

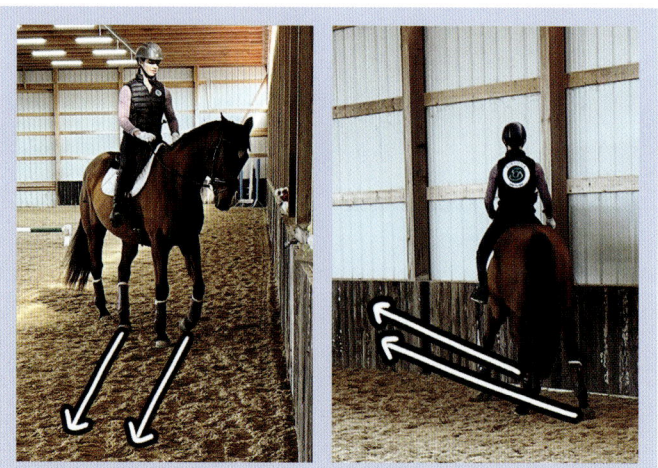

A   B

THIS · NOT THIS

7.5 A & B Outside Forward. This horse, Tulip, is traveling in leg-yield to the right. Due to the left flexion, Tulip's left side is her inside so her left pair of front and rear legs should cross regularly and evenly over her right pair of front and rear legs in an organized and coordinated fashion **(A)**. The outside pair of legs should not ever step sideways, out from underneath the body, as then the inside pair of legs can only "catch up" to them because they are too far away to cross over **(B)**. ●

7.6 Nice Example of Nose to Rail. The horse is straight, the inside legs are crossing over and in front of the outside legs, and flexion is slight. ●

legs step over his outside legs (figs. 7.5 A & B). Maintain his straightness with the outside rein and his suppleness with the inside rein. Be more vigilant about maintaining your outside rein and outside leg so the horse does not turn too perpendicular to the rail or run through your aids (fig. 7.6).

★ **Benefits of Nose to Rail**

1. *Slows a strong or rushing horse.*

2. *Puts the horse more on the outside rein because he can't push forward through it because the wall blocks him.*

3. *Going the opposite direction down the rail positions the shoulder that falls in (see p. 57) more underneath the horse, making the horse more upright and stable.*

4. *Improves transitions for horses that lunge into canter. Practice transition to canter from the nose-to-rail position so he has nowhere to go…and nowhere to go fast.*

5. *Helps the horse cross his inside legs over and in front of his outside legs more.*

6. *Relieves the rider of the need to use the reins, as the fence line or wall does a lot of work for you. Removing any feeling that you need to "pull" to restrain the horse is immensely helpful because pulling on the reins stops the hind legs from coming forward under the horse's body, killing impulsion, energy, connection, and balance.*

7. *Makes it easier to keep the horse straight in his neck and body.*

Two Fundamental Leg-Yield Exercises

Two Fundamental Leg-Yield Exercises

Scan to View
Tail-to-Rail Leg-Yield

Tail to Rail

After riding through a corner, position the horse as if you are about to ride across the diagonal line for a change of direction. Once your horse's shoulders are angled away from the fence line or wall at 35 to 45 degrees, "catch" the horse with your outside rein (the one facing the direction of travel down the long side), saying, "That's far enough," to prevent him from moving forward onto the diagonal (figs. 7.7 A & B). Squeeze the outside rein when his outside front leg is on the ground to delay it there, while you redirect the energy sideways with your inside leg. Rhythmically pushing the horse down the wall with your inside leg (when the inside hind leaves the ground), while squeezing on the outside rein with every stride to remind him not to bully through the contact. At the same time, your inside rein should maintain inside flexion away from direction of travel and keep him soft (figs. 7.8 A & B).

★ Benefits of Tail to Rail

1. ***Adds a measure of control that you might not yet have with your leg to control the path of the hindquarters.***

2. ***Prevents the horse's outside hind leg from stepping sideways out from under the body (only the inside hind leg should step sideways).***

7.7 A & B Tail-to-Rail Leg-Yield (Correct and Incorrect). By keeping the horse's hindquarters on the rail with his shoulders at a 35- to 45-degree angle, he can be even more effectively placed on the outside rein. The inside **(left)** pair of legs will cross in front of the outside **(right)** pair of legs **(A)**. When the shoulders are incorrectly turned at an angle of more than 45 degrees, the leg-yield is incorrect **(B)**. Leg yield is *not* a "side-pass" (going completely sideways without any forward movement).

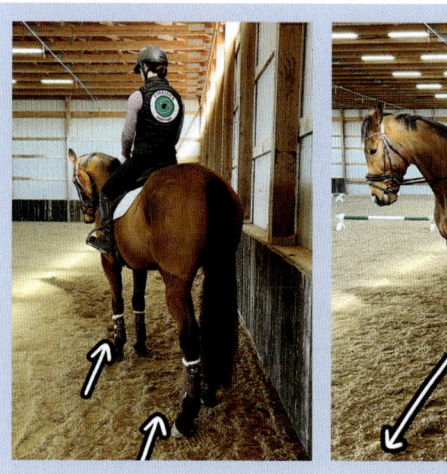

A   B

A   B

7.8 A & B Leg Crossover. In **(A)**, you are looking at the *outside* of the horse in tail-to-rail leg-yield. The outside (left) pair of legs are traveling straight and are underneath the body. The horse is very slightly flexed away from the direction of travel and is straight through the body. The inside pair of legs is crossing over and in front of the outside pair. In **(B)**, you are looking at the *inside* of the horse in the same movement, with the same qualities evident. •

3. **Controls the outside hind leg, which increases the inside hind leg's ability to cross over.**

4. **Stretches the side of the horse that resists (the short/hollow side—see p. 55) when it is placed against the fence line or wall.**

5. **Teaches the horse that an open space in front of him does not necessarily indicate that he should charge through it.**

6. **Helps the rider more easily feel the inside-leg-to-outside-rein relationship.**

7. **Supples and strengthens the hindquarters.**

8. **Gives horse and rider the feel for another lateral movement, as the positioning is similar to a "shoulder-in."**

★ **Important Note**

Be aware that tail to rail and nose to rail work in opposite directions. So if you want to use tail to rail to, for example, push the horse's right shoulder under him, you will need to travel around the arena to the right. The wall in this case is the "outside" and the interior of the arena is the "inside" because of the flexion you will keep. However, if you want to fix the same problem with nose to rail, you will have to travel, instead, to the left, and the wall will be the "inside." It is good to fix a problem with both tools, going both directions; just realize they will be opposite. •

Two Fundamental Leg-Yield Exercises

There Isn't "One" Connection

When you finally feel and maintain connection, you can rejoice, but know that connection, roundness, and throughness **can always be improved upon**, and your horse will become more responsive as you progress. Continue to strive for greater consistency, push, energy, steadiness, autonomy, softness, outside rein, and promptness in response through consistent work.

When everything is working properly, it will no longer be difficult to maintain the connection regardless of gait. Gaits will have a smooth, solid, quiet, energetic, and springy feel. The horse will feel loose, calm, confident, and steadily forward. It is very satisfying when your horse stays stable in the contact and connection. They will improve over time until they no longer come and go, but it's always a work in progress, with new levels of technicality being added as you progress. Staying connected requires more skill than simply attaining it. As new insights emerge, you will re-experience everything you've previously done in a new light. For example, when you finally get the horse's ribs pushed out enough so that the horse responds willingly to a slight aid on the outside rein and that contact feels "live," malleable, and functional, you suddenly and more profoundly understand the phrase "inside leg to outside rein." The horse is flexed in a posture in which the outside rein is like a line tangent to an arc (figs. 7.9 A & B). It is this posture that allows your horse to go "to the outside rein," where the outside rein can communicate effectively.

Using Connection:
It's All About the Outside Rein

Staying properly connected on the outside rein is one of the most important concepts when it comes to controlling your horse and having him become straight and unquestioningly willing. When your horse is "on the outside rein," the outside rein functions as a joystick and you have a control mechanism for steering, slowing, straightening, balancing, and collecting (fig. 7.10). The horse is putty in your hands, because the horse, as Sharon Vander Ziel reminds us, "goes *to* the outside rein, not *through* it." This means that the horse accepts the flexion and bend, stays on the line of travel, and does not drift out past or through the reins.

The outside rein serves as a common language for communication. Being connected enables you to intentionally apply or remove pressure from the reins. We've already established that the horse recognizes when you apply pressure on the outside rein and *moves away from it,* just as he moves away from pressure from your leg. This allows you to steer by using the rein of the direction you *don't* want to go and telling the horse, "Don't go that way," rather than pulling the horse to, "Go this way."

What this means is that, when you are riding a 20-meter circle, your outside rein and leg stop the horse from making it a 21-meter circle. If your horse *does* make the circle larger, then he's *going through the outside rein*. He's not respecting or recognizing its boundary. Remember the circle exercise from p. 62: You should be able to ride several circles while leaving only *one* set of tracks, about a foot wide at most. When there is no discernible, tidy set of tracks, your horse went through the outside rein or fell in a lot, causing the arena to look as though a herd of buffalo ran through.

You *communicate* with that outside rein, you don't pull on it so hard that he turns his head to the outside, or "counterbends." If the horse turns his head toward the outside rein, that rein droops,

7.9 A & B Arc Tangent to Circle. You will suddenly understand the phrase "inside leg to outside rein" when you finally get the horse's ribs pushed out and off your inside leg enough so that the horse responds willingly to a slight aid on the outside rein, and that contact feels "live." You know you have it when you can slow down, change direction, or do transitions without any change in the flexion, bend, or height of the head. The horse is flexed in a way that the outside rein is like a line tangent to an arc **(A)**. Think of the tangent line like a boundary—the horse's neck and shoulders do not bulge past the line **(B)**.

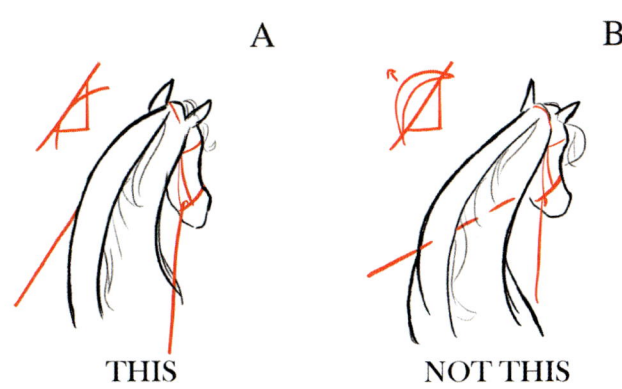

contact is lost…and as Sharon Vander Ziel emphasizes, "The outside rein instantly becomes the new inside rein!"

Use the inside rein and leg to keep the horse flexed sufficiently to prevent counterbending or loss of contact. In fact, the inside rein *gives you an outside rein to use*: the inside curvature of the neck due to slight flexion puts more positive tension on the now stretched outside rein than on the inside rein. This "tension" strengthens the connection, so that when you squeeze the outside rein to signal the horse, he can instantly feel it.

Like a pianist, your two hands—inside and outside—perform different, simultaneous, and interdependent functions. Both require your attention.

…And Also About the Inside Rein…and Leg!

The inside rein is essential because, as just noted, it prevents the horse from turning his head to the outside when the outside rein is used, and the flexion in the poll encouraged by the inside rein/outside rein relationship keeps the horse cooperative. He can't resist you with this positioning because the flexion removes his leverage against you.

Don't "hold" the inside rein; use and release its pressure as needed to supple. Holding is static and your horse will disregard you like he does the girth—a constant pressure most horses learn to ignore. More importantly, remember you will generally get the desired response from the horse during the release rather than the squeeze.

To test yourself, it is useful to have someone competent longe you while you drop the inside rein completely. See if you can get your horse round with

7.10 On the Outside Rein. This horse demonstrates a clear contact on the outside rein. You can also see that the right front leg is crossing over to the left and the left front leg is remaining upright to support the body. The horse is not falling inside with the inside front leg. There is a uniform curvature throughout the horse's body. The horse's ribs are off the rider's inside leg. ●

his body curved properly to the circular track by using *only the inside leg and outside rein.* This diagnostic exercise is excruciatingly revealing, clearly exposing what you cannot do. Be prepared for it to be a fiasco—the horse going the wrong direction or turning his head to the outside—until you figure out how to accomplish correctness with your body. Be patient, calm, and persistent. Once you can do it, your horse *will* end up moving with more scope, quality, and reach with his neck, and you can pick up your inside rein and appreciate just how *little* you really need it in order to keep him flexed and supple. You will become a more judicious, empathetic rider, beginning to comprehend the meaning of "hands independent of seat" because you will have had to use your seat to accomplish this. This alone substantially improves the quality of connection.

If you feel you need to use your inside rein, try your inside leg *first* to push the horse's rib cage out and curve his entire body, like a banana. The leg is a better option on the circle because the inside rein can encourage the neck to bend but not the whole body, causing the horse's outside shoulder to bulge out. For a horse, bending the neck is much easier than bowing the body by rotating the spine and swinging the rib cage. The neck can sometimes be like a flexible straw, with the straw bending only at the corrugated rings, forming a right angle with the horse's body. Try not to let the area at the junction of the withers and base of the neck jackknife. Hold the outside rein steady and *steer the horse's withers* rather than his head. Use your pelvis and legs to "rotate" the saddle away from the direction you don't want him to go.

An Effective Inside Leg to Outside Rein: The Sweet Spot

On DressageToday.com, USEF "S" dressage judge Fran Kehr presents the useful admonition, "I must emphasize that just going through the motions doesn't necessarily give you a correct response. Inside leg to outside rein provides the correct ingredients, but you must determine the recipe. If you have never experienced the proper feel of these aids, have a professional establish the communication with your horse and show you the correct response in your horse's balance, posture, and contact. Then get on your horse and with the help of your instructor, try to recreate that connection until you feel the straightness, improved balance, and contact. In the golfing world it would be called the 'sweet spot.' You must apply these aids until you feel the sweet spot. You will know you are there when you feel an elastic, uphill contact and energy. Until then, unfortunately, you are just motoring around."

To find the sweet spot, ride your horse off the rail so *you* are controlling him, not the fence line or wall. To help yourself know where you are, set flattened disc cones or other low objects for reference points (things the horse doesn't perceive as a barrier) along the long side before you get on. Ride to the "inside" of them so they are on the "outside." Use your outside leg and rein to keep your horse next to them, but always on the inside of them. Say you are riding to the left, so your horse has a left flexion. Your reference ground line will be on your right. Push your horse's ribs to the right with your left (inside) leg. Your outside rein guides the horse by saying, "Don't go to the right; stay going left." If your horse steps to the right and steps over your line on the ground, he'll have "gone through" the outside rein and you won't be in control. Only when he goes "to" and "meets" the outside rein from that aid from the inside leg, but doesn't plow through it, do you have a horse that's straight and connected. It feels more solid and balanced and the contact is unambiguous.

Steering with the Connected Outside Rein

It is human inclination to turn a horse by pulling on a rein. While pulling the right rein to turn your horse to the right and vice versa is instinctive, it can actually cause problems, so we must override our tendency. Regrettably, this habit sticks with us, even when we know otherwise.

When you pull the inside rein to turn in that direction, your horse's head moves to the inside. As a result, his nose in no longer centered in the middle of his chest, equidistant between each shoulder blade, and his outside shoulder will bulge out. This means that the spine is no longer aligned over the line of travel. Moving his weighty head and neck also shifts that weight to the inside shoulder, causing his hips to swing outward. Since he's no longer balanced, he'll resist the turn, or bend his neck too much. He'll lean his body into the turn and become heavy on the forehand.

The sensation of turning to the inside like this is vastly different than when you use the outside rein aid in conjunction with your outside leg to turn to the inside. Because the outside rein prevents the horse's neck from overbending at the base by the shoulders, the horse's spine remains aligned and his legs stay underneath his body, keeping him balanced throughout the turn. This feels noticeably more stable and upright. It also allows the ribs to rotate toward the outside of the curved line of travel and not fall in. The shoulders swing around the hips.

While they aren't the dominant turning aids, the inside rein and leg *do* play a role in turning with the outside rein. The inside rein maintains flexion so your horse doesn't look to the outside when you use the outside rein, and the inside leg continues to push the horse's ribs out. Staying connected through the inside rein is important during a turn, but it is a lighter contact than the outside rein at this time. The inside rein aid is helping put the horse on the outside rein.

Be careful that you don't balance yourself on the inside rein during a turn. Holding onto the inside rein is a hard habit to break because the rider is unaware of doing it. Return to the longeing exercise that let's you practice turning with just your outside aids if necessary (see p. 58).

Limit the amount the neck flexes inward by using the outside rein. The front end of the horse must turn as a unit. However, the outside rein remains sympathetic and elastic, permitting the horse to move freely. When appropriate to provide a release, you only need to yield a few millimeters for the horse to stretch; you want the horse's frame, balance, and rhythm to remain intact. Don't trap him too tightly *or* release him completely.

You Must Ride Each Direction Differently

As you learned earlier in these pages, one side of a horse's body is more willing to stretch than the other. If your horse bends easily to the left, it means that his right side is able to stretch more than the left. The right side lengthens to accommodate the left turn's bend. You must be "firmer" on that outside (right) rein and keep it steadier so the horse doesn't overbend his neck and pop his right shoulder out. If his body easily bends to the left, *so will his neck*—keep it straight.

Going in the opposite direction (to the right in this example), the horse will still want to bend to the left, so he may move counterbent to the direction he is traveling; he'll try to flex left while going right, and lean his right shoulder into the curve. You'll need to ride differently to accommodate and encourage his left side to lengthen by giving the outside rein more than you did when riding in the other direction. Otherwise, restricting the left (outside) rein will prevent him from stretching on the left side. You'll need more weight in the outside stirrup to help him shift his weight to the outside and more push from your inside leg to swing his rib cage out to the left. To get him off the inside shoulder, you can use the inside rein to intentionally move the outside shoulder out farther. Your objective is to assist the horse in lengthening the outside of his body so that he can turn equally in both directions.

★ Caveats

❖ As discussed, riders commonly stabilize themselves with the inside rein, holding onto it while preparing their bodies to use the outside rein. **Pulling on one rein inhibits the hind leg on that side, causing the horse to travel unevenly**. Because of the shortened stride on the affected side, some horses may appear lame ("rein lame"). Good connection requires that the horse pushes evenly with both hind legs.

❖ Resist the urge to use the inside rein for everything. Try inside leg instead. **Legs create rhythm; hands destroy it**.

❖ You will initially ride with your hands controlling something 99.9 percent of the time. You should

transition to using your seat and legs, as when riding a bicycle. On a bicycle, the energy to move forward comes from the legs, while the hands play a very minor role. You can steer and turn a bike using your body even if you let go of the handlebars. By the conclusion of this book, you should aim to ride with only 10 to 20 percent hands, at most.

❖ Many people try to maintain connection by twisting their wrists around, crossing their reins over the horse's neck, or straightening their elbows. **Wearing carpal tunnel gloves** with integrated wrist brace/palmar splints while being longed can be effective in learning how to keep your wrists aligned and still so that your arms move in sync with the horse through fluid elbows and shoulders. When your wrists are unable to gyrate, your connection, torso stability, and pelvic mobility improve dramatically.

❖ Keep your hands in front of you. If your elbows come back past your sides, your reins are too long. Be aware that **reins slide easily and can quickly become too long**. Keep your elbows ahead of your chin.

❖ Pay attention and you will begin to **notice the slightest deviations from correctness**, instead of only the obvious ones. If your horse rushes when leaving a curve to go straight, for instance, feel for that first leg taking that first step of a more powerful surge. (Try this yourself: walk with small steps, then prepare to take a large step. Feel the related thrust?) That's what you must sense in the horse.) That first big step, or raised head, or bulging shoulder, marks the start of a loss of connection and possibly a loss of control. Catch him in that first step and immediately transition to a 10-meter circle. Repeat this until he no longer attempts it, and you will have a horse that always waits for you. Catching deviations early and nipping them in the bud is what gives you the horse you thought you bought!

❖ Your horse must move forward in a consistent rhythm and tempo; this prevents the connection from becoming erratic. To do this, **ride with more leg than hand**. The more you push your horse forward, the easier maintaining and understanding the concept of connection will be for him…but this isn't rushing and running. It is beneficial if your horse has already established a sense of rhythm and tempo.

- If you are wrestling with the horse's neck, then it is likely your **tempo isn't correct**. When it's too sluggish, push the horse forward. Momentum makes things easier. When your horse is running through with very quick, short strides, ride on a circle, pushing him out to meet the outside rein with your inside leg until he slows. When things are good, you will feel the horse moving regularly, confidently, and springily. To keep a steady tempo, sing a song or count in your head. Stay on **your** beat; don't follow the horse's. The horse will follow the rhythm of the tempo you set, especially when you are posting the trot. Take note when the horse drops his neck in relaxation, stretching his nose out past the vertical and reaching—you've probably found the best tempo for your horse's body in that gait, his "working" gait.

- **If your horse isn't forward**, it could be because you're not consistent with your aids or expectations; or you're tense, rigid, or pulling; or the bridle, bit, or saddle doesn't fit; or you're not balanced and independent in your seat. In short, if your horse isn't moving forward, look at what you're doing to cause the inhibition. Your horse can rush, but that is *not* "forward." Rushing indicates that the horse is tense and needs to relax.

- An overachieving horse may try to **lower his head too far** when connected. If you're not prepared for it, the resulting pull on the reins may tip you forward, over his shoulders and neck. Take care not to snatch his head back up. He's doing his best, and he'll come to realize that stretching and reaching is not all or nothing. Only release as much as you want his head to drop. Keep a firm grip on the outside rein and don't let it go any further. Don't pull on it; instead, "freeze" it. Be strong in your core to avoid being dragged forward.

- Horses will often repeatedly drop the outside rein. Be prepared to **constantly check and adjust the contact and connection**, push the rib cage out, and soften the inside rein.

- Early on in this work, **be cautious about the sharpness of your turns and bending lines.** If your horse is green, ride larger arcs. Only ride smaller circles or tighter turns when your horse develops the balance and agility to do so. In dressage, for example, Training Level horses turn on 20-meter circles. Higher up the levels, 15-meter and 10-meter circles are introduced. Really advanced horses are capable of doing 8-meter or 6-meter circles. As

7.11 A–C "Suck Back" and "Run Through." When a horse "sucks back," he is "behind the vertical," bringing his nose closer to his chest and avoiding contact **(A)**. Because there is no connection, he will feel very light but must be pushed forward onto the bit. A horse that "runs through," on the other hand, is "above the bit," sticking his nose out or his head high in the air **(B)**. You need to work on relaxing his tension so he listens to you. Ideally, the hind legs push the horse to reach for the bridle, stretching the topline and lifting the back, resulting in an arched neck with the nose just in front of the vertical **(C)**.

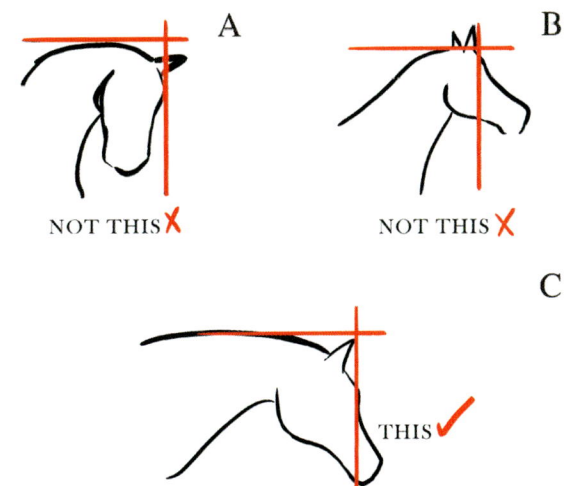

turns become steeper, don't allow your body to collapse through the core or become crooked in the spine. Don't "fall in the well," as rodeo people say, sliding your weight to the inside of the turn.

❖ Connection varies from horse to horse. Remember what we learned on p. 173 about **"suck back" and "run through"** horses (figs. 7.11 A–C)? Knowing if your horse falls into one of these categories helps determine the approach you need to employ to maintain contact. When he "sucks back," it can be deceiving because he feels light in the reins. Indeed, riders seek self-carriage and lightness of response, but in these horses there is *no connection*. The horse's head feels like it is floating. In this case, you need to think of that boat pulling a water skier. The boat has to be moving along pretty well to tighten the line to pull the skier out of the water. If the boat slows or stops, the skier sinks. So you must get the engine going on this type of horse. Ride him a little bit more nose out and forward until he takes the bit. Remember, riding *isn't* about putting the head down; it's about taking the bit forward. A horse that sucks back often "looks pretty" and may seem ideal to the uninformed, but don't be fooled by it. When you have a horse that "runs through," or grabs the bit, pulls, and rushes, work on relaxing his tension so he listens to you, which you can do by slowing his tempo and lengthening his stride. A positive aspect is that such a horse usually has a strong connection that you can easily feel.

❖ Even though the concepts are the same, **each horse feels and reacts differently**. Whereas one horse may be as stiff as a board, the next may be wiggly and unstable; another may be in a hurry, while others may seem to oppose everything you do. The amount of contact may vary dramatically, so you must differentiate what you do to be appropriate for each horse.

❖ **Educate yourself on the proper fit and function of various types of equipment**. Bridles can be too tight or too loose in the crown, browband, cheekpiece (which causes the bit to be too high or low), or noseband. Nosebands make contact with a network of facial nerves. One finger width should separate the noseband from the end of the ridge of bone (facial crest) that runs down each side of the horse's face. Do not allow the noseband to press against the cartilage just above the nostrils at the end of the nasal bone, nor should it be too low. You must account for the fact that horses' tongues vary in thickness. Bits can be excessively thick, thin, sharp, short, or long. A loose, drooping bridle isn't necessarily more comfortable, either! If your horse is uncomfortable or in pain, he'll try to evade or resist.

❖ **Horses do not benefit from draw reins and similar devices.** They hinder both the horse's and rider's ability to learn. In lieu of developing balance and seat functionality, devices encourage riders to concentrate solely on the horse's front end and rely on stronger aids delivered by the arms. Furthermore, when draw reins are used, the horse learns to bend the wrong vertebrae of his neck to avoid pressure on the reins, resulting in the overdevelopment of the wrong muscles. Devices can also be dangerous if your horse violently objects to their use…and some do. Bottom line: It is well worth the patience employed to teach your horse to come forward onto the bit correctly. You will learn a lot from the process and thereby have no need for "crutches" or "fast fixes."

★★ Extensions

❖ The head and neck reaching down and forward in connection contribute positively to the horse's length of stride. **Length of stride is lost when the horse lifts his head** because, to lift the head, the back muscle must contract and, thus, it shortens (fig. 7.12). This, then, allows the belly to drop in front of the hind legs, blocking their forward swing. Consequently, the hind legs are restricted and the stride becomes shorter. As Sally Swift demonstrates in *Centered Riding,* you can experience this yourself by crawling on your hands and knees: Lift your head high and feel your back sink. Your arms will start carrying your weight. Try to move one knee out in front of the hand on that side, like a horse "tracking up," and you will find it impossible. On the other hand, if you bend your head down, your back will round up and your legs can easily swing farther forward—"track up"—between your arms.

❖ It is crucial to be aware of where your horse's nose is in space. It must remain centered in the middle of his chest so that he remains straight and **his neck does not overbend** anywhere along its length (figs. 7.13 A & B). Keep the "bulge" of the muscle in the horse's neck in line with his outside shoulder. This keeps the base of the neck by the withers straight. The base of the neck is the most flexible part of a horse's body, allowing it to bend with the greatest ease. If they bend here rather than at the poll (the least flexible part of the neck), communication is lost and the energy you would have "caught" in the outside rein "escapes" through the outside shoulder, and you lose communication with the hind legs.

❖ Circles help the horse develop suppleness, straightness and balance. Circles are wonderful in this respect because there is never an endpoint where you must stop and interrupt what you are doing because you "ran out of space." When you

7.12 Tracking Up. The horse on the left is demonstrating connection by reaching into the bridle. His hind legs are "tracking up" underneath his lifted abdomen. This means that his hind hoof steps into or beyond the hoof print left by his front foot, indicating that the horse is moving freely through his back. His stride is loose, long and swinging. The horse on the right has no connection. The reins are dangling and his neck is inverted. To lift the head, the back muscles contract and shorten, causing the back and stomach to sag in front of the hind legs, blocking their forward swing. This restriction shortens the stride and his hind feet step short of the front feet's footprints. This means the horse's hindquarters aren't engaged. The difference in the spread of the hind legs is readily apparent. •

decide to transition from a circle to a straight line, notice immediately if your horse stiffens, falls in, or rushes—if he does, go right back to the circle. **The straight line—and especially the transition into it—needs to be as easy and resistance-free as the circle.** If the circle isn't easy and resistance-free, don't try transitioning to a straight track. Be careful that, as a rider, you don't get stiff yourself, or do something different, in preparation for the change of direction, flexion, and bend. You don't want to telegraph to the horse that something alarming is about to occur. Relaxation goes two ways.

❖ **Frequent circles, turns, and changes of direction invite your horse to drop his head and relax.** Relaxation leads to "swing" through the body. You should feel like you're riding a trampoline.

❖ **Ride ovals, which have short straight sections but let you return to a curve to get your balance and rhythm back.** As your horse learns to go straight for more strides without getting off track, you can make the oval bigger. Note that when your horse is on a straight track, things may go wrong, like the horse lifting his head, dropping his back, rushing, or getting crooked.

❖ **Practice riding circles of fixed sizes** until you know the curvature and feel of each by heart. Accurate circles are important because they keep a uniform bend to the horse's body and demonstrate that your horse is responsive to your leg, seat, and rein aids. Riding various-sized circles benefits the horse's balance, suppleness, flexibility, symmetry, rhythm, and strength, all of which

7.13 A & B Don't Overbend the Neck. It is critical to be aware of and vigilant about the position of your horse's nose in space. It must remain centered in the middle of his chest so that he remains straight, even when gently flexed to the right or left. His neck should *not* be overbent at any point along its length **(A)**. The base of a horse's neck is extremely flexible, so it is *very* easy to bend the neck too far inward, putting the nose in front of the inside shoulder, when all you are looking for is correct flexion in the poll. Overbend causes the horse to become crooked, and energy from the hind legs "leaks out" through the horse's bulging shoulder instead of being transmitted to his mouth, resulting in a loss of connection **(B)**.

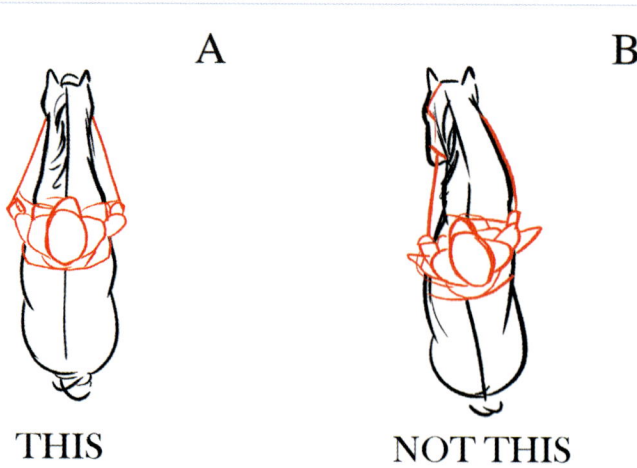

❖ When your horse's entire spine is perfectly aligned over his line of travel (curved or straight), this is referred to as "alignment." **A properly aligned horse is a calm horse.** Because you have positioned your horse so that his vertebrae are in alignment, his head may naturally drop. When your horse's head drops, he acquires the "round" form through his topline you desire. To this end, "round is free"—you are not required to "create it" beyond creating a situation in which this posture is likely to occur.

improve connection. Smaller circles are more challenging than larger ones because the horse must bend and stretch more. Return to a larger circle when the horse has difficulty.

Study Guide

Craft an X Post

Business communication expert and author Carmine Gallo's TED speaker research shows that the brain needs to see the big picture before the details.

"You might have a remarkable idea, but it is imperative that first you show your audience the big picture, how the details interconnect." Gallo says. "The first step to giving a TED-worthy presentation is to ask yourself what is the one thing I want my audience to know (about my company, product, service or idea)?" He suggests creating an X- (formerly Twitter) type post, making sure it easily fits within the 280 character limit of "regular account" post. Gallo notes that this "works for two reasons: 1) it's a great discipline, forcing you to identify and clarify the one key message you want your audience to remember and 2) it makes it easier for your audience to process the content." Gallo prefers the notion of a post because, "From a well-crafted post, I should be able to identify what the product, service, or cause is as well as what makes it different or unique." A short post is powerful because it "can be easily remembered and shared across social networks."

SAMPLE:

- *It is beneficial to build a relationship with your horse from the ground to get a good grasp of who he is and how he reacts. (124 characters)*

- *Riding is a thinking game. (26 characters)*

Study Guide
Craft an X Post

It is helpful for you to try applying his ideas to your riding. Your task is to write an X-friendly post for each of the sections in this chapter that you struggled with the most.

I encourage you to share your "posts" on your own social media and request others to respond with their own. After struggling with this yourself, it is fascinating to see what others have created. Your appreciation for their insights will run deep, and the material in this book will become part of you rather than just be words on a page.

In education, reconstructing knowledge for yourself is known as "discovery learning." These activities, then, enable you to discover what you *know* you know, what you know you *don't* know, what you *think* you know, but actually don't, and what you *don't even know* you don't know…so that you can identify and rectify shortcomings.

When I apply this study guide technique to the riding lessons I teach, I find that my students' self-reflection leads to a significant increase in competent independent practice and a heightened rate of progress.

Your notes

Chapter

TRANSITIONS

08

Maintaining the connection, balance, alignment, and absence of resistance in your horse during a transition is a challenging task. Prior to requesting a transition, it is imperative for both you and the horse to be correct, maintain correctness throughout the transition, and continue riding correctly after the transition. The quality of the subsequent gait is contingent upon the quality of the preceding one.

8.1 Visualizing Connection. The horse should take the bit forward like it's a Frisbee in a dog's mouth. The Frisbee is carried forward with the dog after he catches it. If you were holding a string tied to the Frisbee, you would feel the connection created by its forward momentum.

Once you're reasonably confident in your ability to recognize and establish genuine contact and connection, your next Non-Negotiable is to maintain it while changing direction or gait during your ride ("transitions"). Transitioning from walk to trot is a logical first option because keeping contact and connection is actually easier at the trot and will help you affirm your feel for both. Also, because there is impulsion in the trot, you will better understand the *difference* between contact and connection, as I described in previous chapters. This is only true, however, if your transition is correct and your hands remain steady. If not, it's game over.

It is a complex task to keep your horse connected, balanced, aligned, and resistance-free throughout a transition. It is necessary for you and the horse to be correct *before* requesting a transition, to remain correct *during* the transition, and to ride on correctly *after* the transition. Before transitioning to trot, you must have an organized and connected walk. The quality of the trot is determined by the quality of the walk. Don't sacrifice form to get from one gait to the next. There is no long-term benefit from urgency.

Remaining Connected Through Transitions

To encourage your horse to transition to the trot from the walk, be stable in your core, widen your reins, squeeze your legs, and push your hips forward. Follow with the reins a bit more and squeeze your legs again to propel the horse forward. However much you give with the hand, squeeze a corresponding amount with your calves in order to prompt him onto the bit. The horse needs to remain reaching forward and down and maintaining a soft pull on the bit *before, during, and after* the transition. Imagine the bit like a Frisbee a dog jumps to catch. Once caught, it continues to sail forward with the dog's mouth (fig. 8.1).

Enable Your Horse to "Go"

During a transition, your horse should surge forward with a controlled feeling of impulsion. Accept the surge of energy, imagining someone pushing you on a swing so that you send your body forward with him. Remember to think of your spine like the pole on a carousel horse, upright and stable. Don't lose your balance and collapse on him when he transitions. Falling back on the reins will stifle the horse's forward motion.

It is advisable to do transitions on a circle so you can push the horse's rib cage out with your inside leg. This provides all the benefits outlined in chapters 6 and 7, as well as preventing that "surge" from becoming a "charge" or "rush." Be sure to stay on the line of travel—don't let the horse leave the circle by "escaping through the outside rein." *Keep directing the outside front leg and shoulder toward the inside of the circle with your outside rein, hip (moved forward), and leg.* Your horse's head and body should stay put throughout a transition. Be prepared: the faster the gait, the sooner and more dramatically everything can occur.

Riding Transitions Is Like Spinning Plates

It isn't likely that your horse will make perfect transitions every time, whatever his stage of training. Some horses ignore you, others overreact, and others need you to hold them together in a firm "hug" with your legs until they step off. Your horse's head may come up, sinking his back. He may go too fast, pull himself along with his front legs, or lean onto the forehand. He may go too slowly or he may just walk faster, rather than trot. When any incorrect outcome occurs, *stop attempting the transition and start over.* Don't press on into trot, or continue trotting if he has already stepped into it.

Many riders are either relieved they get the upward transition at all or are so laser-focused on trotting, they disregard how it transpired. You must evaluate the quality of the current gait, the quality of the transition, and the quality of the following gait. Future responses develop from how your horse perceives the parameters associated with these interactions; don't waste this opportunity to set the stage for your horse to realize that there are Non-Negotiables woven into every move he makes, including:

❖ Rein contact must be steady and even.

❖ He must stay supple, symmetrical, and flexible in all parts of his body.

❖ He must stay straight and aligned over his line of travel.

❖ He must be able to bend, turn, stop, move laterally, or transition again at any time.

❖ The tempo must remain steady, appropriate, and forward.

❖ The hind legs must step up under his body, providing support and energy, pushing equally.

❖ He must maintain his balance and keep a consistent length of stride.

These are pieces that can go awry before, during, and after a transition. The more assiduously you attend to them, the more properly your horse will develop, and the more obedient he'll be, simply because he was never exposed to incorrect options. As Thomas Ritter shares in his ArtisticDressage.com blog: "Transitions are hard because they are especially vulnerable to mistakes or changes in the frame and contact because the horse's balance changes from one gait to the next, the energy level changes, and the movement is different." Riding a successful transition requires spinning all these plates simultaneously so the horse doesn't become crooked, lose his balance, or change the contact.

Invest in the Future by Getting it Right, Now…Take Your Time!

Don't rush a transition. Riders get impatient, sometimes wanting to just "kick and go," getting on with the new gait, but transitions are valuable in their own right. The quality and correctness of a transition matters since the quality of any gait is dependent on the transition that leads into it. Transitions are especially fragile maneuvers because the horse's balance needs to change from gait to gait, opening the door to disruptions in contact and straightness.

As with many things, the more time you spend getting something right up front, the less time you will end up spending overall. If you do a poor job of training something from the start, you will end up spending more time correcting it after the bad habit becomes ingrained.

Maintain the Frame

Because the horse must eventually maintain a "frame" throughout everything you want to do with him (see p. 129), you might as well start by not allowing him to change it when transitioning from walk to trot. As mentioned, it is important for the horse not to lift his head because it inverts the neck, drops the back, and braces the body with tension. This results in a loss of contact and forces his hind legs out behind him, thereby preventing him from stepping up under his belly where they need to be for balance (fig. 8.2). When the hind legs are "out behind," confirms Thomas Ritter, they "can only push the body mass horizontally forward, which results in a horse that's on the forehand and running away from the aids."

Using Clear and Consistent Aids

A quick reminder about the consistency of the rider's aids when asking for transitions: The rider needs to be methodical and patient with giving only the cue that you want to use until you get the response that you seek. We likened this process to Morse Code back on p. 100—use only one signal for a transition to trot so that your horse doesn't ever have to guess what you want. When asked, many riders realize they can't articulate what their signal to trot actually is, or even recall what they did the last three times they asked for a trot transition.

8.2 Out Behind. This hose rack depicts a horse with the hind limbs trailing out behind. When riding, this causes a loss of contact and connection. Because the horse's hind legs are "out behind" where they cannot bend and, as a result, are not properly flexed underneath the body, the croup is raised and the horse is visibly "downhill" on the forehand in this image. Consequently, the horse must move quickly forward to maintain balance. Even in an iron silhouette, you can sense the majority of this horse's bodyweight is supported by the forehand. ●

Decide which aids you want to use to ask your horse to trot and never vary from that sequence. A possible example could be:

❖ Create a more energetic walk so that there is enough energy to propel him to a trot in the *first* stride. Do this by pushing his belly over so that he can swing the hind leg further under his body on the side you just pushed. Your inside leg also activates the hind leg on the same side and causes it to leave the ground more quickly, so trotting becomes an option. (Do not "dribble" into a trot by walking faster until he trots.)

❖ Be sure he's reaching forward into the bridle. (Give an inch and push him forward onto the bit with your calves.)

❖ Flex him inside and again push his ribs out with your inside leg. This also acts as a forewarning to him that something is coming, so you don't suddenly ambush him with a kick and expect a trot transition out of nowhere.

❖ Ask him to trot when his outside front leg is on the ground. Since the trot is a diagonal gait, this means he'll push appropriately with his inside hind leg when you ask. To get the timing right, you can say to yourself, "Trit, trot," saying, "Trit," when the *inside* front leg is on the ground, and then emphasizing "Trot," when the *outside* front leg is on the ground. Watching the horse's shoulders, say, "Trit, trot," a few times until you have a rhythm and are mentally and physically prepared to transition the next time you say, "Trot."

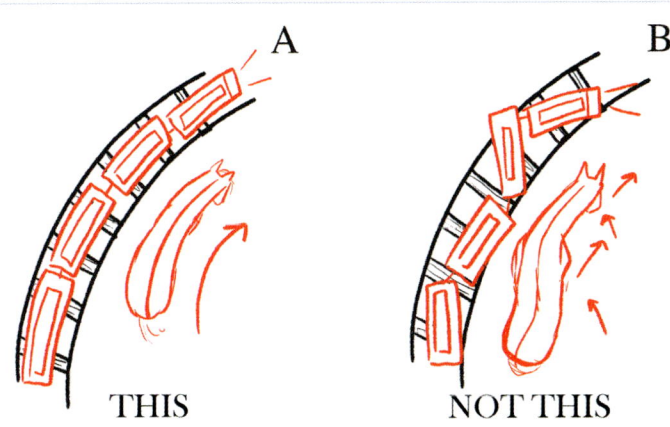

8.3 A & B Derailed. Remember the monorail we discussed earlier in the book (see p. 146)? During transitions, the horse must align his vertebrae over his pathway of travel. Whether this pathway is straight or curved, the spine must overlay it directly, like a train on its track **(A)**. When the horse is crooked, he becomes "derailed" **(B)**. "Off his track," he blocks his own movement and cannot go forward.

❖ Squeeze with both calves, push your hips forward, and allow the inside rein to give forward.

2) If all went well, trot on!

You can use any arrangement of these aids you like, as long as you do the *same thing every time* and your horse understands what you want him to do. Don't put your horse in the position of having to guess what you are asking of him. Furthermore, make sure you go directly into the kind of trot you want so that he doesn't have options. Be definite. Have your horse ready before you ask for the transition. He needs to have contact, be reaching, soft, and eager. If "before" has any errors or changes, abandon the transition and prepare your horse again. "Before" *must* be correct. During the transition, nothing changes but the gait. After the transition, the horse has to remain steady without going faster, getting tense, falling back into the walk, or raising his head. ("Before, during, and after" is important for *everything* you do in riding.)

In dressage trainer Beth Baumert's *When Two Spines Align: Dressage Dynamics*, the author astutely points out that riders normally think of aids as asking a horse for a *specific action*, but that successful riders use aids for *specific purposes*:

❖ **Preparatory and shaping aids** prepare the horse for action by putting him in front of the leg.

❖ **Listening aids** see if the horse is ready to respond.

❖ **Action aids** ask the horse for action when the horse is ready.

Baumert continues: "An effective rider's position sculpts the horse so he's in the balance that maximizes his ability to perform. Once that's accomplished, the rider 'listens' to the horse to see if he feels like he's ready to go. Only then does the rider make the request for action." Because of the preparation, the horse isn't surprised. Because the rider prepared and listened, she can be fairly sure that the horse will respond well.

On the other hand, a less-skilled, passive rider may unknowingly interferes with the horse's balance and movement; doesn't notice mistakes; or reacts emotionally to what the horse does, which makes the transition worse. My instructor,

Know Where the Horse's Legs Are

IN chapter 6 (p. 159), we talked about how, at the walk, your legs can feel the horse's rib cage swinging alternately left and right, like the Viking ship ride at an amusement park. I've emphasized how this motion is crucial from a biomechanical standpoint in order to "clear space" for the advancing hind leg to step well up under the horse. The rib cage swings toward the hind leg that is on the ground pushing the horse's body forward, and away from the hind leg that is in flight. Then, that leg will land and the rib cage will swing the other way.

Your left calf is pushed left when the ribs swing left to make way for the right hind leg to come forward (which means the left hind leg is on the ground). Your right calf is pushed right when the ribs swing right for the left hind leg to come forward. Learn to unerringly feel this, so that you know which hind foot is on the ground and which is in flight. Put your hand on the horse's hip as you walk, or have someone on the ground call the hind strides out to you, until you can accurately identify which hind leg is where. Eventually, you will be able to recognize the motion in your body. (Note: Be careful not to grip tightly with your legs because this inhibits the horse's ability to swing freely.)

It is vitally important to understand this because timing of the aids is everything. Remember, when you use a rein aid when a foot is on the ground, you keep it there for a fraction of a second longer so you can encourage the horse to bend the leg further, slow down, change gaits, and keep the leg under the body. When you use your leg when the horse's leg is in the air, you can encourage it to move laterally (cross over the other) or take a longer stride. Using a rein or your leg in time with a selected leg of the horse gives you incredible control over the horse because the horse is physically able to do what you ask only at that precise moment; it is biomechanically impossible at any other time.

Think about the trot—a two-beat gait in which the legs move in diagonal pairs: the right front leg and left hind leg move together, and vice versa. This means that while one diagonal pair of legs is on the ground, the other diagonal pair is in flight. Posting on the correct diagonal, you sit when the outside front and inside hind legs are on the ground (the inside front and outside hind legs are in the air). You can easily see when the outside front leg is on the ground because you can see the horse's outside shoulder sweeping back toward you. If you want to ask the horse to do something, such as a transition, you must know when the leg you need to control is on the ground or in the air.

8.4 A & B Rib Cage Blocking the Leg. To move forward, the horse's ribcage must rotate to the right in order for the left hind leg to advance, and vice versa **(A)**. When a horse is crooked, his ribs and abdomen swing in the incorrect direction and obstruct the hind leg, preventing it from moving forward and potentially forcing it to the side **(B)**. (Note: The horse in the illustration looks "fatter" to indicate the rib cage is rotated closer to the viewer.) As a result, the horse "blocks" his own movement by literally getting in his own way. To remedy this, the rider can assist the horse by pushing the rib cage away when she feels it pressing against her leg. ●

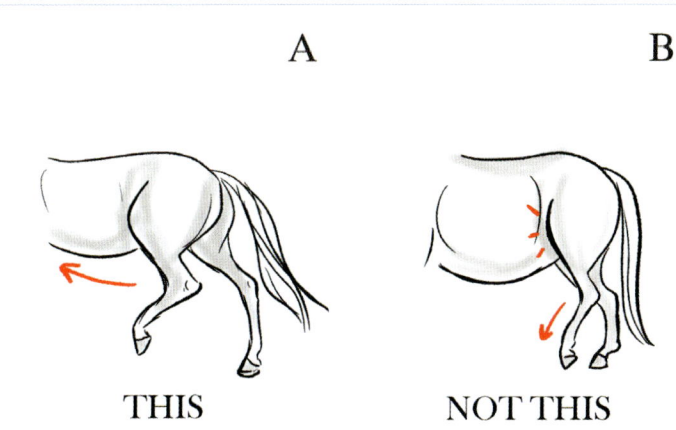

Sharon Vander Ziel, advises the rider "not to enter the horse's drama," and Mary Wanless concurs in her teaching with, "Your correctness must overcome the horse's wrongness."

The Horse Must Be Straight

A horse will be more willing to trot from walk when his nose is centered in front of his chest, equidistant between his shoulders. This positioning aligns his vertebrae over his pathway of travel, wherever his feet are taking him (figs. 8.3 A & B). Whether this pathway is in a straight line or on a curve, the spine must travel directly over it—remember that monorail on its track (p. 146)? In riding, the word "straight" is used to describe this state of travel. Straightness of the spine is important because, when the horse is crooked (his head is in one direction, his neck another, his shoulder bulging left or right, his hindquarters curled in), it is likely that his rib cage is obstructing a hind from swinging forward or forcing it to out to the side. The horse is, thus, "stuck" or "blocking" his own movement (figs. 8.4 A & B).

Horses aren't born straight or symmetrical. Nor do they analyze where their body parts are on the line of travel, so they need your guidance to free them up to move more easily. It is up to you to figure out where your horse's asymmetry is, and to remedy this crookedness as much as you can so that he can travel as efficiently and balanced as possible, *especially* in transitions.

Once a horse is straight, he's physically out of his own way, and he can "surge" forward into trot without inhibition. When you set your horse up properly, you don't need to force him to transition because he's physically able to go;

8.5 A & B Parallel Shoulders and Hips.
To facilitate a clear transition to the trot, begin on a circle and push your horse out onto a larger circle with your inside leg. Stepping sideways and forward causes the horse's hindquarter joints to bend more deeply, encouraging the hind legs to spring directly into trot, without just walking faster. It is essential that the horse's shoulders and hips remain aligned and move out together **(A)**. When the shoulders or the hips lead, the horse's position becomes angled, leaving the circular track **(B)**. This method is applicable to any transition. •

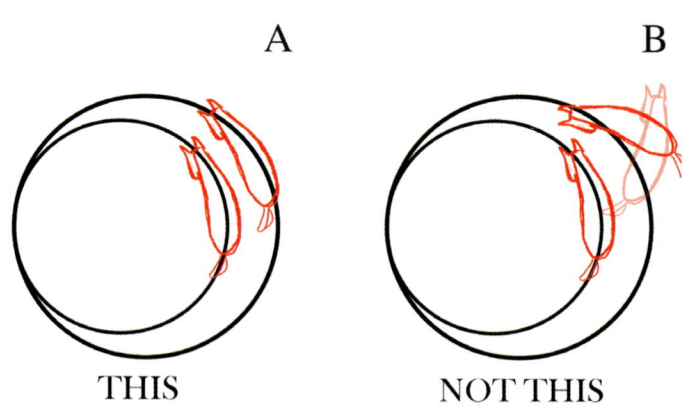

you actually just *allow* the transition. Horses, as flight animals, are designed to "go." When they don't want to "go," they are most likely crooked or confused, and you need to fix that.

Encourage the horse to lower his head and reach forward before your transition. It indicates that his spine is straight because he can't drop his head when his spine is crooked. Transition directly from the walk to the trot without allowing the horse to walk faster or hurry into the trot. Rushed (short, choppy and more frequent) strides result from tension or lack of balance, and the necessary "engagement" (bending of the joints) and stepping under of the hind limbs doesn't occur. He needs to go directly from a good walk to good trot.

To make the transition to trot easier, start on a smaller circle and push your horse out with your inside leg onto a larger circle (figs. 8.5 A & B). Doing this moves the rib cage out of the way of the inside hind leg, enabling it to step up under the body for an effective first thrust in the trot. As you ease off on the inside rein, your horse will want to spring into a trot of his own accord. This is because, when you asked the horse to go sideways and forward (spiraling out), it caused the joints of the hind legs to bend more. Bent joints want to straighten. When they straighten, that's the spring you need to step naturally from walk into trot. The up transition is actually inviting to the horse because he *wants* to straighten his legs.

Keys to Clear Transitions

A mantra I frequently express is that "trot and canter are gaits, *not* speeds." Horses shouldn't associate "faster" with either of these gaits. Running your horse into either gait by going faster *isn't* what you want. The converse is also true: don't slow down until the horse falls into a lower gait. *Make clear transitions.* Be patient and invest the time it takes to develop quality upward and downward transitions. When you work on it regularly, every transition will come with increasing understanding and confidence as he becomes sure of what you want.

First "Up" Then Forward

When you perform a transition, you always want to feel the horse *lifting up* and *then* going forward; most transitions just go forward. A good transition should feel like the horse's back is coming up under you first because, ideally, the hind legs are stepping under the body to push first, and only *then* do you feel *forward* motion occur. You don't want the front legs to pull the horse along in a downhill trot. Think, "Up first, then forward," (*especially* when transitioning to canter).

Newton's first law of motion states that things in motion tend to stay in motion unless acted upon by an outside force, so a horse moving quickly on his forehand will begin that way and remain so unless the rider becomes the outside force and actively intervenes. That intervention is *connection*. Connection enables you to use a squeeze on the outside rein to slow him down, shifting his balance back to the hindquarters so that the forehand comes up, rather than just speeding forward. By the same token, stay out of the horse's way when he is trotting well. Don't interfere with inadvertent motions so that he falters frequently.

Stabilize Your Hands

Scan to View Hands Still When Posting

One of the most difficult aspects of staying connected is maintaining the connection before, during, and after a transition. When trot is involved, you may be posting, which can cause your hands to move up and down with you, jostling the bit in the horse's mouth, forcing him to avoid it. The horse can't be expected to keep a steady contact if you don't!

To learn to stabilize your hands, practice in front of a mirror. Find a chair or another object you can place your hands on at about waist height. Position yourself so you can see yourself from the side. Then squat and stand repeatedly, imitating the rhythm of posting. Keep your hands resting on the object; notice that your elbows bend and straighten as you go up and down while your hands remain in one location (figs. 8.6 A & B).

Having been told, "Keep your hands still," many people freeze their arms at their sides, which causes the hands to move up and down with the body. Watch in the mirror what happens when you lock your elbows to your sides and imitate posting. You will see your hands moving up and down with your body, coming off the chair. They no longer occupy the same position relative to the object. In the saddle, this would mean your movement would bang the bit up and down in your horse's mouth.

It is a good idea to evaluate the quality of your posting. Have someone video you so that you can see if you are riding as you intend, since perception is often inaccurate. It is surprising how many people don't realize that their hands actually *do* rise and fall with their posting! Mary Wanless expounds on this in more detail, citing Noel Burch's Four Stages of Competence psychological learning model:

> *Being unconscious of your incompetence...means that you don't know what you don't know. When you don't know what you don't know, you don't know what there is to know.... But people become conscious of their incompetence and begin to realize what it is that they didn't know, and this can be a shock. People say, "I've been doing rising trot for thirty years and you're telling me I'm not doing it well?" Yes, I am. I'm telling you that you've automated some ways of doing it that aren't great, and we need to go back to the drawing board. So becoming conscious of your incompetence can be a nasty shock, but it becomes an 'aha moment' where you realize what you do...once you realize what's gone wrong, that's the gateway to the next stage where you become*

A

THIS

B

NOT THIS

8.6 A & B Stabilizing Hands. To learn to stabilize your hands when posting, practice in front of a mirror. Position yourself so you can see yourself from the side. Place your hands on an object that is about waist height for you. The correct height of the object allows your elbows to be bent when your knees are bent, so that your forearms are parallel to the ground. Imitate posting by squatting and standing repeatedly. Because your hands are resting on a stationary object, notice how your elbows bend and straighten as you go up and down. Your hands are *still* relative to the object, as they need to be when riding. The bending and straightening of the elbows allow your hands to remain in one place so the bit remains steady in the horse's mouth **(A)**. Notice what happens when you go up and down with your elbows locked to your sides. Your hands will rise and fall with your body **(B)**. They are no longer stationary in relation to the object. That means you would be banging the bit up and down in your horse's mouth as you post. •

consciously competent on how you change those patterns. If you didn't have that aha moment, you couldn't begin the next stage to build the new patterns of behavior.

Quality Control

It is a well-known rule of thumb that "the quality of your gait is only as good as the transition, and the quality of the transition is only as good as the gait before it." It is nearly impossible to fix a gait after a bad transition; it becomes a landslide of errors that can't be corralled. It is pragmatic to start over, focusing on maintaining the good gait you got from the good transition. This is of fundamental importance: if you continue to ride the horse incorrectly, not only will it develop the wrong muscles, he will think that what has happened is what you want and that he's doing it well. This creates a mountain of problems to overcome. If, however, you are perpetually conscientious about the quality of transitions, your horse will learn that there is only one proper way to transition, and it will become habitual for him.

I've mentioned how people are frequently so relieved that a transition has occurred that they cease actively maintaining the trot's quality, causing it to deteriorate. Concentrate on maintaining the forward and downward reach after the transition to the trot, so the horse understands that he must continue to "go." Maintain a rhythmic posting so that the trot is not erratic; the horse should match your tempo, not vice versa. Allow him to carry the trot for a few strides on his own a few steps after the transition, when you feel that things are stable and consistent. Initially, refrain from trotting for an extended period for three reasons:

- Left alone, the trot will tend to fall apart and you don't want the horse to remember that as the last thing he did.

- You need the opportunity to practice more transitions.

- Your horse will get too tired. Performing is more difficult when he is tired, so the exercises you are doing together will become less enjoyable or engaging for him. He is incapable of producing quality work when he is exhausted or uninterested; therefore, the exercises you are doing become pointless, and he may even turn or revert to undesirable behaviors. As your horse becomes fitter with more correct training, it will become easier for him to maintain his good posture ("frame") for longer periods of time and through multiple transitions. You should always end on a positive note.

Consider the "after" phase of an upward transition to trot. Very quickly, this "after" becomes a "before" because you will either want to make another transition, make a turn, or perform a particular movement. This means that you are about to do something new, that has its *own* "before," "during," and "after." So, most "afters" are really "befores" for whatever you are going to do next. Ensure that you do not attempt any type of movement or transition unless the trot is satisfactory.

Downward Transition to Walk

Now let's talk about a downward transition. Given we have just gone from walk to trot, it makes sense to consider returning to walk from the trot.

8.7 Canter Stride. The canter is a three-beat gait that consists of: Beat 1, one hind foot; Beat 2, a diagonal pair; and Beat 3, the remaining front leg, followed by a suspension phase where all four legs are in the air. In this photograph, the left hind has set down for the first beat, the diagonal pair of the right hind and left front are just setting down for the second beat, and the right front leg will set down for the third beat when it reaches its full stride extension. The right front leg is the "leading" leg. You can feel the beats as you ride: Beat 1 is when the horse's front end rises and you are lowered in the saddle. Beat 2 occurs when your seat is pulled forward, as depicted in this image. Beat 3 feels like you are moving downhill. •

Before asking for the walk transition, make sure the trot is connected, soft, forward, and in a good frame. Begin by squeezing gently on the outside rein, timed with the backswing of the horse's outside front leg as the hoof touches down, simultaneous with sitting in the saddle during the correct posting diagonal (if doing a rising trot). Do this twice as a notification that a transition to walk is imminent, and make the transition on the third stride. Think, *Sit, sit, walk*, as you squeeze a third, longer time on the outside rein and stop the motion with your lower back. This avoids ambushing the horse with a sudden, unexpected jerk on both reins, and it also allows you to make a transition when and where you want it, such as precisely at a letter in a dressage test. Note that for a downward transition to walk, you don't *have* to time it with the outside front leg: experiment with sending the signal as the hoof touches down in each of the four legs.

If something goes wrong *during* the down transition (the horse inverts his neck, throws his head up, becomes tense, or pulls), return to the trot (widen the reins and squeeze with your legs), and try again once composure is restored. The horse should not interpret down transitions as a time to "quit" or collapse his frame. Nor should you! Many riders crumple when they down transition, thinking they are "done" or because they are tired. When riders give up, horses follow suit. Your horse shouldn't think that "dribbling" from a trot into a sluggish walk, or even stopping, is acceptable. Be diligent about this now, or you will have a problem to solve in the future when an energetic, "marching" walk is required. You must be prepared to do something else after transitioning to the walk...when it becomes a "before."

After the transition, the horse should maintain a good, forward walk, without pulling down, jerking his head up, or stopping. His frame and energy should not change; only the footfalls change, from two beats to four. The walk is as important as the other gaits and deserves equal attention. Move on to the next exercise only after you have walked some distance so the horse expects to "walk on" after the transition.

It takes self-discipline to ride a correct downward transition every time, but it is well-worth the front-end investment of time and determination to ensure yours are reliable and consistent. These initial efforts at firming up this Non-Negotiable lay the foundation for future training success and proper physical development of the horse.

Canter Transitions

The canter is a three-beat gait consisting of one hind foot, a diagonal pair, and the remaining front foot, followed by a suspension phase in which all four legs are in the air (fig. 8.7). The original hind foot then returns to the ground to repeat the sequence. To properly transition upward from the trot to the canter, signal the horse to canter when his *inside front leg comes forward* (or when you should be sitting if you are posting). Because of the diagonal nature of the horse's footfalls, the inside front leg moves forward simultaneously with the outside hind in the trot, and therefore will set down in the first beat of the correct canter lead.

Watch the front legs and say "can-*ter*, can-*ter*" with the "can-" timed to the outside front leg moving forward and the "-*ter*" timed to the inside front leg moving forward. Signal the horse to canter (your outside leg sweeps back as your inside hip comes forward) when you say "-*ter*." You can repeat "can-*ter*, can-*ter*" as many times as necessary until you easily recognize and feel confident of the timing. It is useful to do this first while longeing your horse (see p. 64), so you can *see* the footfalls and become familiar with the timing before working on your transitions.

Another clue for when to signal the horse to step into the canter is, when posting, timing "can-" with the rise of your post, and the "-*ter*" when you sit (inside front leg coming forward and outside front foot on the ground) and signal with your leg. The "-*ter*" is emphasized because that's when you give the aid. The "can-" gives you a mental preparatory moment. You may need to say "can-*ter*" to yourself for several strides in a row to give yourself time to mentally prepare and physically coordinate for the transition.

It is immensely beneficial to look at slow-motion video of walk, trot, trot-canter, and walk-canter transitions. Watch the front legs closely and say "can-*ter*, can-*ter*"; then, observe how the hind legs fall in relation to that. With the proper timing, your horse will easily canter from trot or walk. When you *don't* get the timing right, he'll just trot faster, take the wrong lead, or scramble into canter through several strides.

Downward Transition from Canter

To come down from the canter to the trot, feel the "1-2-3" rhythm of the canter: Beat 1 feels up, Beat 2 pulls your seat forward, Beat 3 feels down. Count to yourself, feeling "*1*-2-3, *1*-2-3..." To help orient your timing, push your heels down (very slightly) on every "1" beat. Give two smaller preparatory squeezes on the outside rein in conjunction with Beat 1 across two strides to alert the horse that you want something, and on the third squeeze, be firmer and hold longer until he changes gait to trot. The reason you do this on Beat 1 is because Beat 2 is a diagonal pair—and *voila*, your horse is now in trot, a diagonal

Two Canter Signals

There are two schools of thought regarding how to request the canter: with the outside leg or the inside leg. The conventional outside leg aid drives the horse's outside hind leg forward and stimulates it to thrust into the canter. However, when you ask your horse to do movements like haunches-in or half-pass, you use aids from the outside leg, and some believe the horse may misinterpret them as a canter aid. To prevent confusion, some horses are taught to canter from the rider's inside leg, or the rider pushing her inside hip forward.

"Which of the two canter aids?" is a much more complex topic than this simple explanation, but it provides a little insight into why you may learn the canter aid two different way. •

gait. As you can see, the timing of the aid is important, because if you were to ask the horse to trot on, say, Beat 3, when the front foot is down and he's about to enter the suspension phase of canter, the horse isn't physically situated for the trot's footfall sequence.

To come to the walk from canter, ask for the down transition on Beat 2.

★ **Caveats**

* **The lessons you are about to learn in flexion and half-halts (chapters 9 and 10—pp. 229 and 259)**, will provide helpful tips for improving transitions, as well as the quality of the trot. The reason that transitions in general, and in particular the transition from walk to trot is presented *before* they are in this book is that:

  •• It is much easier to feel and maintain contact and connection in trot because the horse moves the bit and reins forward more discernibly.

  •• Because the horse's head doesn't bob at trot (as it does at walk and canter), it is a great gait to practice getting and staying connected.

  •• Both horse and rider are better engaged with a lesson when they do more than walk.

  •• Half-halts are easiest to understand when you use them for downward transitions, so you need to be able to transition up to trot in order to have something to slow down from, and you need to be teaching your horse to do it well, even when it is not your focus.

- **Do transitions on curved lines or circles**. When traveling in a straight line, horses are more likely to become tense, go faster, raise their head, and lean to either side. Circles are advantageous because:

  - They never end, so there is no threat of a straightaway that necessitates a change.

  - The horse cannot brace his neck when turning.

  - It is easier to step forward and sideways to spiral in or out, moving closer to or farther from the center.

- **Before a transition, riders frequently foreshadow their intent** by shortening the reins, becoming tense, or leaning forward. This alerts the horse that something is about to change, and as a result, he will alter his position and mental state in anticipation. Therefore, it is essential that you identify what you routinely do in preparation for a trot, regardless of whether it is necessary, and either eliminate that action or repeat it at the walk until that movement from you no longer generates tension or anticipation in the horse.

- Make it a priority to **attend to the "during" and "after" of a transition**. "Kick-and-go" riders only pay attention until the transition has occurred, thinking their job is done once the gait changes. The horse then falls apart for anything else you might want to do after that. Keep your horse together. He relies on you for continuous guidance.

- **Immediately correct any deviations**, such as loss of balance, rushing, or straightness, while the deviation is still 1 percent. Otherwise, the deviation will grow beyond your ability to salvage the situation. When your horse has a propensity for a particular behavior, pay close attention to the preceding events so that you can identify and correct the underlying cause. Each horse is unique, so familiarize yourself with your mount and ride accordingly. Some horses exhibit different issues in each direction, so it may feel as though you are riding two different horses, one to the right and one to the left. *Learn your horse* so that you can accommodate and mitigate his idiosyncrasies.

❖ **Remember to ride "back-to-front"** with giving hands from a stable core. Invite your horse to reach, and encourage the driving force from behind to do its work.

❖ Resistance can be caused by **dental or physical problems**. If a resistance persists for an extended period of time or your horse changes behavior inexplicably, it is time to consult a medical professional.

❖ **Avoid drilling endless** transitions so you don't create burnout in your horse. Don't be discouraged if you don't achieve your goal in one day. Find a good stopping point. Tomorrow is another day.

❖ Natasha Althoff shrewdly observes in her Dressage Mastery Academy manual, Course 2, Part 5: "**Transitions are an amplifier of where you are in your training**. It is possible to tuck the horse's head and 'look' on the bit… but the transitions won't be good. It isn't possible to fake your way through a transition. However, if you have transitions that are round and soft and nothing changes…I guarantee you that the rest of the work is also good, as you must have the rest of the work good first before the transitions can be good!"

★★ Extensions

❖ To have a good transition—or a good *anything*—**the horse's legs must be underneath him**, not escaping out to the sides. Think of a dinner table versus a picnic table. When the horse has "a leg under each corner," each supporting an equivalent amount of body weight, both horse and rider feel balanced (figs. 8.8 A–C). When one or more of the horse's legs are angled out to the side of his body (like the slanted legs of a picnic table), the horse's movement is rough. (You may be accustomed to your horse feeling this way and unaware of how much more enjoyable he can be to ride!) If needed, review the discussion on p. 102 where I discussed getting the horse's legs under him.

❖ **Use mirrors**. If the arena where you usually ride doesn't have them, you can purchase several full-length mirrors and hang them side by side at one

8.8 A–C Lateral Balance. A horse with lateral balance has his legs underneath him **(A)**, not out to the sides of his body **(B)**. When viewing a straight, laterally balanced horse from the front or the rear, you should only be able to see the two front legs or the two hind legs, as the other two legs should be obscured by the legs closest to you **(C)**. When more than two legs are visible, the horse's legs are not directly beneath him. For the horse to make a good transition, or do anything well, his legs must be under him. In this picture, Jim Koford guides Envoy in excellent straightness and lateral balance. •

end. Have a helper on the ground find the best height to affix them for optimum viewing when you are in the saddle. (Give your horse a chance to look at the mirrors so that the "mystery horse" doesn't frighten him.) Walk toward one of the mirrors in a straight line, and watch whether your horse wobbles left or right out of the frame. That's your first hint that he isn't stable or straight. Keep an eye on his legs. When your horse is going straight, you should only be able to see his front legs in the mirror, as they should obscure the view of his hind legs. This is an excellent opportunity to experience how straight feels. If your horse steps to the side with any leg, feel what that feels like so you can recognize it *without* a mirror, and practice correcting it with your seat, legs, and reins so you can see what is effective and know when the correction has been successful. Next, walk toward the mirror and execute the upward transition from walk to trot and downward transition to walk while keeping an eye on the alignment of the legs. Keep your horse's feet underneath him at all times from now on to maintain this new advantage.

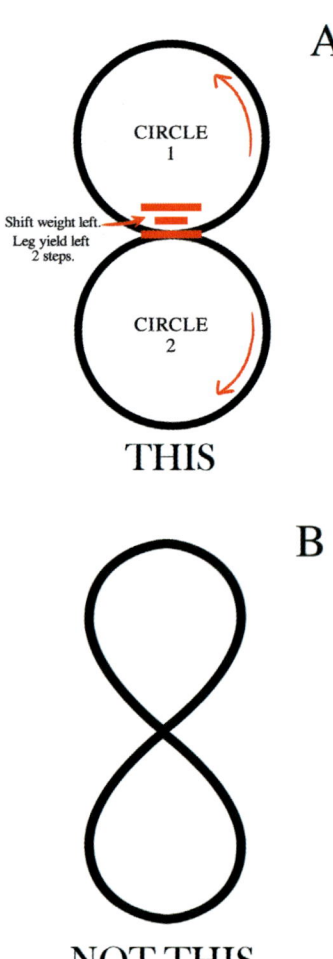

8.9 A & B Correct Figure Eight. Riding a figure eight in a specific way can help your horse achieve the "lift" that provides the impulsion in "go." When traveling to the left, as you approach the midpoint of the figure eight in the first circle, shift your weight to the left, toward the inside of the circle you are leaving. Leg-yield the horse left to shift his weight into his left hind leg while taking a couple of straight strides between the circles of the figure eight. As you leg-yield, change his bend from left to right **(A)**. Master the pattern at walk before attempting trotting and cantering. For variation, you can halt, transition up or down, or remain in the gait you are in when you change direction. Maintain the alignment of your horse's shoulders and hips. Do not cut across the figure at an angle or fail to produce correct circles **(B)**. This is not correct. •

❖ **Use the figure eight to teach your horse "lift-before-go."** If you are circling to the left, leg-yield your horse to the left as you approach the center of the figure eight, where you will go straight a couple strides. This means that you need to shift your weight left (toward the inside of the circle), change the flexion and bend (in preparation for the new circle to the right), and push him left with your right leg into the inside of the circle you were just on (figs. 8.9 A & B). As you change direction, transition from walk to trot (or trot to canter, if you and your horse are ready) to help you feel the "lift" attained by shifting the horse's weight in this way, putting his weight on the "new" outside pair of legs (in this example, the left). Thomas Ritter says to remember the order as follows: "Shift the weight, change the bend, change the direction." It can be helpful to actually say this phrase out loud as you do it.

❖ **Improve your horse's attentiveness and alacrity of response to transition aids** with the following exercise: Trot six strides, walk one stride. Trot five, walk one. Trot four, walk one. Trot three, walk one. Trot two, walk one. Trot one, walk one. Then, reverse the sequence back up to six. It may take some time to master this transition pattern, which is jam-packed with "befores," "durings," and "afters." Don't fight with your horse to get it right. You'll know you've made progress when you and your horse can do it with relative ease.

❖ **Continue in the same gait after a good transition** and perform additional movements or exercises so your horse learns that he can relax in a gait after the transition.

- **Keep your horse mentally fresh** by practicing transitions on a trail ride.

- When your horse is going reliably, **experiment with different „size" trots**. Find the trot stride that feels most natural to your horse, and label it your „working trot"—this is your horse's natural, moderate, energetic trot (for English riders). Then ride one and two notches shorter, more collected and one and two notches longer, more extended, so you have discernible trot paces to work with later. What you *never* want is a rushed, quick, speedy trot with short, choppy strides, or a dragging gait that goes nowhere.

- When posting, concentrate on controlling the downward motion of your seat as if the saddle is made of fine china. It is the rider's responsibility to „control the down" so that you **do not crash heavily down onto your horse's back** every time you sit. Furthermore, you should not be "standing" or exerting any effort on the "up" because the horse's stride should push you up.

- At any time, revisit the groundwork and longeing we discussed at the beginning of this book (pp. 000 and 000). Working with your horse on the ground will provide insight into what you are doing now and make the groundwork more meaningful. They go hand in hand.

Managing Head Height

Trotting your horse on a circle with his head at varying heights is a good exercise for both horse and rider. The horse learns to work in different frames and the rider learns to maintain the same connection with different length reins (fig. 8.10). Consider three different frames:

1. *Low ("stretchy")*.

2. *Medium (the natural carriage for your horse's physique)*.

3. *High (advanced/elevated from the withers)*.

The stretchy, low frame is useful for encouraging your horse to reach for the bit (see chapters 6 and 7), testing his understanding of how to maintain connection, and stretching out back muscles. When you ask him to stretch, make sure your horse is actively reaching and not just letting his neck fall. But beyond improving connection and stretching, it is not optimal for a horse to perpetually go long and low. Because he is carrying his weight on his front end and moving "downhill" in this posture, his front legs are subjected to an excessive amount of stress. As you progress together, you must therefore "lift the neck" to a medium or high frame and transfer his weight to the stronger hind limbs.

To raise the neck, do it in gradual increments by shortening your reins, as if you were moving your horse's head up a staircase, one step at a time. Shorten your outside rein, hold it stable at the shorter length, and urge him forward. Because the outside rein controls the height of the head and neck, start

Managing Head Height

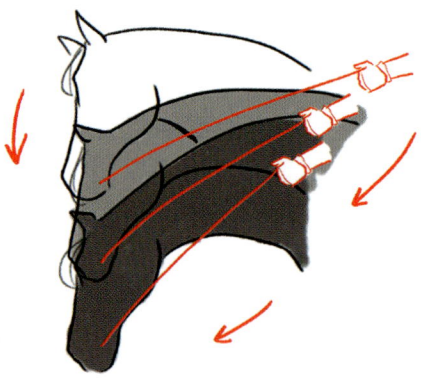

8.10 Head Height. You and your horse must both learn to maintain balance and connection at varying head heights because appropriate height of his head varies, depending on the activity or level of development. You and your horse must be well-versed in, and comfortable with, all of them so that you never miss a beat when conditions change. Your horse must discover how to alter his head height without accelerating, decelerating, altering flexion or bend, or resisting. As the rider, you must master rein control at any length. •

by shortening the outside rein—gently pull it up a little with your inside hand above your outside rein handhold. Then hold the outside rein at the new length, and adjust the inside rein to match. This allows you to keep contact on both reins at all times so that you don't interrupt the connection. Let your horse find his balance and consistent connection at each new head height level before moving on to the next, until you reach the medium height frame where your horse likely feels most comfortable. This can take minutes, or days, depending on the horse. Spend time at each level until your horse develops the strength and balance necessary to carry himself there.

Be careful not to let the tempo fluctuate. Horses tend to speed up when the head is down and slow down when it comes up. Alternatively, try maintaining the same head position while changing the tempo, but never change more than one thing at a time. Such exercises are the first steps in teaching your horse to become adjustable in a variety of contexts.

Depending on the circumstances, being able to easily raise and lower your horse's neck at any time to adjust his frame is useful for several reasons:

1. *An alarmed horse will raise his head on a rigid neck and prepare to flee. To avert this impulse, the horse must respond unquestioningly to a rider's request to relax and lower his neck while maintaining connection and focus on his work.*

2. *It's a good test to see if your horse understands that you wish to maintain the same connection regardless of where the head is positioned.*

3. *It's a first step toward showing your horse that he can do whatever he's asked at any time, in any gait, direction, or frame, with correct basics and without hesitation, in order to progress to more advanced work.*

4. *You can tell which level your horse finds his balance the easiest. In early stages of training, when the horse's head is lower than is comfortable, he will be on the forehand, and when it is higher, he may go above the bit and lose the contact. He'll eventually learn to manage all head heights without anxiety, resistance, or changes in rhythm, but it is helpful to know his initial comfort zones.*

8.11 A & B Active Reach. When a horse reaches for the bit with positive tension, impulsion, and energy, he voluntarily moves the bit forward and down. This can be observed in the muscular arch of his neck and how far his hind legs step under his belly **(A)**. How far his neck moves forward and down is determined by your permission. To maintain the horse's energetic reach when you give the rein, drive him forward proportionally so that his reach remains constant, with no dangling reins and no loss of energy and thrust. Your contact should be equivalent to what is produced by the horse's hind legs, and should result from what you ask for with your legs. You will feel him surge forward; this is good. There should be no need to pull back on or adjust the reins to maintain the contact and connection because the horse should always "take" as much as you "give." For the horse to be connected, he must actively reach, rather than passively allow gravity to pull his head down **(B)**. Merely lowering the neck has nothing to do with reaching forward. It is just a passive posture in which the horse falls onto his forehand and becomes unbalanced. ●

THIS

NOT THIS

5. *The horse should start training with his head low to allow the withers and back to rise, but as he gains strength, you can bring his front end up, lowering the hindquarters. As he develops, he will be able to carry more weight behind without compromising the lift in the back muscles.*

6. *This is a good exercise for the rider because it teaches you to maintain contact with any length of rein and to control how high or low the head goes by learning to use the outside rein to place it at the desired height. The horse's neck is higher when the reins are shorter and lower when the reins are longer. Many riders find it difficult to feel the connection on a longer rein because the horse's neck has more play, and if he moves it up even slightly, the rider can end up with a lapful of reins, losing connection. To keep the connection as you change head heights, be prepared to widen the reins quickly and push the horse forward. Then shorten the reins by sliding the outside rein through your hand first, then the inside rein.*

What is the "right height" for your horse? As noted, he will prefer to carry his head at a "comfortable" height. The most important aspect is that he remains relaxed, straight, and in the contact. Every horse is different. If your horse is already naturally low-headed or tends to pull on the bit, you don't need to emphasize this position, as long as you have control. Breed characteristics also play a role. Breeds with necks set on high (more upright), like Saddlebreds or Morgans, will have a higher natural neck carriage than breeds with necks set on lower (more horizontal), like Quarter Horses.

Managing Head Height

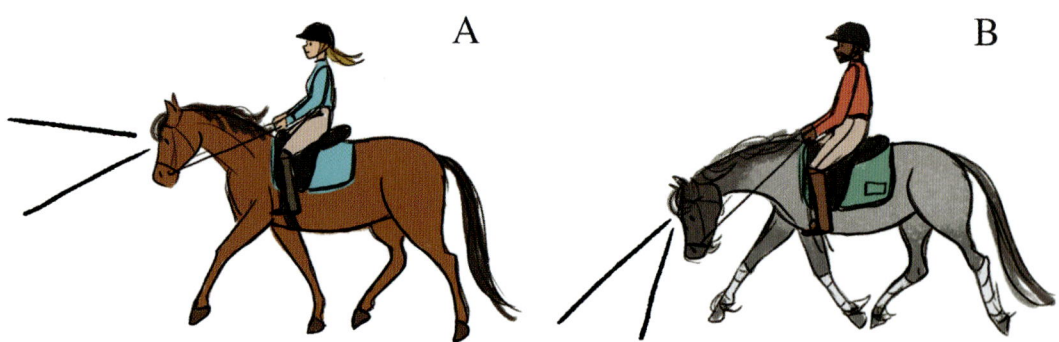

8.12 A & B Impact on Vision. A horse raises his head to focus his attention on objects in the distance and lowers it to consider objects a few feet away **(A)**. When we ask the horse to be in a frame, we remove his ability to analyze what might be in the distance, using all his senses, forcing him to concentrate on what is immediately in front of him **(B)**. As a prey animal, giving up the ability to scan the horizon for danger is a significant sacrifice, demonstrating his trust in the rider. •

The frame that best suits the horse's build will be what you ultimately seek at this stage.

Because altering the height of the horse's head affects his vision, it is prudent to have a rudimentary understanding of how horses see and how this affects their behavior. Because horses' eyes are larger than humans and on the sides of their heads, they have almost 340 degrees of vision, but their acuity (ability to focus on details) is far worse than ours. They make up for a large range of blurry vision by raising their head to analyze movements and objects at a distance, using all their senses, and lowering their heads to consider objects that are closer (figs. 8.12 A & B). Also, because horses' eyes are on the sides of their heads, they have blind spots where things seem to disappear and reappear, like right under their noses (one need to lower the head) and right behind them. (The book *Horse Brain, Human Brain* by neuroscientist Janet Jones explains equine vision extremely well, if you are interested in knowing more.)

When you ask a horse to lower his head, you remove his ability to focus his attention on distant objects. As a result, your horse may suddenly raise his head if he is alarmed by a movement or sound he perceives in the distance, since his instinct tells him he needs to identify whether it is a danger. The upshot is that, in order for the horse to remain in a frame and keep his head at a set height of the rider's determination, he has to give up his ability to see and understand his surroundings and put his trust in the rider. •

Study Guide

Prior Questions

AS a teacher, when I introduced a new concept in science class, one of the most useful techniques I used regularly was to tell my students to take out a sheet of paper and write down half a dozen questions—or however many that came quickly to mind—that they would want the answers to before they took a test or did a presentation on that topic. Then, we would share the questions aloud so that other students might gain even more insight into the topic by hearing the thoughts of others.

SAMPLE:

Topic to Present: *How to Get the Horse onto the Outside Rein*

Questions to Answer First:

❖ *Why is the outside rein important?*

❖ *How can I tell if the horse is on the outside rein?*

❖ *How does flexion toward the inside create the contact on the outside rein?*

❖ *Can I put too much pressure on the outside rein?*

❖ *Can I put too much pressure on the inside rein?*

Study Guide

Prior Questions

❖ How can I tell if my horse is avoiding the outside rein?

❖ What role does my inside leg play in helping to get the horse onto the outside rein?

❖ How do I know when to "give" on the inside or outside rein?

Answering these questions clearly will make a huge difference in your understanding and ability to explain to others how to get your horse onto the outside rein—and therefore, also your ability to actually *do* it. The questions help you discern what you do understand and what you still don't know. By doing this exercise, you can see the interrelationship between the quality of your thinking and the consequent success in learning how to communicate with the horse and riding well. You understand the concepts through thinking the content through on your own.

Try this with any of the topics from any chapter in this book. Ask questions that you think you might know the answer to, and then challenge yourself to extrapolate on the answer you gave. Find answers to the questions you still don't know the answer to. You may surprise yourself at what you do and don't know because having to articulate your thoughts in words or on paper often reveals what your mind might be taking for granted. ●

Your notes

Chapter

FLEXION

_09

When the horse's poll is flexed properly, his head readily moves in that direction. Only the area of the throat where his neck meets his head is flexed; the middle and lower parts of the neck do not bend.

9.1 A & B Flexion of the Poll. This refers to the movement of a single joint ("poll") in the small area behind the horse's ears where the skull connects to the neck. Flexion is defined as a slight turn of the head **(A)**. It is not the same as bending the neck or body anywhere along its length **(B)**. •

A
THIS

B
NOT THIS

The word "flexion" has multiple applications when applied to horses and riding.

❖ "Flexion" is defined as **the bending of any joint**; when joints "flex," the angle between the bones involved in that joint becomes smaller. Joints absorb shock when they bend. Propulsion is produced when (leg) joints straighten. The horse cannot move comfortably or fluidly without healthy joints, and increasing their ability to "flex," particularly in the hind end, is a primary goal of correct movement under saddle.

❖ **Flexion of the poll** refers to the movement of a single joint, the poll, which is located behind the horse's ears and connects the skull to the neck. (The poll is a protrusion from the back of the skull, and the joint in question is the one between the skull and the "atlas," or "C1.") Flexion in this case is simply the slight turning of the horse's head. Flexion of the poll does not imply bend in the neck vertebrae; only the skull moves (figs. 9.1 A & B). Poll flexibility is required for relaxation, spine maneuverability, and willingness in the horse. At the poll, there are three directions of movement:

• • *Longitudinal flexion* brings the horse's chin toward the underside of the neck, in the same way that humans nod their head, "Yes."

• • *Lateral flexion* closes the angle between the cheek and the side of the neck, flexing the joint side-to-side, similar to us shaking our head to say, "No."

• • *Rotation* (twisting) causes tilting of the head.

9.2 A & B Flexed vs. Inverted. A soft, compliant horse is the goal **(A)**, not a stiff, resistant horse **(B)**. "Inversion," as seen in B, is a result of retraction of the neck and must be eliminated in every gait and maneuver.

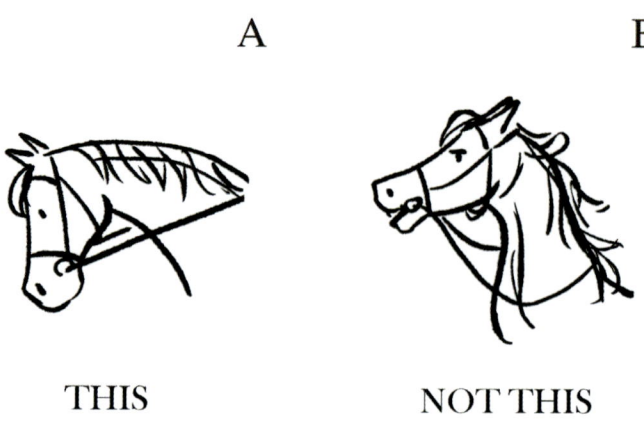

When the side-to-side flexion changes from left to right, it is often possible to observe the "nuchal ligament" in the crest of the horse's neck "flip." This reflex action indicates whether flexion is present and when it changes. (Note: Some horses have a conspicuous ligament flip, while others may have a barely perceptible tic.)

❖ Flexion **through the body is called "bend,"** which is generally a uniform curvature from poll to tail. Bend includes both the "inside" (concave) and "outside" (convex) curvature of a horse's body (think of a banana). To enable the horse to reach around a turn and maintain his line of travel while bending, the muscles on the inside of the turn are contracted and the muscles on the outside are lengthened, or stretched. "A correctly bent horse will have correct flexion, and a correctly flexed horse will have correct bend," explains trainer Sharon Vander Ziel. She continues, "Faulty bend, however, is bend only in the neck, or bend in the wrong direction."

This chapter focuses primarily on poll flexion because it is essential to keep the horse soft and willing. Understanding the significance of flexion, what it accomplishes, how it feels, and how to access it takes time. Do not accept that what your horse feels like to ride *now* accurately depicts riding; flexion enables you to modify the experience significantly! The sooner a rider learns to distinguish between a soft poll, neck, and horse, and a rigid one, the more rewarding riding becomes (figs. 9.2 A & B).

Flexion Is Kryptonite for Tension and Resistance

When a horse is learning, he often has negative tension in his body, which causes muscles and joints to lock up. Trainer Sharon Vander Ziel points out that "if one joint is locked, they are all locked." So you need a means of dispelling this tension. Flexion can be thought of as "kryptonite" to stiffness and resistance: when a horse is flexed at the poll, he physically can't resist because *his leverage is taken away*. Varying the position of the poll is like pushing the spring button in the base of one of those vintage puppet toys, causing the strings to go slack and the puppet to collapse (fig. 9.4). Likewise, flexing the poll removes and prevents stiffness.

Olympic team sports therapist (for both horses and riders) Jo-Ann Wilson further explains the importance of poll softness and flexibility:

> *Although the poll area is relatively small compared to some of your horse's other muscles, it is key to his freedom and ease of movement. If you think of your horse's motion as a wave that originates in his hind end and flows through his body and neck, you can see that the poll is the point at which the wave ends: The energy flows all the way from the hind leg to the head. If the poll is tight on one side (or both), it interrupts the completion of the wave. The effects of this interruption may*

"Inside" vs. "Outside"

As you have already discovered in these pages, when working with horses, there is a key distinction between the meanings of the words "inside" and "outside": "inside" isn't always on the side closest to the center of the arena and "outside" isn't always nearest the rail. The "inside" is always the direction in which the horse is bent or flexed. It has nothing to do with where you are in the ring. Therefore, it is possible that you could ride your horse bent toward the rail, and the rail would be on the inside. Also note that if, when using your outside rein the horse turns his head that way, the "outside" is instantly no longer the outside! Since the horse has changed his flexion or bend, that side now becomes the "inside."

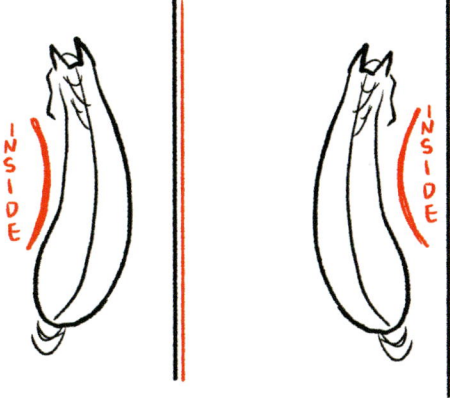

Bend of horse determines "inside," NOT the wall

9.3 Inside vs Outside. The "inside" of the horse is always the direction in which the horse is bent or flexed; it has nothing to do with where you are in the ring. The inside is the "concave" or shortened side of the horse. The "outside" is the "convex" or lengthened side that must stretch around a curve.

9.4 Flexion Overcomes Resistance. When the spring plunger in the base of a vintage puppet is depressed, the tension of its internal string is released and the puppet collapses. Similarly, flexing a horse's poll removes his leverage for bracing his body so that he is soft in the rider's hands. Like the string that runs through a puppet's body, the horse has a series of muscles that run from poll to tail. Because the poll is situated at the front of this system, it is referred to as the "gateway to the spine." The flexibility of the poll determines whether the rest of the horse is stiff or flexible, and its proximity to the bit in relation to the rest of the system determines whether your rein aids reach the horse's back and hind legs. It is fortunate that the horse's poll is conveniently located in front of you so that you can easily see it to control the horse, knowing that the remainder of his back will function as it does. Because of this, you can "see what you're riding." •

show up as problems in other parts of your horse's body. For instance, if simple muscle tightness in the gluteal muscles or the hamstring inhibits your horse's freedom of movement in his hind end, he will tighten in his poll to balance or compensate for this lack of freedom of motion behind.

When the poll is supple, it is easy to flex the horse's head in either direction, but the horse's neck and body should remain straight. It is quite an epiphany to discover just how much, and how frequently, your horse braces his poll (and neck and body) and becomes rigid in one area or another. It is normal to "soften" him frequently. When your work with your horse ensures he no longer stiffens his body, he gets that "light," "soft as butter" feel that correctly trained horses offer (and which we talked about on p. 134) and is wonderful to ride. What does this mean? It means that when you squeeze gently on a rein, your horse's head follows that rein just as gently. He doesn't get stiff, pull back, raise his head, get tense, or resist. It's like opening or shutting a door with well-oiled hinges: it swings freely.

The Role of Flexion in Connection

Once your horse has learned contact and connection, it doesn't mean that he'll autonomously remain connected like a car in "drive" until you take it out of gear. To the contrary, your horse has a mind of his own and may not want to do what you ask. He may become distracted by a captivating or scary incident, or he may become tired. In any case, he'll lose connection repeatedly if you don't know how to prevent the loss of it, or know how to get it back quickly. Flexion plays a significant role in maintaining and regaining connection.

You do more complex maneuvers than simply walk and trot in a straight line while riding. At the very least, you have corners to negotiate, gates or doors to pass through, and you may wish to ride in a circle or serpentine, and any number of other figures. Because horses respond instinctively to such challenges (or distractions) by stiffening or "bracing" the neck or entire body, any of these activities can disrupt connection, making it difficult to do them, or making riding feel a way you don't really want it to (hard, uncomfortable, frustrating). When a horse has a stiff neck and shoulders, he's not connected. He's not listening to your aids.

As horsemanship trainer John Lyons stated in his Aug 31, 2005, *Practical Horseman* article, "Head Position Matters":

> *Few things are as frustrating as trying to reason with a horse whose head is up in the air. The problem goes beyond aggravating to unsafe when he's acting goofy and not letting you call the shots. There's no steering, slowing, or stopping. When a horse's head is high, it's as if his brain is experiencing a certain type of static. If the horse could talk, it seems the only word he'd say is no. But when he drops his head into what we'd consider a normal position, he calms down. In fact, we call the "head down" cue the "calm down cue" for that reason.*

Therefore, you need a tool to recover and maintain your horse's attention, cooperation, and calmness in order for him to remain connected and functional on the outside rein, and in the frame and head height you desire (see p. 221). That tool is "flexion." Flexion is the key to maintaining a soft, willing, and connected horse. When the horse is flexed, it is difficult for him to raise his head or misbehave. Once you understand how to achieve and maintain flexion, you will reap its incalculable benefits and never ride without it again. I cannot emphasize enough how worthwhile it is to persist in comprehending and mastering this Non-Negotiable, as a soft, non-resistant horse that respects the outside rein is a delight to ride.

To the Outside Rein, Not Through It

One objective of flexion, as we touched upon in earlier chapters, is to bring the horse *to the outside rein*. You can feel that connection, and when it happens, he will respond easily and readily to the outside rein. It's glorious! Once you are able to *get* your horse to the outside rein, however, you must learn to prevent him from "blowing through it." You must "catch the connection" in your outside rein and keep the base of his neck straight in order to prevent him from "buckling out" at the withers and straying from the line of travel (see figs. 7.9 A & B, p. 187).

Flexion Requires Persistent Attention

Most horses require a bit of persistence to achieve correct and consistent flexion. The necks of horses are robust, and they can wield them like steam shovels. As a "fight" reflex to resist rider requests and to take the reins away from you, the horse may swing his neck like a male giraffe sparring. As a "flight" reflex, he may pull it forward and

Flexion and Bend and the Outside Rein

When working on a curved line of travel, like a circle, flexion of the poll must relate to bend in the horse's body. Bend should result in the same degree of body curvature from the horse's ears to its tail. Because you have put so much effort into learning how to create this curve by pushing the rib cage out and sensing the connection in the outside rein (see p. 188), you may be thrilled with your horse once you reach this status. The insidious issue is that, even when your horse is bending correctly, he may be drifting, even slightly, outside of your circle, thereby enlarging it. This indicates that he is still "escaping"—he is still going through the outside rein. Because you accept it unknowingly, he believes it's what you want.

When circling to the left, for example, the horse's right/outside (front and rear) legs likely step to the right. As a result, even if you believe you're maintaining his spine over the imaginary line of the track, it's far more likely that you have drifted...and you're not aware of it. Therefore, setting up flat soccer cones on your circle or laying a lead rope on the ground and doing a circle in front of it while avoiding stepping over it can be an eye-opening experience. You may find remaining within a boundary extremely challenging. Consider an ice skater performing crossovers during a turn: the crossover keeps the skater on the line because the outside leg moves inward, preserving the circle's arc, and the inside leg keeps the skater upright. The same is true for horses on a circle: the outside front leg should be directed toward the interior of a turn, not away from it, to give the impression that the horse is crossing

rush. If he "freezes," he may raise it like a periscope to look around. Regardless of the situation, his neck and body become rigid, rather than his poll flexing softly. To maintain or regain control of the horse, a mechanism (that goal of flexion) is required to prevent stiffness and refocus his attention on you and what you are asking.

Using the Warm-Up to Develop Flexion

In her book *Dressage for the Not-So-Perfect Horse*, FEI 5* dressage judge Janet Foy recommends the following for producing the softness and attention for which you aim:

> *The horse needs to be ridden in a position where the warm-up can do him the most good. The topline muscles must be stretched and loosened correctly in order to carry the energy from the hind legs to the contact. Each horse needs to have a warm-up tailor-made just for him. Why? Horses have different types of bodies, necks, balance, and, of course, temperament. This may sound like strange advice, but "wherever" your horse likes to be physically speaking... well, you need to change it to warm him up. If he wants his neck high, it should be low. If he wants it low, keep it higher. If he's lazy, make him hotter. If he's tense and fast, slow him down. In other words, whatever the horse wants to do by nature, change it!*

Consequently, if your horse is stiff or resistant, the primary objective during the warm-up should be to make him soft (flexible in the poll). If you warm up without flexion, you risk developing the wrong muscles and practicing mistakes. According to an old adage, every second on a horse is either spent training or un-training him. Because your horse does not comprehend the distinction between the "warm-up" and the "work phase" of your training session, the warm-up can occasionally become the work, encompassing the entire ride if necessary. Reward your horse and boost his confidence by stopping early on days when he performs well, flexing without resistance or evasion. Tomorrow is another day.

What are some things you might want your horse to do that he'll resist? Anything and everything! Getting him to the outside rein (he goes through instead); changing directions (he stiffens and leans); walking a straight track with a little flexion (he walks like a drunkard); staying on the rail or coming off the rail (he wanders); transitioning to trot (he raises his head and pushes with his chest). If you ask for something and the horse stiffens and resists, you don't have the flexion you need to prevent it. Indeed, until you learn to recognize the signs of resistance, you might not even realize when it's happening.

Some horses resist strongly, and it is readily apparent. Some horses exhibit subtle forms of resistance. However, regardless of the size of the resistance, its over in the same way as the skater—right legs step left, and left legs step right. To accomplish this, maintain an open outside rein and direct it toward the hock when squeezing the rein (half-halting—see p. 261) when the outside front foot is on the ground. Keeping that leg grounded for an additional second prevents your horse from moving laterally (you are saying, "Don't go that way"). Maintain the flexion by periodically squeezing the inside rein to ask, "Are you soft?" This is an essential sensation to discover and pay close attention to. When you are able to contain this without tightening the horse's neck—he must still drop his head and be relaxed while reaching for the bit—your horse will feel incredible to ride.

When you first start working on this skill on the circle, keep your outside rein low and open and push with your inside leg. On the inside, he must remain flexed and soft. Your horse will most likely try to go faster, step farther to the outside, stiffen, raise his head, twist his neck, or lean on the reins. Don't get involved in his struggle. Just stay on message until things improve. This could take minutes or weeks, depending on the horse. Make sure to reward him when he tries. ●

existence is a problem. When you begin to notice stiffnesses and resistances, you will become able to identify more of them, originating in all areas of the horse's body. The goal is to flex just a little, but you may have to do more—known as "suppling"—until the horse understands and yields.

Suppling to Achieve Softness

To initially remedy a stiffness (often caused by the inability of unfit muscles to stretch) and start on the road to the subtlety of flexion, you may need to begin with "suppling." Suppling is a temporary training technique that encourages your horse to be soft and pliable rather than rigid or antagonistic. How do you know if your horse is soft or if you need to supple? When you squeeze the inside rein, his head should move freely, like a bobble-head dog in the back window of a car on a bumpy road. He should easily yield to you. If he doesn't, or pulls in the opposite direction, he needs suppling. How do you do it?

Scan to View Introducing Suppling to the Horse

* Flex the horse's head toward the inside while turning in a small- to medium--size circle (this **encourages the horse's muscles on the outside of his body to stretch**, preparing him for work), using your inside leg to involve his entire body in the bend needed to follow the curved line of travel (not just the neck) and to keep him moving forward. It is *essential* that the horse bends through the rib cage. Push the ribs out (see p. 188). Turn your shoulders to the inside. Be sensitive to the size of the circle you ride because smaller circles require the horse to stretch more. Don't ask for more than your horse can do comfortably.

* Don't let the outside rein sag, forgotten; however, **the outside rein must maintain enough elasticity to allow the horse to flex and bend to the inside, as well as stretch the outside of his body.** Don't be so immobile so that you prevent him from doing what you ask. You will be able to tell if you are too rigid because the horse may counterbend or become agitated. Sometimes, in the earliest stages of training or retraining a horse, you may need to use just the inside rein and let the outside go until your horse can do what you ask. You will feel him loosen up and swing through his body. He may move briskly as he loosens; this is fine. Allow him to put his head at the height at which he can do this comfortably—it will probably be low.

Then, you can gradually resume contact on the outside rein—just enough to ride the horse "how he should be ridden" while staying balanced. Too much and you will unbalance him again.

❖ Keep your outside elbow close to your ribs to act as a "side-rein" to **stabilize the base of the horse's neck, preventing his outside shoulder from protruding** and enabling him to step off the line of travel (for example, when circling to the left, his right legs stepping to the right and out from underneath the body). Learn to recognize and prevent this deviation, no matter how slight, when riding. The outside rein will keep the horse's shoulders aligned with his hindquarters, while the inside rein will keep the horse's head, neck, and jaw in the correct position for an inside flexion (going *to* the outside rein, and *not* through it). Remember to envision directing the left front leg of the horse to the right and the right front leg to the left. This assists in the outside front leg crossing in front of the other during a turn, while keeping the inside supporting leg underneath the withers to keep the horse upright and not leaning. When the rib cage is asked to shift to the outside, the horse's legs must not step out from under the body in that direction. It is helpful to think to yourself, *Ribs right, step left*, or *Ribs left, step right*. The horse won't actually step in the opposite direction, but the imagery will assist you in redirecting the legs to stay on the path of travel. Try this yourself: Walk next to a straight line (like a broom handle) and push your ribs in one direction, but don't step over the line. Step forward, not sideways. The body doesn't leave the line of travel, despite the rotation of the ribs.

❖ **Maintain a supportive outside leg so that your horse cannot swing his hindquarters outside** the circle's line of travel to escape the resulting body curvature. Many horses will swing their haunches out when asked to bend, so the rider must be prepared to prevent this with a firm outside leg. This use of outside aids keeps the horse's haunches aligned with his shoulders and maintains the horse's travel direction. The shoulders and rear must move sideways in tandem; neither can advance before the other.

❖ If you need to "block" either the shoulders or hindquarters from leading and drifting out past the confines of your line of travel, **direct the outside rein toward the outside hock**. One of my instructors gave me an effective way of thinking about this, saying: "Use the rein on the side of the direction you *don't* want to go and the horse can't go that way. It's like closing a door in his face." However, this is where flexion becomes imperative: If you don't have inside flexion and you use the outside rein, the horse will turn his head to follow that pull and look to the outside. This is why, when using an opposing rein, you must maintain flexion in the opposite direction so that the horse doesn't counterbend.

❖ Once you feel suppleness on the inside, continue in the same direction but **switch to suppling your horse to the outside**. This means you will *intentionally* be counterbending him! This has three benefits: 1) Your horse needs to be equally supple on both sides of his body regardless of which way he is going, 2) this will push his outside shoulder underneath his body and he will become more upright and stable, and 3) it can be effective when your horse has trouble bending in one direction (circle him in the easier direction first, and then counterbend while still going that way).

Eventually, you will be able to determine the exact amount of suppling that elicits the softness, flexion, and bend you seek, without having to be dramatic. At first, it may take quite a bit of strength to bend even his neck (the most bendable part of the body), whereas, when he's supple, you should be able to flex his poll without meeting any resistance, and whether you are bending his body or not, as if his head was attached with a slinky. Ideally, with a well-schooled horse, you will just need to move a finger to remind him to be pliant. Sharon Vander Ziel suggests, "Think of your wrist joint as the horse's poll/jaw. Move your (inside) wrist like you want the horse's poll to move." When you get to this stage, this advice is nothing short of miraculous. When the poll moves easily with your wrist, your horse will likely present a lovely frame and be very rideable as the result of his newfound softness, with connection to the outside rein. It is important that the horse keeps taking the bit forward for connection; this can never be forgotten or abandoned. This whole process takes time and will likely continue to present a challenge during every ride. It will get easier as time passes, but you can never abandon requesting it.

Scan to View Proper Flexion and Suppling

Common Mistakes When Suppling

Many riders don't realize when they are employing "toxic measures," so you must be intentionally mindful about how you are suppling. Thomas Ritter sums this up well, noting that aids are intentionally named "aids" as opposed to "interferences." This makes sense because aids *benefit* the horse while not interfering with him. So, make sure you're actually helping the horse and not making matters worse. Here are some common mistakes to be on guard against:

❖ Don't bend the horse's neck to an extreme degree so that his nose touches your foot. This takes him off balance. Remember, the goal of suppling is to attain flexion in the poll, *not the base of the neck.*

❖ Pulling only one rein causes the neck to overbend, forcing the opposite shoulder to "pop out": if you pull the left rein, the right shoulder pops out and the horse's body "jackknifes," and vice versa. When this happens, the horse's right leg will step over to the right, compounding the problem, and the horse

9.5 Jackknifed. When you pull on one rein, this causes the horse's *opposite* shoulder to bulge the other way, creating a jackknifed position with his neck. This causes the horse to become crooked, making it difficult to maintain connection. This also causes the horse to move away from the direction you want to go. For example, if you pull the left rein, he will "pop out" his right shoulder and move to the right, even though you are trying to turn him to the left.

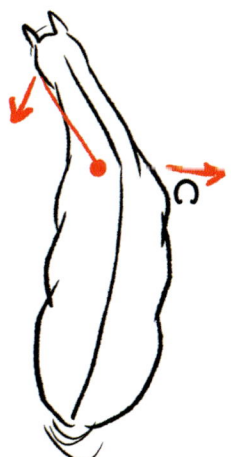

will follow that shoulder *away* from the line of travel (fig. 9.5).

❖ Don't "wag" the horse's head from side to side by see-sawing the reins, repeatedly pulling one way, then the other.

❖ Don't get frustrated and yank on a rein to punish the horse. Abusive hands are never acceptable.

❖ Incessantly pulling on the inside rein is the most common issue I see in students. Many riders unconsciously rely on the inside rein to maintain their stability. Often, when asked to use an aid, the first thing a rider does is grab the inside rein for leverage and balance *before* applying the requested aid. This only teaches the horse to lean on that rein, leading the rider to believe the horse is pulling on her.

❖ When using a rein, do not cross your hand over the withers as if you were playing a violin. Crossing your hand over the withers to the opposite side of the horse serves only to overbend the neck at its base. Left hands remain to the left of the horse's neck, while right hands remain to the right. Do not touch the horse's neck with the reins.

❖ As riders learn to overcome the novice tendency to "forget the outside elbow," allowing it to repeatedly relax forward of its own accord, resulting in a floppy outside rein, they pass through an overcompensating phase of being too rigid and pulling back. This rigidity restricts the natural movement of the horse's head and neck, causing the horse to feel trapped and unable to escape the discomfort. Thus, it is imperative that the rider is attentive to maintaining a considerate, elastic contact that follows, but doesn't disappear. This has to be a priority in the progressing rider's mind.

❖ Don't hold the horse's head in position. The horse needs to carry his own head.

❖ Trainer JP Giacomini reminds us, "Suppling must never become the source of a loss of impulsion or direction."

9.6 Ideal Flexion. Flexion occurs only at the poll (the atlas joint) and works like us nodding our head "yes" and "no," turning only the head up or down or to the left or right, without allowing bend in the neck. A small rotation or shift in position of the head is all that's needed for flexion. If a straight horse is like twelve noon on a clock, correct flexion to the left positions the head "two minutes before noon," while correct flexion to the right places it "two minutes after noon," according to trainer Yvonne Barteau. Any more is too much. ●

Establishing Correct Flexion

In correct flexion, only the horse's jaw is turned slightly in the direction of the flexion, and the head yields willingly. The head does not tilt or twist; it simply moves freely in response to a gentle invitation on the inside rein. If your horse's head does not move freely, he is rigid. If the head tilts, he is evading (you can tell this is the case because the ears will not be parallel; one will be lower). Expect stiffness to return in varying degrees as you work on this skill and that you will likely need to adjust it on a regular basis. Do not assume that if you "fix it," it will remain fixed. Even with the most highly trained horses, every rider is constantly working on flexion.

"Two Minutes Past Noon"

Scan to View Flexing Two Minutes Before and After Twelve

In her book *The Dressage Horse Manifesto*, Grand Prix dressage trainer and competitor Yvonne Barteau describes flexion in a way that is simple to comprehend and visualize: "Imagine your horse's neck and head emerging from the center of his chest at 'twelve noon'" (if there were a clock on his withers and you were looking down from above). Everything to the left of that is "left positioning," while everything to the right is "right positioning" (fig. 9.6). You are doing extremely well if you can eventually get your horse to flex to the left "two minutes before twelve" or to the right "two minutes after twelve." Due to the fact that each horse has a unique body, you might determine if you need "three minutes" instead of "two." Additionally, your horse may not be symmetrical, so you may need to flex more in one direction than the other to achieve identical results on both sides. Remember the neck, particularly at its base by the shoulders and withers, remains straight. *Only the poll is flexible.* Even though your outside rein maintains this straightness, it is not held rigidly and indefinitely to keep the horse in position. Be sensitive and elastic at the elbow so that the horse can reach down while maintaining his straight posture. You must give, observe how your horse responds, and make adjustments as needed.

"Tiny Suppling"

In essence, flexion is "tiny suppling." Once the horse understands the cues for suppling (see p. 238), a simple indication that it is desired should be sufficient to prompt him to flex and soften. Flexion involves maintaining the connection on the outside rein while opening or suppling the inside rein. Again, like playing a piano, each hand has a unique and separate function: the hand positioned in treble clef plays melodies, while the other, in bass clef, plays accompaniment. Likewise, the rider's inside hand maintains the softness and flexion while the outside rein intentionally regulates how much the inside rein can bend the neck (although not so restrictively that the horse feels trapped by it). In addition, the opening flexion of the inside rein (combined with inside leg) pushes the horse's neck and shoulders to the outside rein so that the rider can use the outside rein for half-halts to balance him, manage the tempo, or keep the outside shoulder from bulging out (see chapter 10, p. 259, for a detailed discussion of half-halts). The inside rein also prevents the horse from looking to the outside when the outside rein is used. For example, say the outside rein is the left rein—you don't want the horse to look to the left when you use the left rein. So you use the inside (right) rein to keep him flexed to the right and push him *to* the left (outside) rein. Then you can use the left rein to tell the horse to slow down, turn, or prepare for a transition. As trainer Sharon Vander Ziel, states, "There is no outside rein without the inside rein."

Each of the rider's hands may also function in different rhythm. The inside hand can be thought of as using eighth or sixteenth note-length signals ("Stay soft; look this way") directed more "upward," while the outside rein uses quarter or half note-length signals ("Slow down; turn") directed more downward toward the horse's hocks. At first, this ambidextrous coordination can be challenging for a rider. You will likely make clumsy adjustments through gross motor movements until, with practice, you develop the dexterity and sensitivity for finer movements. Eventually, you will learn to feel small resistances, stiffenings, and counterbendings in the horse, and catch them quickly, so that overdone corrections become a thing of the past. A quick press of the inside leg and a tiny restriction on the outside rein will be enough to correct the more sophisticated horse-and-rider team.

Because the horse is innately crooked and bends the same way going both directions (see p. 190), you will need to apply your aids differently each direction. Going one way (usually to the left), you'll need to maintain better contact on the outside rein so the neck doesn't overbend to his hollow (left) side. The right side of the body is receptive to stretching; however, when you *go* to the right, you must be more elastic and forgiving on the outside rein (left) so that the left side of the horse's body can stretch more, which it doesn't want to do. You will need to use more inside leg to ensure that the right shoulder doesn't fall in. The goal is to gradually develop the horse so that his flexion in each direction becomes symmetrical and you don't have to do such drastically different things to accommodate him.

To assist your horse through this developmental stage, position your inside hand to indicate where you want his nose to point. When he flexes, be firm on your outside rein—as if you are a human side-rein—so that he stays put, and then gradually, a millimeter at a time, ease off on the inside rein so that you don't lose him and have to start over. Do not completely let go of the inside rein so that it becomes slack. If you let go too quickly and too much, his head will pop up or he will immediately look outside. The horse requires orientation and a gradual release of pressure with an elastic feel.

Rein Length Serves a Purpose

The flexing rein asks for flexion, and the non-flexing rein concurrently limits the amount of flexion to prevent overbending. The length of the outside rein *determines which part of the neck gets suppled or flexed.* A longer rein allows the neck to bend for suppling; a shorter rein keeps the neck straight and encourages flexion of the poll.

When asked, the horse must also be ready and willing to flex in either direction. It is also critical that the horse continues to take the bit forward for that connection you have been working on (see p. 127). This can never be sacrificed, so you may need to alternate between "widen/squeeze" and "suppling/flexion." Savvy interplay between the two reins keeps the horse soft to the inside, and connected on the outside rein. To experience this counterbalancing effect yourself, try to feel with your left hand, through the reins and bit, what your right hand is doing, and vice versa. Don't think of the reins as two separate reins; instead, think of them as a single, continuous loop, like a necklace (see exercise on p. 157). Note what it would feel like when you let one end sag: the connection between your hands would disappear. Feel for this sensation when riding, but imagine the bit in the middle and the effect you have on the horse's mouth and tongue. This imagery will help you maintain that connected feeling at all times and reminds you to think of the bit, reins, and your hands as communication tools.

Scan to View Overbending and Different Lengths of Rein

Evasion and Resistance

The horse will likely initially object to the flexed posture because he wants to do what is easy. To get out of or avoid the flexion and bend, he may look outside, pop his outside shoulder, put his head in the air, jut out his underneck, or brace against your request for all he's worth. Supple him to the inside until

9.7 Flexion in the Poll and Bend Through the Body. This picture depicts perfect flexion, balance, and bend through the body, from the poll to the tail. The ribs are clearly "out," not falling in toward the center of the circle or pushing against the rider's inside leg. The horse is staying on the curved path specified by the rider and is not drifting out. The shoulders and hips remain in alignment. ●

he's soft, connected, and flexed through the poll and bent through the body (fig. 9.7). You will repeat this process countless times, but each time it should become less dramatic until the proactive maintenance is barely noticeable. Don't let the horse's resistance bother you. Just keep repeating the message until he learns it is easier to do it right. Repetition is a powerful persuasive technique.

Your horse will evade or resist until he understands, decides it is easier to comply, or his body adjusts to the new movement methods. Until then, he will continue to resist. He may do so aggressively at first, but less so as he progresses—or as your skill, tact, or response timing improves. If you understand that his resistance is reflexive and follows a predictable pattern, you will not be surprised, frustrated, intimidated, or scared. You will be ready.

"Opening" the Rein: Overcoming the Urge to Pull

It is easier for a horse to relax the poll when the neck is lowered, which is one of the reasons why this book introduced "widen and squeeze" and an invitation to lower the head and reach before I dug deeper into flexion in this chapter.

When you "open" a rein, you move it away from the horse's neck *without* pulling back on it (fig. 9.8). (Alternatively, a "lift" can work, as well.) To understand how to do this (and to overcome the involuntary default of pulling back), I introduce the concept while longeing my student and her horse. I instruct the rider to "place the inside rein over the longe line." This isn't literally possible because the longe line is attached to the bridle or cavesson and extends to my hand from there, but it compels the rider to open the inside rein in an attempt to reach that extreme (the far off longe line) and develops a new brain connection in the rider to give forward. As a result, the horse generally provides the desired response (reaching forward, flexing to the inside), so the rider gets positive reinforcement from the effort and continues to use the technique from thence forward. Being on the longe line is also beneficial psychologically because riders don't have to worry about controlling the horse and can instead focus on themselves.

Another effective strategy is for me to raise one of my hands while standing in the middle of the

9.8 Opening or Lifting the Inside Rein. "Opening" the rein means moving the rein away from the horse's neck in the desired direction. By opening the inside rein, you invite the horse to take the contact. Note: You can also raise the inside rein to get a better response when you ask for flexion. If necessary, opening and lifting can be combined.

arena and invite the rider to reach for it with her inside hand. As a result, the rider shifts her opening hand to the side and forward, rather than pulling back, and the tension on the reins remains constant.

The opening rein's primary advantage is that it guides the horse's nose in a direction without the rider pulling back, ensuring the hind leg can step under his body. Since opening the rein will ask the horse to turn, the opening rein is on the inside of a curved line of travel. Consequently, this also asks the outside of the horse to stretch so that, gradually, his left and right sides become more symmetrically flexible and ambidextrous. The inviting open rein has other uses, worth mentioning here:

❖ Horses tend to move with their haunches misaligned, and opening the rein can assist in straightening them out by guiding the shoulders in front of the hips.

❖ The opening rein is often used on young or green horses when introducing them to steering.

❖ You can open the outside rein to invite a horse that is falling in to step out, into the open space. Simultaneously shifting your weight into the outside stirrup helps get the idea across. This is a useful technique when introducing leg-yield (see p. 176).

❖ Opening the inside rein can stop the horse from falling in by shifting the weight from the inside shoulder to the outside shoulder.

It may help to think that widening the reins, which you now know how to do, is merely opening *both* reins. Opening both reins applies even pressure on the horse's mouth from both sides, directing the horse's nose to the center of his chest and straightening his spine. As both horse and rider gain experience and conditioning, the need for the opening rein (or needing to open it as much) decreases.

Accommodating Muscle Fatigue

As with any fitness regimen, the horse needs breaks to rest his body. Don't ride him in flexion for more than a few minutes, or even strides, at a time, initially. Allow him to become accustomed to using new muscles, and then give him a long rein and a pat as a reward for compliance. Let him relax and then "put him together" again. Ride him for a few strides at first, then maybe one circle, and so forth. Over time, he'll build up endurance and be able to carry himself and perform new maneuvers in this manner.

Furthermore, it is critical that he is in this posture, with flexion, and that he is soft and rhythmic before you attempt to make any transitions (see chapter 8, p. 200). If he resists during a transition, stop the transition, flex and soften him again, and try again when he's relaxed and listening. While it is important to practice flexion in transitions and in all gaits, don't overdo it in one ride. Allow him time to get in shape as you work on new skills. You don't want to make him dread or resent being ridden.

Restoring Flexion Throughout a Ride

Scan to View Flexion into Transitions

You will likely have to address physical tension from scratch in each gait, in each direction, as well as before, during, and after every transition. You may find that you must do this every day during warm-up. A stiff poll and neck resistance isn't something that goes away. You will find that you must remind the horse many times during every ride. This is normal. But he'll feel *great* to ride when he softens his poll, relaxes his body, becomes round, and takes longer, smoother strides, all pushing evenly from behind. No one will need to tell you that you have succeeded because your horse will feel springy, swingy, and soft. At first, such a moment might be fleeting, so don't miss it. Your entire notion of riding will change in that instant of enlightenment. Don't be disappointed if you don't feel it again right away; it will return.

I have what I refer to as the "Thousand Rule": You achieve something. Then, after 999 more attempts, you feel it again. Then after another 998 attempts, again. Then 997, and so on, until whatever it is you're attempting to accomplish becomes consistent. You accept that your horse's cooperation swings like a pendulum. Momentarily, the stars align and everything is perfect—your horse is soft, connected, and rhythmic, and riding is effortless. The pendulum then swings to the opposite extreme, where the horse resists and becomes unbalanced once more, as he either tires or refuses to do it because it is difficult. You reaffirm your aids; he concedes, and the pendulum swings back. However, it swings to a lesser and lesser degree with each repetition as your horse's resistance lessens and he grows stronger.

As your horse becomes physically fit and accustomed to following your cues, resistances and corrections become minimal, and you spend the majority of your time enjoying a consistent ride. This persistent consistence—or consistent persistence—is the essence of training and applies to everything you will do with your horse. Recognizing this pattern of events helps you manage your expectations during a ride, removes the element of surprise from what your horse may do, and keeps the rider calm and methodical. When you can predict and perceive the changes in the pendulum's swing, you recognize the progress that you are making.

Until a rider comprehends (it's an epiphany!) the subtleties and outcomes of suppling and flexion, there will be a lot of trial and error. The rider might be too hesitant and get no results, or may overdo it and need to dial back. Eventually, as you gain a glimmer of understanding, you will also gain insight into what your horse put up with while you were clueless! We all have to learn. Riding is about self-reflection—thinking about your riding while you are riding *in order to improve your riding*. Bring compassion to your riding naiveté. Riding isn't about ego, or proving to yourself, to your horse, or to others how tough or good you are. Riding is a partnership.

Putting the pieces together to achieve flexion is a huge turning point for both horse and rider. Like contact, it is a bottleneck through which you must pass in order to experience an extraordinary world of communication with your horse on the other side. You literally become a new rider because you realize how unconsciously incompetent you have been up to this point, but you also understand how to do less and get so much more. You become more intentional, you can feel when something isn't right—and know what to do about it. You know who your horse is, and you no longer ride offensively, relying on force without comprehension. As trainer Beth Baumert states so effectively in her book *When Two Spines Align*:

> *Although control over the flexion seems like a small matter, it is one of the single most important aspects of your ride. Without correct flexion, it is impossible to have correct alignment and bend, so it's impossible to have a correct connection or collection. Without correct flexion, half-halts don't go through, and transitions are ineffective. Correct flexion is nearly invisible, but the educated observer can see it and the educated rider knows if she has it or not.*

"Single most important aspects of your ride." It can't be overstated what an effect flexion has on the horse. Mentally, the horse becomes accommodating, trusting, and respectful. Physically, the horse becomes soft and relaxed, and his gaits become springy and rhythmic. And you are able to tap into the amazing communication afforded by the half-halt (see the next chapter—p. 259). It is an *entirely* different ride. And it really does exist!

★ Caveats

❖ Remember to separate the functions of your two hands in your mind by thinking of manipulating the reins as akin to playing the piano: **two hands performing separate but complementary tasks**. It's important to keep track of what each hand is doing. In the case of flexion, once you have established contact, yield the outside rein forward just enough to accommodate the slight shortening of the inside rein and allow the flexion.

❖ If you **overbend the base of the neck by the withers**, your horse will lose straightness and balance by popping out his outside shoulder. When on a curved line of travel, he will no longer have equal bend throughout his body, from poll to tail; instead, he'll look more angled, bent like a jackknife at the shoulder. Turning is more difficult in this jackknifed position because the horse will lean and step to the outside of the circle, heading off on a tangent to the circle you are no longer on because he's veering more sideways than forward. At the very least, your circle will have grown in size and will no longer be round.

❖ Furthermore, **perpetually pulling a rein** (it takes two to pull) can be avoided if the rider simply does not do it. Consider a person sitting with her elbow on the table, chin on hand. What if I remove the table? Since the chin no longer rests on anything, the neck must now support the head. It is the same with the reins.

❖ Temporarily bending the neck to stretch the outside neck muscles to establish flexion is beneficial, but keeping it bent for too long is detrimental. **Supple only enough to loosen the poll, then stop.** Pulling on a light switch longer or harder won't make the light brighter. Once the light is on, it's on…

❖ If your horse's head and neck are more than three minutes before or after noon, he is overbent. People who are first learning to use flexion tend to ride at 11:45 or 12:15 and are unaware that they have too much forced bend instead of a buttery soft responsiveness followed by release. **Overbending the neck is harmful** and the opposite of what you are intending to achieve.

❖ The term **"rubber-necked"** refers to an overbent neck when the horse's body does not turn to follow. Instead, the horse keeps going straight or even in the opposite direction, "through his shoulder." This tends to be associated with a horse that is out of control and fleeing.

❖ **When suppling,** apply the same amount of pressure as the horse, which might feel like a lot. You can overcome any response by pushing him sideways on a circle with your inside leg while softening the inside rein. Strong resistance from the horse should not last long. If it does, or if the horse becomes upset or stressed, seek qualified assistance in determining the cause of the resistance.

- **Too-long reins permit the horse to bend at the base of the neck, which is easier for him than bending at the poll, so the horse defaults to this position whenever possible**. Maintain your outside rein so that the neck remains straight and only bends at the poll. However, despite the need to keep the horse's neck straight, remember not to trap the horse with a tight rein. Be elastic, accommodating, and empathetic with your outside rein. It can't droop, but doesn't have to be unalterably stiff. Flexion should not be forced.

- Dressage Olympian and coach Debbie McDonald tells her students to occasionally pat the horse with the inside hand, which causes riders to instinctively give the inside rein without question. The horse should maintain flexion on his own, or through reminders from the rider, with the leg, while reaching for the bit and remaining connected from behind. If the inside rein "gives" and the horse moves his head to the outside, it means the rider has been pulling or holding the inside rein.

- You will need to figure out **how long or short the outside rein needs to be** when you ask for flexion, especially if the horse bends his neck in any place other than the poll. While it might not be a reaction you want, it may provide useful information. Where exactly *can* he bend? Where is he the stiffest and most resistant? Ideally, with work on bending lines, you should mobilize the entire neck so that residual stiffness in one area does not impact another.

- The **base of the neck, where it connects to the horse, must be stable and solid** for riding. If it liberates from the shoulders and becomes crooked, the outside shoulder will pop out and the connection with the hind legs will be lost. They will get strung out behind or step out from under the body to either side. As described by Thomas Ritter, "As you go from the base of the neck to the poll, the flexibility has to increase. Like a tree, the neck should be the broadest and most solid at the base/trunk and become more slender and elastic at the top." Some horses are built this way and are easy to ride because of it. However, horses usually come with a variety of conformation challenges. Horses with short necks are thicker at the poll and are therefore more difficult to ride on the bit; horses with thin, long necks tend to be very unstable at the base. It's easier to supple a stiff neck than to stabilize a thin one.

- When suppling the poll, **some horses re-stiffen so quickly, bracing repeatedly**, that you may be tempted to believe that you are doing something incorrectly or that the exercise is ineffective. Persist. It will come. Overcoming the horse's resistance will result in a softer horse. Suddenly, the horse will finally yield, and it will feel incredible as he "melts" in your hands. Even if it's only for a split second, once you feel it, you *know* it's possible and understand what you're looking for. You'll keep practicing until it's "how you ride," at which point you'll refuse to accept anything less. It will take some time, but when your horse understands, he will be relaxed and happy.

- **Don't become emotional over your horse's stiffness or resistance**. The horse's muscles are not yet limber and supple or he doesn't understand what you are asking. It's not personal.

- **Watch for "tells" that you are about to lose softness and flexion.** Your horse might lift his head, speed up or slow down, pull on the reins, abandon the contact on one or both reins, leave the line of travel, or become crooked. Ask yourself what happened *just before* the loss of flexion or the appearance of resistance. The sooner you notice that something is about to happen, the more quickly you can take preventive measures. Once you recognize a pattern, you can predict it. A pattern will never be resolved if you are unaware of it. Typically, horses have patterns.

- When suppling, **be careful not to end up see-sawing on the reins and "wagging" the horse's head back and forth.** Allow enough time between softening attempts to avoid developing a "wag." Because a release of negative tension in the horse typically occurs after the rider "gives," allow the horse a few seconds to process and react to each suppling effort. When you move quickly, the horse has no chance to react. Rapid bending and releasing doesn't improve performance.

- When the horse does what you ask, *leave him alone*. This means you no longer give aids; you remain neutral in your body. **Don't fall into the trap of "living in the fix" or constantly correcting** the horse, whether he needs it or not. Learn to recognize when he is soft and responsive and leave him alone for a few strides. Instill confidence in your horse by rewarding him with a release from pressure.

- One of the most useful pieces of advice that trainer Sharon Vander Ziel shared with me is, training is **"not all the aids all the time."** When you use all the aids at once, your horse will be unable to distinguish between them, or determine which order to follow. Additionally, your entire body will be tense. As you seek flexion and learn to manage your reins, keep this rule in mind.

As riders learn the significance of the outside rein and become determined to prevent it from becoming lax, **they often experience a phase of keeping it too restrictive.** You must also learn to follow the horse with it—give when necessary, don't give too much, and don't trap the horse by holding him in. Think of moving both hands in the same direction, like bicycle handlebars.

- **Flexion in a horse can vary greatly each direction.** You may feel as if you are riding one horse in one direction and another in the opposite direction.

9.9 A & B Head Tilt. Don't confuse a head tilt with proper flexion. When tilting, horses usually tip their nose to the outside and drop the inside ear. Head tilt can occur for a variety of reasons, including a lack of suppleness in the poll. If your horse only tilts his head when ridden (not in the pasture), it is most likely due to excessive use of the inside rein while riding. In proper flexion, ears, eyes, and nostrils remain parallel to the ground, while the head remains perpendicular to the ground.

A

BACK

B

FRONT

This is typical. Commonly, one side is more difficult than the other, just as humans are either right- or left-handed. Take note of what needs to be done on each side and ride the horse accordingly. As your horse becomes more symmetrical in his posture, he'll ride more similarly both directions.

❖ **Look at your horse and how he stands and moves without a rider.** Some horses carry their heads askew due to a physical problem. Perhaps a previous rider had an idiosyncratic seat and the horse adopted an awkward posture in order to compensate. If you notice that his head and neck are awry, contact your veterinarian, equine physical therapist, or chiropractor to analyze his body and potentially treat him before your training advances.

❖ Your horse may **tilt his head** when you supple or ask for flexion, which is incorrect (figs. 9.9 A & B). A stiff or inflexible poll can contribute to head tilt. To remedy, try releasing the rein corresponding to the head tilt, changing the flexion to the opposite direction for a few strides, sending the horse forward, or using the other rein to bring the head back to the center of the chest. Tilting the poll may also occur when the horse's feet aren't under his body. Put each leg under the body (mirrors can help—see p. 218) by straightening the horse or stepping sideways (in leg-yield—see p. 176), and see when the horse's ears become level again (uneven ears are an indicator of head tilt). Whichever repositioned leg resulted in removing the head tilt is the offending one; monitor it going forward. Other contributors to head tilt include the corresponding hind leg not stepping up, a poorly fitted saddle, or bad teeth. Consider having your horse examined for pain or discomfort, and possibly treating him with equine massage or chiropractic care.

- **The poll is often the last part of the horse to become supple.** Once the poll releases, the horse will be more forward and responsive.

- It takes time to train postural changes; they do not occur overnight. Even though it is beneficial, it still requires physical effort. Keep early rides short until the horse becomes more physically fit and accustomed to carrying himself differently. Examine where your horse has been perspiring. **Where he is sweaty often indicates which muscles worked hardest**: His neck? His stifles? His hindquarters? You want the hindquarters to be sweaty; not the neck.

- **Persistent resistance can be an indicator of pain, and bridle or saddle fit may be the cause.** Ideally, you should address the horse's physical health and comfort and assess tack fit at the outset of acquiring a horse to minimize discomfort and training issues going forward. The bit can be uncomfortable if it is too long or too short. Check the corners of your horse's mouth. Are there cuts? Rubs? Does the bit sit in the right place in the horse's mouth so it doesn't bang his teeth? Does the bit have rough edges? Is it too thick or too thin? Is the browband too tight? Is the noseband too low? Back pain can affect how your horse carries his body, especially his head and neck. When a saddle is girthed or when the rider's weight is added, the

Be Aware of the Nuchal Ligament

The nuchal ligament is an important part of how correct riding works. It attaches at the poll and runs along the neck, just beneath the mane, to the withers, where it joins the supraspinous ligament, which continues to the sacrum (fig. 9.10). This connects the poll to the pelvis, uniting the horse's front and back, and explains the adage that with horses, if you have a hip problem, you probably have a poll problem, and vice versa. Because the nuchal ligament has finger-like projections that attach to individual cervical vertebrae in the horse's neck, when the neck reaches forward and flexes, the ligaments pull the spinal processes of the withers forward, causing them to open like a fan, thereby helping to raise the back.

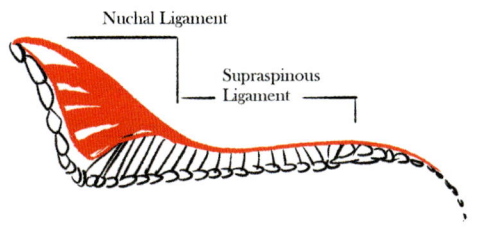

9.10 Nuchal Ligament. The *nuchal ligament* links the poll to the pelvis via the *supraspinous ligament* thus uniting the front and back of the horse. It supports the head and neck of the horse.

Be Aware of the Nuchal Ligament

As discussed on p. 232, the crest of the horse's neck will "flip" over from one side to the other if you begin with a proper flexion and then switch to a proper flexion in the opposite direction. Some horses have a noticeable mane flip, while others have a very subtle twitch in the neck. It is easy to identify because it resembles the sudden muscle jerks that some people experience when falling asleep. I find the "nuchal flip" useful for students to identify when they truly have flexion. When used as a warm-up exercise, either mounted or un-mounted, the "flip" also relaxes the temporomandibular joint (TMJ), causing the jaw to become supple and the horse to become softer. The horse's neck must be straight to perform the flip, with only "two minutes past noon" flexion at the poll.

fit changes. The withers are compressed by a saddle that is too wide because it sits directly on them; a saddle that is too narrow pinches. Changing saddles may make all the difference, so learn DIY saddle-fit techniques or invest in a qualified saddle fitter to determine whether your saddle is appropriate for your horse.

★★ **Extensions**

❖ Sharon Vander Ziel says you can **monitor flexion** by looking for the base of the horse's outside ear being ahead of the inside ear, or it "leading the way." The outside ear should always "arrive first." Observing the horse's salivary gland is another way to check flexion. It's typically a large gland, about the size and shape of a hotdog (in some horses, more like a green bean), located along the jawbone, toward the ear (fig. 9.11). The salivary gland is displaced and made visible when the horse flexes. You can manipulate the fascia around the salivary gland to loosen it, making flexion easier for the horse: by loosening the fascia, the jaw can slide more easily underneath the gland, preventing it from becoming pinched between the jaw and neck.

❖ Asking your horse to **flex before you get on** can be beneficial. This gives him the opportunity to understand what you're asking, and it's similar to stretching in

9.11 Salivary Gland. A horse's salivary gland can range in size from that of a green bean to that of a hot dog. It is located just behind the jawbone, toward the ear. Observing the salivary gland is another method for detecting flexion: when the horse flexes his jaw correctly, the salivary gland shifts and often becomes visibly more prominent. •

Scan to View Flexions from the Ground

that you can work out the tension before riding. While standing in front of your horse, grasp the bit with both hands and ask him to yield to the left and right, slowly and slightly. Keep the outer ring of the bit steady. Initially, he may raise his head and neck in surprise or resistance, particularly in the stiffer direction. You will be able to observe the nuchal ligament "flipping" when he is correctly flexed (see sidebar and p. 253).

❖ As you gain proficiency with flexion, switch to **using more leg than hand** to achieve it, keeping your hands steadier. And, as your horse learns to maintain poll flexion, shorten the inside rein and use your inside leg to push him onto the outside rein (see p. 159). Then, communication becomes very subtle, as your horse will respond readily to a light squeeze of your outside hand and will readily slow down, straighten, or rebalance as needed. Eventually, you will get to where most of the flexion is occurring from your inside leg. If it seems you still rely on your inside hand too much, experiment with riding with both reins in the outside hand. Push the horse into flexion with your inside leg. It's simpler than you think and produces good results from the horse. Because there is no inconsistency from two hands providing contradictory information, holding the reins in one hand keeps the bit very stable.

❖ Like connection, flexion can be elusive, transitory, and evolving. Regardless, you must establish and maintain consistent contact and flexion every ride for the rest of your life. That's what the **warm-up** is for. Every time you ride, you must re-establish contact and re-invite him to flex. When your horse consistently accepts both, then other work can begin.

Study Guide
Summarizing Excerpts

IT is beneficial to summarize information in your own words since it reveals how well you understand it. Additionally, by relating this knowledge to your own experiences, you come to understand the importance of the new information.

Read the excerpt below and:

❖ **Rephrase each sentence.**

❖ Apply the key points to all the Non-Negotiables. For example: Consider this key point: **The rein aid is never used without the leg aid.**

Now consider how this key point applies to:

❖ *Go*

❖ *Get Connected*

❖ *Stay Connected*

❖ *Transitions*

❖ *Flexion*

❖ *Half-Halt*

Study Guide
Summarizing Excerpts

Whereas the aid for flexion in the poll is often considered the domain of the inside rein aid, flexion also comes as a result of bending from the rider's leg. The rein aid for flexion is given by the inside fingers and wrist. But the rein aid is never used without the leg aid. The effectiveness of the leg aid should always be greater than the restriction of the rein aid so the horse keeps stepping to the rein.... Obtaining correct flexion requires a "feeling for flexion," which is quite subtle. Anytime the goal is relaxation (of the poll and jaw) the action needs to be soft. Imagine feeling your horse's tongue. That will encourage sensitivity, which in turn is likely to create a supple poll and correct flexion... Although control over flexion seems a small matter, it is one of the single most important aspects of your ride. Without correct flexion, it is impossible to have correct alignment and bend, so it's impossible to have a correct connection or collection. Without correct flexion, half-halts don't go through, and transitions are ineffective. ●

* From *When Two Spines Align: Dressage Dynamics* by Beth Baumert, and reprinted with permission.

Chapter

HALF HALT

10

A half-halt is a versatile aid that positively influences a horse's way of going. It enables a rider to prepare and notify the horse to perform any of a variety of functions. The result of a half-halt is that the horse continues moving forward, while his hindquarters gather and his hind legs flex more underneath his body.

10.1 The Universal Tool. Lifting, collecting, balancing, shaping, turning, slowing, signaling transitions, refocusing attention, and preparing the horse are all functions of the half-halt. Through such half-halts, Jim has lifted, collected, balanced, shaped, and is turning Envoy, as seen in this image.

The Universal Tool

The "half-halt" is the fundamental, multifunctional, and indispensable aid for *everything* in the saddle. It's like a joystick that you use to change gait, adjust tempo, alter stride length, prepare for anything (before, during, and after), transfer weight back, straighten, refocus, maintain rhythm, turn, lift/collect, energize, activate, create impulsion, control lateral movement, improve way of going, and more (fig. 10.1). As trainer and coach Jane Savoie said:

> *You use [a half-halt] every time your horse needs a reminder to pay attention to you, either because he's distracted by his surroundings or because you want to warn him that you are about to ask for a new movement. You give a half-halt to rebalance him every time he is heavy on the forehand, leaning the wrong way around corners, yanking at the reins, sticking his head up in the air, feeling stiff in his body, or is otherwise resistant and uncomfortable to ride.*

It is imperative for you to have a rudimentary understanding of the half-halt and its timing in order to be able to influence your horse effectively, especially when he becomes too strong or too low. You need to learn the aids for the half-halt; how, when, and why to apply them; how to tell if they are effective (and what to do if they aren't); how often you need them; what to do with your body; and what the half-halt does in your horse's body.

Although I've mentioned it at times throughout these pages, the half-halt is discussed in more detail at the conclusion of this book because the implementation and recognition of its impact require sufficient familiarity with the Non-Negotiables covered in the previous chapters. A half-halt cannot exist without its ingredients: forward motion, connection, and transitions or flexion. The half-halt is comparable to frosting on a cake: if there is no cake, there is nothing to frost.

Half-Halts Are Part of Your "Horse Code" Language

Remember how I explained how the aids function a little bit like Morse code or sign language in that they facilitate communication between entities when the spoken word isn't an option (see pp. 100

and 205)? I use the Morse code analogy because, for instance, rhythmic touches on the reins or squeezes on the horse's sides—like tapping on a telegraph or flashing a light on and off—signal the horse that you are "talking" to him. Morse code also implies that there are breaks in between the signals (for example, dot dot dash) so that you aren't pulling on the reins or squeezing without release in a long, monotonous tone, which would be ineffective. A very important part of the half-halt is the *give*, which is the break in the signal. With most aids, often you get the response from the horse when you give and release pressure, rather than when you are contacting the mouth through the reins or his back through your seat.

This "language" between the horse and rider is a combination of seat, legs, and hands. When used in concert, these elements can produce the half-halt aid. Half-halts *inform* the horse; they don't create the action you are requesting. In this way, they are like road signs: they benignly inform you to do something (yield, stop, turn, slow down); they don't grab your car and wrestle it into a position.

What half-halts *do* create is *opportunity*, by putting the horse in the suitable positioning and mindset for optimal response.

Why Call Them Half-Halts?

Unfortunately, the name "half-halt" is perplexing. It's not necessarily about halting the horse, and you're not really doing "half" of anything. Many riding terms come from imprecise translations, primarily German and French. In her blog on her self-named website, Yvette Koth—German dressage trainer, writer, and translator "for all things equine"—points out that the term "half parade" is the origin of the term half-halt. She states:

> *In English, we ask for the half-halt (halbe Parade) or a halt (ganze Parade). But there is a lot of confusion about the half-halt as it's often reduced to a squeeze with one or both reins. The halt is seen more as a movement than an aid. For the Parade, also called "the mother of all aids," you will first apply your weight, then leg aids, riding from back-to-front toward the passively resisting hand... Thinking of the Parade as a series of aids in a particular order involving your entire body will help you influence your horse correctly.*

A half-halt, then, is a concurrently coordinated application of the rider's legs, seat, and hands; an aid that uses the whole body, that informs your horse that you are about to ask for something new, what that is, and when and how to do it. The half-halt is a communication tool like the turn signal on a car. The turn signal alerts other drivers that you intend to do something so that your actions are expected. In the same way, preparatory half-halts serve to forewarn your horse that some action is about to be required of him: *Pay attention.*

There are numerous applications for half-halts, depending on their function. Nonetheless, they are all conveyed in the same manner.

The Role of Flexion in Half-Halts

In preparation for a half-halt, you must have flexion (see chapter 9, p. 228). The softening effect of the inside rein and leg that creates the flexion preserves the resulting steady connection on the outside rein and keeps it "live." Flexion is necessary for the outside rein to remain taut, enabling you to communicate the half-halt and enabling the horse to perceive your signal. This "liveness" is important because it indicates that your horse is listening and ready, so that when you momentarily restrain the outside rein, and your body, he responds.

Let's review the example I've used throughout this book: if you want to go from a (posting) trot to a walk, you could do a three-count transition preparation, with two short squeezes of the outside rein, followed by a longer third squeeze timed with the touchdown of the outside front leg and a stilling of your back that says "walk now." The two gentle advance signals tell the horse that something is coming so that your walk request isn't a surprise; it's expected: *Prepare. Prepare. Do.* The aids for the half-halt are also likely to straighten the base of the horse's neck and balance the horse—one half-halt provides several concurrent beneficial aids.

Timing of the Half-Halt

The *timing* of the half-halt is important because it tells the horse which thing you want him to do and gives him the signal when it is biomechanically possible for his body to comply. One example, in the trot to walk transition just described, is to half-halt on the outside rein when the outside front foot—or the one you want to influence—is touching the ground in order to keep that foot on the ground a moment longer, which slows the horse. (Try it yourself: walk along and then freeze your foot on the ground. You will slow down and lose momentum.) The resulting pause gives you time (split second) to tell the horse the *next* thing you are asking him to do—in this case, change your gait. You can easily see this timing by watching the outside shoulder come forward, just like checking for your correct diagonal. The moment during posting when you sit is when the outside front leg is on the ground and when you should apply the half-halt. Over the course of three strides of the outside front leg, the aid sequence for the downward transition trot to walk is *half-halt, half-halt, walk.* If you try to half-halt when the outside front leg is in the air, it will be a useless aid, affecting nothing. You can't stop a leg that is in flight.

German dressage trainer Hubertus Schmidt offers more insight into the why the outside rein is used in the half-halt: "A right half-halt adds weight to the right hind leg, and the same is true for the left. It's important to realize this because on any bent line or movement with bend, the horse's inside hind leg naturally carries the most weight. To balance the horse so he carries equal weight with each hind leg, the rider half-halts with the outside rein." Therefore, when the horse is correctly on the outside rein and balanced with half-halts, it is easier for his inside hind to swing under because it is not so weighted down.

Aids for the Half-Halt

Your body (ear, shoulder, hip, heel) must be in correct vertical alignment, allowing you the freedom to aid as necessary while not impeding the horse's ability to perform the desired response. Variations of the aids specify what a half-halt signifies, but the following generic elements are fundamental to all half-halts:

- **Leg** to drive the horse forward because a half-halt requires energy.

- **Seat** for pushing or retarding motion, and absorbing energy.

- **Inside rein** to supple and **outside rein** to convey the mission of the half-halt.

You may also utilize other parts of your body to enhance or differentiate a half-halt, such as:

- Sitting taller to "carry yourself" more and allow the horse's back to rise into the space left by the seat.

- Stilling your seat to stop pelvic follow-through and slow or stop the horse.

- Bringing your shoulder blades closer together so it feels as though you are bringing your armpits closer together behind you to influence the reins *instead* of your arms.

- Imagining the reins as a bracelet that circles from the bit around your lower back muscles to use the back muscles to affect the reins instead of using your biceps to pull (*don't* become rigid in your back so that you bounce).

- Closing fingers to communicate to a sensitive horse.

- Using the wrist to create activity, not to restrict (alternating driving with your seat and bending your wrists in toward your belt buckle creates energy and activity in the horse).

- Doing a "Head half-halt" by pulling your head straight back slightly with the muscles at the back of your neck (imagine someone giving your pony tail a quick pull).

- Using your core to push forward to steady hands by tightening your tummy (squeezing the core) and squeezing the inner thighs as your hands just continue to ask your horse to stay round.

- Maintaining the positive tension in your torso with your "stabilizing muscles" (your *transverse abdominals* and *gluteus medius*) so you remain upright and centered without swaying any direction.

Examining the Ingredients

The mechanical sequence of aids to create a generic half-halt is not complex:

- Start by closing both your legs to send the horse forward.

- Your seat/pelvis absorbs the motion of the horse and lifts to make room for the horse's back to come up.

- Steady your outside rein to contain the horse (or catch his energy) to signal him.

- Use your inside rein (and leg) as needed to keep the horse flexed inside and soft, depending on how he responds.

- However, *unpacking the knowledge behind each of these components* is what makes the half-halt a potent combination of aids.

Before, during, and after *any* maneuver you ask your horse to perform, he must remain as correct as possible: connected, straight, forward, yielding, and rhythmic. The same is true for the half-halt. When you use it, he should not lose any of these qualities. In fact, they should improve. If any are compromised, you must regroup and start over. *You* must also be in good order: upright, centered, strong in your core, and steady, with elastic contact. You also cannot lose any of these before, during, or after the half-halt. Note that because the half-halt is the aid used to connect, straighten, and ask for other qualities of movement, the concept is a bit of a Catch-22, a chicken-or-egg situation: the horse must be prepared for half-halt, but the half-halt is what prepares the horse. Regardless, working on any of these aspects contributes to the horse's overall improvement. Let's examine each individually:

Forward

This creates energy and creates connection. The *leg aid* is a forward-driving aid and is the dominant component of a half-halt. It drives the hind leg under the horse, closer to his center of gravity, which supports the horse's body and provides time for the joints to flex to absorb shock and produce impulsive energy when they push to straighten. Your horse needs to be willing to go energetically forward off a nudge from your calves or a drive from your seat. Refresh this notion by gently asking the horse to *go*. If he goes, reward him; if he doesn't, follow up with stronger leg or a touch of the whip until he associates the gentle squeeze of your leg with moving forward with alacrity and energy. Your horse needs to have a "forward thinking" mentality. He needs to keep going until you ask him to stop. He should never be allowed to quit of his own accord. He needs to go more forward if you ask for that. He shouldn't rush, just surge more powerfully. You can transition this to coming from your seat by pushing your hips slightly forward, following the same process.

Outside Rein

This catches energy and communicates. When you use the driving aids to ask your horse for more energetic forward impulse ("go"), it doesn't mean go faster. Instead, "catch" this energy in the outside rein as soon as you feel the horse take it forward by closing your hand on the rein and keeping your arm steady, instead of following. Don't pull; it's just "not giving." In this way, the horse removes the slack, not you. This is the essence of "back-to-front" (see p. 120).

Inside Rein

This maintains flexion and maintains softness. The inside rein is the tricky part. It is imperative that you *do not* hold the inside rein for your balance, to brace against in order to use the outside rein, or for any other reason. The inside rein needs to be mobile and is employed based on your horse's response to the outside rein. It asks for flexion and keeps the horse from looking to the outside when the outside rein is used. How much inside rein is used depends on the amount of resistance your horse offers. If your horse is soft and yielding, you won't need much. If your horse resists, you need to reply in kind, until he understands his positioning. The inside rein may be used reactively, but you can also apply it *proactively* to prevent the loss of flexion or softness for a more harmonious ride. Always try using the inside leg *before* the inside rein.

Strength

The amount of *strength* required to perform a half-halt depends on what you're doing or how sensitive/insensitive your horse is. For example, down transitions require more energy than up transitions so that the horse continues to move in an uphill fashion and does not collapse on his forehand. Skipping gaits (walk/canter, canter/walk, trot/halt) necessitates more energy input than transitions from consecutive gaits (walk/trot, trot/canter, walk/halt). Depending on the horse, you may need multiple "strong" half-halts to elicit the desired response, or you may need to vary your emphasis on the leg, seat, or rein aid. A high-strung horse may require more seat and rein, while a sluggish horse may require more leg and seat, with very little rein. Eventually, as your horse gains understanding, he will become more responsive and cooperative, reducing the amount of work you have to do. Remember to release after or between half-halts to either create an opportunity for another one or to reward the horse's try.

Repeat

Through methodical repetition, the horse learns that half-halts are a form of communication and that they indicate that he should do something. Your horse may initially resist you in some way or fail to understand. Then, you soften him by wiggling the inside rein to loosen his poll, create flexion, and try half-halting again…and again until you get the desired response. For example, if he goes too fast, half-halt in time with the outside front leg until you feel him come back to you and slow down; or half-halt going up into a trot transition so that he stays balanced. Half-halt for everything. It is said, "You can't half-halt enough," and I find that's true! You will eventually progress from using it indiscriminately to using it deliberately. That comes with experience and understanding.

Dosage

Understanding which aids to prioritize, in what order to implement them, and at what intensity is crucial for the success of the half-halt. All the aforementioned options depend on what you want your horse to do, or what you wish to prevent or avoid. Do you plan to transition up or down? Do you need to shorten stride? Is your horse running away? Ignoring you? Spooking? Pulling on the reins? The temperament/reactivity of the horse also determines what kind of and how much half-halt you execute.

I recommend making a chart of all the things you want to do and experimenting with the basic half-halt components, as well as the supplementary options, to determine which combination and dosage of each component works best for you and your horse. Be methodical: list the maneuvers you wish to perform along with the half-halt variation and dosage used for each. Then, make a list of the things your horse does that you *do not* want him to do and note which version of the aid is the most effective at stopping or preventing that behavior. Thus, you will have a distinct tool for each issue, and the horse will understand your intentions.

Isn't There a "Too Much"?

You really can't half-halt too often. I know people worry about this and even count how many should occur during a given dressage test, but trust me, it is more important that you learn how to use them. I used to worry about my horse thinking I was a ceaseless nag, given you don't want to overly use other aids for fear the horse begins to ignore them, but I haven't found it to be a concern with half-halts. Eventually, you will sift out which half-halts are effective and when to do them. The only way to get to that point of understanding is just to try them. Use them for everything. One day, you will feel that epiphany of *what you got for what you did*.

When I first learned to use half-halts, I just half-halted regularly for a while—say, five times down the side of an arena at a trot, asking him to slow down. While I don't recommend purposeless half-halts, you will get better at the mechanics from repeated practice and, like learning to feel which hind leg is on the ground, you will eventually recognize a sensation you can identify and replicate. In my case, I was able to notice that the horse got straighter, more compliant, and waited for me. The important thing was that I could feel an effect and it was repeatable, once I noticed it.

Ask yourself questions as you ride: *What if I use a half-halt now? Now? Now?* After experiencing enough of them, your horse begins to "proactively" listen. And after achieving success with one horse, your half-halt skills can be applied to all other horses. Indeed, with each new horse you ride, you will become more effective much sooner, and you will be aware of it. Horses are happier when you understand what you are doing and they understand what you want them to do. Understanding half-halts will benefit your riding exponentially.

Half-Halt Stages
Before the Half-Halt

As with any maneuver, make sure your horse is in good order before attempting a half-halt: he should be aligned, rhythmic, loose, flexed, and connected. Prepare him for the half-halt by driving him forward energetically onto the outside rein. Do this enough so that you have a clear, steady contact and connection in your outside hand, so that he will be able to detect your momentary restriction there when you apply it. This restriction, described well by Jane Savoie, is "slightly more than the maintenance pressure you have…in your firm but gentle feel of his mouth." Your legs and seat generate the energy that is gathered and regulated by the outside rein. Touch the outside rein a couple of times in conjunction with the outside front foot setting down to alert the horse that a half-halt is coming. Don't ambush him with a sudden aid.

During a Half-Halt

In the first half of "During the Half-Halt," as you apply that restriction or squeeze to the outside rein, a lot of data feeds into your body from the horse. It is at this point that you will need to determine how much of which component of the aid you need to use more or less of. More outside rein? More leg? More inside rein flexion? Less of any? Did he slow down? Did he try to run through? Did he get crooked? Did he suck back? Making these instant decisions plays a big role in determining the efficacy of the half-halt for whatever you are using it for.

10.2 The Mechanics. Mechanically, a half-halt is the sequential application of the leg/seat driving aids plus a softening inside rein and a brief restraining outside rein aid to connect with, communicate with, and balance the horse. More importantly, it is a *feeling*! You can feel the half-halt "catch" in the hindquarters, similar to a sprocket in a gear. When this occurs, the horse flexes his hind legs deeper underneath him, lowers his croup, gathers energy, and raises his shoulders. As his back raises and lifts you, you can feel a powerful wave of energy propelling you both forward, like a surfboard on its way toward shore.

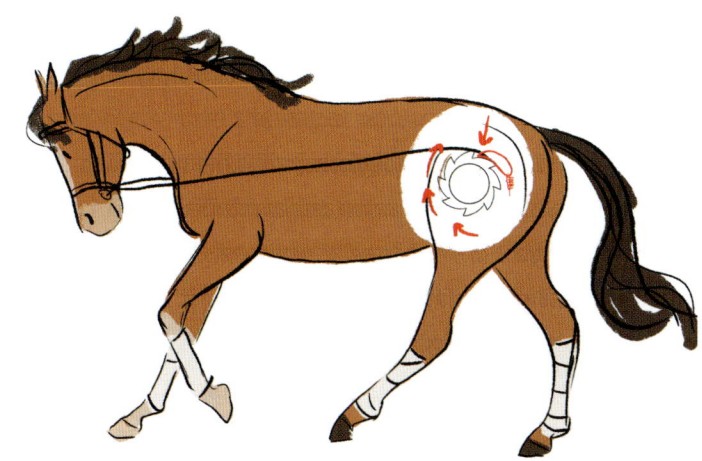

In the second half of "During the Half-Halt, when your horse complies, his neck will usually drop or become slightly longer, reaching forward. His hind legs will come under him more, the shoulders lift, the horse becomes more compact, he will get straighter, and his back will come up. When the horse is on the bit, you can use the outside rein, and he feels it, and his response allows you to connect the rein to the hind leg. You can feel the half-halt "go through" when there is a momentary pause as the hind leg stays on the ground a second longer, flexes deeper, and the shoulders come up. You can feel the half-halt "catch" in the hind leg (fig. 10.2). The horse gets easier to ride—he is much less bouncy because his hind joints are absorbing the shock from impacting the ground, not your spine.

After a Half-Halt

After the half-halt, relaxing the signal is actually the completion of the aid. According to Jane Savoie, it "is as important as the aid itself because it is the horse's reward." Be prompt in your release, but this means only to remove the restriction, returning to "maintenance contact." Don't "throw the reins away" because the point of the half-halt is to connect, balance, and improve the horse. If you totally release to slack, all your effort is down the drain.

All you need to do is release the pressure. The horse will feel and understand this. People have a tendency to give too much, too quickly, as if they are flicking a fly from their hand. A slow and small release is sufficient but preserve the connection and send the horse into it with your leg. However much you give, you must send the horse forward, so don't give more than you can manage. Think in millimeters rather than inches. Otherwise, you will experience a loss of connection and slack in the reins. Then you'll have to start over by reconnecting.

It doesn't take much to get the job done.

In her book *Dressage 101: The Ultimate Source of Dressage Basics in a Language You Can Understand*, renowned coach Jane Savoie says, "Relaxing your aids tells the horse that this is what you want, 'the instant you step through to my hand, the aid will be finished and you will be rewarded.'" She adds that it is good to relax even when you can't tell if you've accomplished anything because the horse might have

10.3 "Scoop Into the Mitt." To understand the half-halt, imagine wearing a baseball mitt as breeches and using your seat/lower back to scoop up the horse's hind end with the mitt. When your seat/mitt pushes the horse's hind legs forward under him, you capture the resulting forward surge of energy by closing your hand on the outside rein, so the horse does not interpret your driving aid as a signal to run. When the horse yields to the action of the outside rein, as opposed to resisting by inverting, his neck and body arch upward into a new shape. Because the outside rein is steady and does not pull, the horse discovers that he can still move, that the barrier of the outside hand is not impenetrable, and that he can become softer and rounder. As a result, his body now moves forward in a more swinging motion, connected to the hand. This is referred to as "through." You will feel like you are sitting over the hind legs and the entire horse is in front of you. The horse offers no resistance, is balanced and elastic, and is connected to the rider in this new world. The half-halt is the ticket to the horse you thought you bought. •

responded, and he should be rewarded, regardless. In my experience, this is a good idea because the horse often responds during the "give" (or reward) phase. This is probably because it takes a second for the horse to respond, or your own softening in the give enabled the horse to do what you asked. Regardless, even if your horse didn't respond, you still have to stop half-halting in order to start a new one.

If you find you need to increase the intensity of the half-halt in order to get a response, Savoie expands, "This is the half-halt and it's not going away. In fact, it will become increasingly more insistent until you begin to step to through to my hand. However, the instant you begin to step through to my hand, the aid will be finished and you will be rewarded." He learns that he has other options besides resisting (fig. 10.3).

Consistent Connection is Critical

Critical to the success of the half-halt is that you maintain a consistent contact and connection on the outside rein that neither dangles nor pulls. While you are learning the tactile finesse of creating and maintaining a sensitive connection with the outside rein and your horse's response to it, you will come to develop a feel for the nuances, or dosages, necessary for his evolution into giving and softness. With more practice, you will get a feel for the frequency, duration, and intensity you need to use on the outside rein to get the desired response. Dressage Olympian Robert Dover describes it thus: "If your horse slows down, you have too much 'halt' (outside rein) and not enough 'half' (driving aids). Or, if your horse speeds up when you half-halt, you have too much 'half' and not enough 'halt.'" You need to correlate the timing and degree of your driving aids to the closure of your outside hand. Too much or too little of either is detrimental.

With regard to "getting through" to your horse with a half-halt, this can be tricky. You must know what you want to achieve (slowing down, balancing, getting his attention, turning) and you must recognize the instant your horse begins to respond correctly. If you think in terms of the *before, during,* and *after* of the maneuver you have in mind, and you half-halt in preparation, and then you half-halt during and you half-halt after, you might approach the status of half-halting enough! Just as your riding coach is talking constantly to you during a lesson—or you are reading all the words in this book!—you must continually relay and receive information from your horse.

How Can You Tell If the Half-Halt Worked?

Your half-halt was successful when you get what you wanted, or an approximation thereof—the trick is to be able to tell that your horse attempted to comply and to reward him for his effort. You want your horse to comprehend and feel confident so he will attempt the same effort again and strive to improve.

If at first you feel like coordinating a half-halt, or recognizing whether one even happened, is next to impossible, that's okay. Keep trying. If it takes a thousand tries, it takes a thousand tries. If your horse isn't responding (which is possible), it's probably because he isn't listening, doesn't know to listen, has difficulty doing what you are asking, or you two are out of sync and he is confused. Watch that as the rider, you aren't holding a rein for too long, too rigidly, or collapsing forward and letting your outside elbow wave around like a flag in the wind, or getting the timing wrong. Practice all of these while keeping a close eye on yourself. It will improve once you have yourself under control.

You will get better at the skill, and one day, your horse will respond in a way that you will notice (he probably responded before and you missed it). He'll feel softer, straighter, easier to control, easier to sit on, more steady in tempo, with his legs staying underneath his body, pushing evenly, maintaining an even pressure on both reins, and ready to do what you ask at a moment's notice. He feels like he's "coming back to you," and almost like you are riding him up a staircase. You can actually feel the half-halt going all the way through his body to his hindquarters. He'll be more round, aligned, springy, forward, and relaxed. The horse has "let you into his back." It will almost feel like magic. At the very least, an epiphany! You'll definitely know you are on to something. He'll feel like you thought he ought!

Now you are in a position to see that getting connected, staying connected, doing transitions, maintaining flexion, and half-halting are all simultaneous and interdependent. Improving one makes another better. All together they combine to create that "live" outside rein that allows you to communicate with your horse through the half-halt. Fluency isn't something you are going to learn in one day. Experiment with using the outside rein, get familiar with its nuances, and analyze the response your horse gives to the half-halt. Your understanding, feel, skill, and comfort level will improve over time, and your horse's response will improve as well.

Until a rider comprehends the subtleties and outcomes of suppling, flexion and half-halting, the horse will have to endure a lot of trial and error. The pendulum of gross motor movement will swing from hesitant to overdone. So, bring compassion with your riding naiveté. Remember that riding is a partnership in which you are both learning. You are on a quest together.

★ Caveats

When any of the **aids** for half-halt are ill-timed, too strong or too soft, or out of sequence, the half-halt doesn't work.

- **Correct timing for the half-halt is important**. If you miss the timing of any aid, or the release, you will be compelled to make a larger correction after the fact, as opposed to giving a small, proactive reminder before the situation becomes unrecoverable.

- When utilizing the half-halt, it is essential to **keep the horse "thinking forward."** You may need to continue pushing him forward before and after the half-halt so he doesn't slow down or lose energy.

- If you **bend the horse's neck too much** to the inside, you are using too much inside rein and not enough outside rein to counter it. And vice versa. Make sure your horse's nose doesn't turn past his left or right shoulder.

- If your horse's **neck becomes too compressed** (nose to chest), you pulled back before or during the half-halt aid.

- If your horse is crooked, particularly if his **haunches curl inward or outward**, you are applying unequal pressure with your legs or they are in the wrong position. When riding straight, your legs must be parallel to one another. Your inside leg should be at the girth and your outside leg should be just behind the girth when riding turns or circles.

- Avoid being rigid. A **rigid body** compels the horse to slow down. Rigid arms and hands never soften, give, or follow. Gripping legs squeeze the horse without release. All of these factors will cause your horse to resist, brace, or avoid your aids. When you are stiff, you are unable to relax to reward or begin again.

- Don't begin with powerful aids. Start with gentle ones, increasing the intensity only if your horse ignores you. **Use stronger aids to reinforce light aids.**

- **Maintain an upright, vertical posture**. Leaning back to half-halt induces the horse to stiffen or hollow, causing the head and neck to rise.

- When using a rein, **keep your seat down in the saddle** on the side where the rein is being used. Reach for the ground with the soles of your feet. Don't become tense and draw your legs up so that your femurs become parallel to the ground. Do not brace one limb to support the use of another.

- Be conscious about **not sitting too heavily**. Create space for the horse's back to come up by lifting your pelvis with the horse's motion (similar to "twerking," except it's a forward/upward thrust of the pelvis). When you sit too deeply, the horse becomes uncomfortable: he sinks his back, raises his head, and lowers his abdomen, and his hind

Explore the Half-Halt with Your Horse

Since half-halts are the "universal tool" that regulate things like tempo, stride length, rebalancing, collecting, and much more, there are a variety of ways to employ them (that is, the "one aid, one response" rule I espoused earlier in the book may not hold in this case). You may find that some work better than others for either you or your horse, or for a given maneuver.

Newsflash: half-halts aren't limited to the outside rein. Horses are individuals and you may find that a horse "didn't read that little book" and may respond more willingly to a half-halt from the inside rein, from both reins, timing the half-halt when a different foot is on the ground, pushing "your belt buckle to the sky," or pressing down on one or the other stirrup iron. Sometimes, just surprising a horse with a new approach gets his attention. Furthermore, horses modify their behaviors from time to time, one signal may not be appropriate at one moment but works the rest of time, or you may find he responds differently traveling in the other direction. As a rider, you must be an attentive, creative, and systematic problem-solver in order to adjust your training to their needs. ●

legs go "out behind." In this posture, the horse is biomechanically unable to respond, and the rider sabotages any chance of success.

* **Don't hold and pull** on the reins. This causes the horse to pull, lean and brace. It takes two to pull, so don't be the one who starts it.

★★ Extensions

* Once you figure out the half-halt, you must **use it with your horse at all gaits** and maneuvers.

* To assist the horse in being on the outside rein, it is easiest to **start with lessons on a circle**. Going straight is more difficult because it is easier to rush or veer off course. Whenever you experience difficulty on a straight track, return to the circle until you regain control.

* Your horse must learn to **do all transitions without lifting his head** before or during the maneuver.

* It may be easier to introduce the half-halt by asking your horse to go forward and back (**accelerate and decelerate**), since you have to have something forward to come back from. Going from "big" to "small" is natural; going from "small" to "smaller" is tricky. Ask your horse, "How small can you go without transitioning into the lower gait?" Do this in stages, asking for even smaller steps as he catches on.

* **Use the nose-to-rail leg-yield to teach the horse** the concept of "going forward through your closed outside rein" to become rounder, or "closed up" (see p. 182). When the horse learns he can step sideways and still remain contained, he learns that he actually can move without running through your connection.

* To do a half-halt with finesse, **the hand becomes immobile (steady)** rather than following the contact, similar to how a pendulum swings back and forth and then pauses for a fraction of a second. This brief resistance (a freeze, not a pull) from the following hand is caused by the rider's seat and back, rather than by pulling the arm back past the body. One of my instructors referred to it as a "full body close." Don't clamp your elbow to your side rigidly, but "firm your back" with enough resolve to transmit your intent. You'll learn how much "firmness" your horse requires to respond.

* **Try a "head half-halt":** move just your head back momentarily, as if someone caught your ponytail.

* **Half-halts create activity in the horse and increase impulsion and expression.** An exercise you can try to feel activation is to "push" with your seat (when you feel a hind leg come forward, push your hip more forward on that side and alternate your legs to push the horse's belly away every stride) for four strides, then bend both wrists in toward your belt buckle four times and repeat. You will feel the swell of energy, the lengthening of the stride, the elasticity of the gait, and the suppleness of your horse's back; all stemming from his desire to go forward. Stay relaxed and don't be intimidated by this sensation. Learn to appreciate it because it is necessary for quality riding.

In Thomas Ritter's December 2017 blog entitled "Growing Pains," he offers reassurance for dealing with so many new learning experiences:

> *After a number of years I realised that these **periods where I felt like I couldn't ride at all meant** that I was about to learn something new and important and that I was about to have a breakthrough. I also realised that each version of my seat and aids could only take me to a certain level. In order to break through to the next level, I had to disassemble myself completely, like an engine that doesn't run well, examine every single piece, discard the broken ones that no longer work, replace them with new pieces, and then reassemble everything and then try to get used to the new feel, the new balance, the new muscles I was using, etc. Since the new muscle coordination is still foreign at first, it can happen that we actually do ride worse for a little while, until this new coordination becomes the new normal.*

Study Guide
Fundamental and Powerful Concepts

A person who has influenced me significantly throughout my life, philosophy and critical thinking professor Dr. Gerald Nosich, describes "fundamental and powerful concepts" as those "core ideas used to organize other ideas and unlock important questions, insights, and discoveries." Dr. Nosich's theory of fundamental and powerful concepts guided my decisions regarding what material to include in this book and how to group it into the Ground Rules and Non-Negotiables. As suggested by another wise friend, musician and author Dr. Frank Messina, the book frequently revisits the fundamental concepts, keeping them in the foreground throughout to serve as constant reminders of what is most important in riding.

❖ Think about what you have read in this book. What ideas may be even more basic than the Non-Negotiables, from which every other idea derives? Which resonate most powerfully with you? What insights did you have? What questions came to mind? What discoveries did you make?

❖ The half-halt is introduced at the conclusion of this book because the implementation and recognition of its impact require sufficient familiarity with the Non-Negotiables. A half-halt cannot exist without forward motion, connection, or flexion. However, it can be argued that forward motion, connection, and flexion cannot exist without half-halts; therefore, half-halts should have been presented much earlier in the book. Reassemble the order of the book's fundamental and powerful concepts in way that makes the most sense to you.

Study Guide
Fundamental and Powerful Concepts

❖ *Now consider how this material helps you better understand the fundamental and powerful question posed by the book:* **HOW TO RIDE THE HORSE YOU THOUGHT YOU BOUGHT.**

Conclusion

AS you internalize the Non-Negotiables to the point where they become an instinctive part of your thought process, and you improve your ability to read your horse, you will know what you want from the horse, whether you have achieved it, and how well you've performed. When the Non-Negotiables become deeply ingrained in you, so that you use them automatically and your horse reacts accordingly without hesitation or resistance, then the techniques are utilized in all gaits, arena patterns, and maneuvers. The goal is to be able to *handle your body in the same composed, coordinated, and methodical manner, regardless of how much physical disruption the horse's movements cause you*—whether he's trotting, cantering, spooking, doing a shoulder-in, jumping, or changing directions.

The best riders are *always* paying attention to the Non-Negotiables, tweaking things minutely to make them *just that much better.* Indeed, you will discover that once you understand one idea, others tend to follow in a rush. You will learn to apply what you know to any situation. The more you learn to *feel*, the more you will be able accurately identify little anomalies. Soon, you will be on that path to continuous improvement, riding the horse ~~you thought~~ you bought.

This!

In this photograph of a stunning Lusitano stallion, classical dressage trainer Jean-Philippe Giacomini demonstrates how all of the non-negotiables contribute to a complete performance.

The horse is forward, connected, demonstrates flexion, and has responded to half-halts so that he is collected, balanced, and moving with impulsion. Through proper training, the horse is expressive while remaining calm.

He is the horse we all want to buy.

Appendix I

Glossary of Terms

The following excerpt from the USDF Glossary of Judging Terms reproduced with permission of USDF ©2018 United States Dressage Federation (USDF). All rights reserved. Reproduction without permission is prohibited by law. USDF is not responsible for any errors or omissions in the publication or for the use of its copyrighted material in an unauthorized manner.

- **ABDUCT:** To move a limb away from the horse's midline.

- **ABOVE THE BIT:** A head position in which the horse avoids acceptance of the contact by putting the muzzle forward and upward, also usually retracting the poll.

- **ACCEPTANCE:** Used in reference to the horse's willingness to allow the maintenance of a steady contact, the application of the aids, and/or the placement of the rider's weight. Absence of evasion or resistance.

- **ACTIVITY:** Energy, vigor, liveliness - especially with reference to the motion of the hind legs.

- **ADDUCT:** To move a limb toward or across the horse's midline.

- **AGAINST THE BIT:** The horse presses against the bit with a rigid or unyielding neck/poll/jaw.

- **ALIGNMENT:** 1) Referring to the horse, the lining up of the horse's body parts from tail to poll. One of the four aspects of straightness (the other three are parallelism to line of travel, parallelism to line of reference, and directness of line of travel). 2) Referring to the rider: a) Vertical alignment refers to the side view of the rider in which the ear, shoulder, hip, and heel are in a vertical line. b) Lateral alignment refers to the front or rear view of the rider in which the weight appears to be evenly distributed on the left and right sides and the rider's body does not collapse in the waistline/core in either direction. c) Rotational alignment refers to the orientation of the front of the rider's body relative to the horse's line of travel or line of reference.

- **AMPLITUDE:** Magnitude of range of motion. Same as *Scope*.

- **BALANCE:** Relative distribution of the weight of horse and rider upon the fore and hind legs (longitudinal balance) and the left and right legs (lateral balance). In dressage training, the horse learns to move with the base of support narrowed laterally and shortened longitudinally, which makes the balance less stable but at the same time makes it more mobile (especially the forehand) and susceptible to small external influences (of the rider).

- **BASICS:** The basics form the correct foundation of the progressive training of the horse, independent of the execution of specific test movements. The basics include: pure rhythm with suitable tempo; relaxation/suppleness/elasticity/looseness; correct contact/connection; impulsion, straightness, and longitudinal balance suitable to the level and exercise—in other words, all the criteria of the *Pyramid of Training/Training Scale*. Correctness of the basics is indicated by the preservation and/or improvement in: the purity and quality of the gaits and paces; the gymnastic ability and physique of the horse; and the horse's attitude and rideability.

- **BEAT:** Footfall of a hoof or a diagonal pair of hooves that strike the ground virtually simultaneously. The timing of the footfalls determines the rhythm of the stride. The walk has four beats per stride (only two of which are emphasized beats perceived by the rider), the trot has two beats per stride, and the canter has three beats per stride (only one of which is the emphasized beat perceived by the rider).

- **BEHIND THE BIT:** An evasion in which the horse retracts or shrinks back from the bit/contact. The head may or may not be behind the vertical.

- **BEHIND THE LEG:** Slow to react to the leg, or sluggish or unwilling to move energetically forward, especially while accepting the contact/connection.

- **BEHIND THE VERTICAL:** With the horse's face viewed in profile, the front of the horse's nose falls behind a vertical line dropped from the top of its forehead. The horse may or may not be behind the bit.

- **BEND:** The laterally curved position in which the horse's body, as would be viewed from above, *appears* to form a uniform arc from poll to tail. Components of bending include lateral flexion at the poll, stretching of the outer side of the body, lowering of the inner hip, and adduction of the inner hind and outer fore legs (see *Flexion* for more in-depth discussion of the elements of bending). Examples of faulty bend are: bending only in the neck, bending only at the base of the neck, or bent toward the wrong direction.

❖ **BIOMECHANICS:** The application of the principles and techniques of mechanics (the branch of physics that deals with the motion of material bodies and the phenomena of the action of forces on bodies) to the structure, function, and capabilities of living organisms. (Webster)

❖ **BLOCKED:** Impaired in the connection due to sustained muscular contraction, creating rigidity.

❖ **BPM:** Beats per minute, as may be measured by a metronome.

❖ **BRACED/BRACING:** The horse defensively setting/ holding its muscles contracted against an opposing force or an expected opposing force, such as the rider's disturbing legs, seat or hands.

❖ **BROKEN NECKLINE:** The position of the neck in which there is excessive longitudinal flexion at the joint between the second and third cervical vertebrae, so that the topline of the neck does not form an even, smooth arc and the poll is not the highest point of the skeleton.

❖ **CADENCE:** The marked accentuation of the rhythm and emphasized beat that is a result of a steady and suitable tempo harmonizing with a springy impulsion.

❖ **CARRIAGE:** The posture of the horse, most easily evaluated when viewing the horse's profile or outline from the side.

❖ **CENTER OF MASS (OR GRAVITY):** The point at which the mass of the body can be considered to be concentrated, and around which its weight is evenly distributed or balanced. The horse's center of mass is located at the 13th or 14th rib and just below the line from the point of the shoulder to the point of the hip. This puts it below the seat of the saddle. In collection, the horse's body rotates around the center of mass.

❖ **CHEWING THE BIT:** The movements of the horse's mouth—gently and softly mouthing the bit—showing mobility and relaxation of the jaw and causing secretion of saliva for a "wet mouth." Not to be confused with snapping, clacking or grinding of the teeth.

❖ **CLARITY/CLEAR:** The correct rhythm (sequence and timing of the footfalls and phases of a gait). Often used in relation to maintenance of the correct rhythm of the gaits before and after a transition.

❖ **CLEAN:** Referring to a flying change, the change of lead is from a pure canter on one lead to a pure canter on the other lead. A clean flying change takes place during the suspension phase, without trot steps or disunited strides.

❖ **CLOSED HALT:** A posture at the halt in which the horse is secure in balance with a shortened base of support achieved by positioning the hind legs forward underneath the body.

❖ **COLLECTION (BALANCE AND LIGHTNESS OF THE FOREHAND FROM INCREASED ENGAGEMENT):** The horse shows collection when he lowers and engages his hindquarters, shortening and narrowing his base of support, resulting in lightness and mobility of the forehand. He shows shorter, but powerful, cadenced steps and strides. The increased elevation must be the result of and relative to the lowering of the hindquarters. (See *Pyramid of Training* for complete explanation.)

❖ **CONFIDENCE:** The boldness and self-assurance with which the horse performs, and the trust in his partnership with the rider.

❖ **CONNECTION/CONNECTED:** State in which there is no blockage, break, or slack in the circuit that joins horse and rider into a single, harmonious, elastic unit. A prerequisite for throughness.

❖ **CONSTRAINED:** Forced or compelled against the will - the horse's forward or sideways movement, bend, and/or execution of the required exercise not appearing voluntary.

❖ **CONSTRICTED:** Limited by constraint, restraint, or sustained muscular contraction. Held together, forcefully shortened, or physically tight.

❖ **CONTACT (CONNECTION AND ACCEPTANCE OF THE BIT THROUGH ACCEPTANCE OF THE AIDS):** The energy generated in the hindquarters by the driving aids must flow through the whole body of the horse and is received in the rider's hands. The contact to the bit must be elastic and adjustable, creating fluent interaction between horse and rider with appropriate changes in the horse's outline. (See *Pyramid of Training* for complete explanation.)

❖ **CORRECTNESS:** The straightness of the action of the limbs (e.g., faults would be winging, paddling, twisting hocks). Not the same as *Purity*. Dressage judges deal with correctness only indirectly, that is, to the degree that it affects the purity or quality of the gait. Correctness is addressed directly in breeding classes.

❖ **COUNTER CHANGE OF HAND (USEF DEFINITION):** A movement containing two (2) half-passes and the horse should be straight for a moment before changing direction.

❖ **CROOKEDNESS:** Aspects of crookedness: 1) Misalignment of the horse's body parts from tail to poll (e.g. popped shoulder or twisted neck). 2) On straight or curved lines, lack of parallelism of the horse's longitudinal axis to the line of travel (e.g. haunches left or right of centerline or circle line). 3) In two track/lateral work, lack of parallelism of the horse's longitudinal axis to the line of reference (e.g. haunches leading or trailing in leg yielding). 4) Lack of directness of line of travel—the horse deviating or wandering left and/or right of the desired path of travel (e.g. as in weaving).

❖ **CROSS-CANTER:** The fore and hind legs are on different leads. Same as *Disunited*.

❖ **DEFINITION/DEFINED:** Used in reference to transitions between paces (within a gait) to indicate a well-demarcated change in length of stride.

❖ **DISOBEDIENCE:** Willful determination to avoid doing what is asked, or determination to do what is not asked.

❖ **DIAGONAL DISSOCIATION (ALSO DIAGONAL ADVANCED PLACEMENT OR DAP):** The hooves of a diagonal pair of limbs (in trot or canter) do not contact the ground at the same moment. The dissociation may be hind-first, which is also called positive DAP, or front-first, which is also called negative DAP. In the trot, hind-first dissociation is usually associated with the horse being uphill. In canter, hind-first dissociation occurs, for instance, in the bounding canter of a young horse and in the pirouette canter.

❖ **DISUNITED (CANTER):** The fore and hind legs are on different leads. Same as *Cross-Canter*.

❖ **DOWNHILL:** Poor longitudinal balance, with failure to elevate the withers and/or lower the haunches. Same as *On The Forehand*.

❖ **DRAGGING:** Refers to dragging of the hind feet or inactivity of the hind legs or failure to lift the hooves clear of the ground.

❖ **ELASTICITY:** The ability or tendency to stretch and contract the musculature smoothly, giving the impression of stretchiness or springiness.

- **ELEVATION:** Raised position of the forehand (head, neck, *and* rib cage). The neck is elevated from its base with the poll as the highest point and the face slightly in front of the vertical.

- **ENGAGEMENT:** Increased flexion in joints of the hind legs during the weight-bearing (stance) phase of the stride, lowering the croup relative to the forehand, enabling the back to assist in elevating the forehand, and providing a springboard for upward thrust/impulsion. Engagement is carrying power, rather than pushing power. At canter and piaffe, there is additional flexion at the hip joints and also greater flexion at the lumbosacral joint, which contribute to the horse's ability to lower the haunches. Note: Engagement is not flexion of the hocks or "hock action" when the leg is swinging forward (as seen most clearly in gaited horses and hackneys), nor does it describe the forward reach of the hind leg under the horse's body.

- **EVASION:** Avoidance of the difficulty, correctness, or purpose of the movement, or of the influence of the rider, often without active resistance or disobedience (e.g. tilting the head, open mouth, broken neckline, etc.). Bit evasions are means of avoiding correct contact with the bit.

- **EXERCISE:** A designated task that may include movement(s), transition(s), figure(s), and/or pattern(s) to be performed at designated gaits and paces and sometimes at specific places in the arena, e.g. 20-meter circle at working trot, half-pass at collected canter, or simple change of lead.

- **EXPRESSION:** Increased impulsion, with harmony, balance, lightness, and cadence, giving artistic or dramatic effect.

- **EXTENSION/EXTENDED (WALK, TROT, OR CANTER):** At trot and canter, a pace that shows maximum length of stride, frame, and phase of suspension. The uphill balance is greater than in the lengthening pace. The tempo remains nearly the same as in the collected pace. At walk, a pace with maximum length of stride and frame, and showing the natural longitudinal oscillation of the neck (while still remaining on contact). The hind feet touch the ground clearly in front of the prints of the forefeet.

- **FALLING IN, FALLING ON INSIDE SHOULDER, FALLING OUT, FALLING OVER OUTSIDE SHOULDER, POPPED SHOULDER:** Lateral deviation of the forehand/foreleg(s) associated with a loss of balance.

- **FIGURE:** Geometrical component, such as a circle, change of rein, or figure of eight. A figure is not the same as a movement. Refer to *Movement*.

- **FLEXIBILITY:** Range of motion of joints and the ability to move the joints freely. Also described as *Suppleness*.

- **FLEXION:** In the limbs—articulation of a joint or joints so that the angle between the bones becomes smaller. At the poll, there are three directions of movement, the first two of which are described as flexions and involve motion of the atlanto-occipital joint: direct or longitudinal flexion brings the chin toward the underside of the neck; lateral flexion closes the angle between the cheek and the side of the neck; rotation (twisting) occurs at the atlanto-axial joint and causes tilting of the head. In the rest of the spine, movements occur in the same three directions as at the poll: flexion-extension (rounding-hollowing); lateral (left-right) bending, and twisting. The combination of these movements creates carriage, bend, displacement of the rib cage, etc.

- **FLUENT/FLUENCY:** Flowing or moving smoothly and easily. Same as fluid.

- **FOOTFALL:** A hoof striking the ground.

- **FORWARD:** Moving or tending to move toward the direction in which the horse is facing (in contrast to sideways, backward, or standing still); it does not indicate *how* he gets there. References to specifics such as impulsion, energy, freedom, reach, length of stride, into the contact, responsiveness to the leg, and tempo more accurately express *how* the horse should proceed in a forward direction.

- **FRAME:** The outline of the horse, which should change according to the length of stride (shorter frame for collection, longer for extension) and which shows degree of uphill versus downhill carriage.

- **FREEDOM:** The reach, scope and lack of constriction in the horse's movement.

- **FREE WALK:** A pace in which the horse freely lowers and stretches out its head and neck, and shows the natural longitudinal oscillation of the neck. The hind feet touch the ground clearly in front of the prints of the forefeet, with strides longer than in the medium walk. Can be performed or required on a long rein (maintaining contact) or a loose rein (with a loop in the rein—no contact).

- **FROM BEHIND:** Shorthand for "energy/activity/thrust from the hind legs" (as in "needs more…'from behind'").

- **GAIT:** Characteristic limb coordination pattern recognized by the sequence and timing of the footfalls. Gaits used in dressage are walk, trot, and canter.

- **HALF-HALT:** A momentary effect of the aids that increases the attention and improves the balance of the horse.

- **HARMONY:** Used in reference to the relationship between the horse and rider, the partners' positive physical as well as mental/emotional connection, showing rapport, trust, and confidence in one another and resulting in a sense of synchrony, contentment and unity.

- **HASTY:** Refers to the tempo (strides per minute) unless otherwise noted.

- **HOLLOW BACK:** Sagging or depressed back caused by slackness of the back and belly muscles (passive) or by sustained contraction of the back muscles, impeding swing and elasticity (active).

- **HORIZONTAL BALANCE:** A longitudinal balance between downhill and uphill.

- **HOVERING TROT:** See *Passage-Like Trot*.

- **HURRIED:** Refers to the tempo (strides per minute) unless otherwise noted.

- **HYPERFLEXION (ROLLKUR):** Exaggerated flexion of the horse's neck, with a low poll and the face far behind the vertical. There is a spectrum from humanely riding the horse behind the vertical to forcefully or aggressively riding the horse in a hyperflexed position and/or sustaining the hyperflexion for more than a few minutes. There may be a gray area between the acceptable and the abusive that is a matter of judgment.

- **IMPULSION (ENGAGEMENT AND THE DESIRE TO GO FORWARD):** Used to describe the transmission of an eager and energetic, yet controlled, propulsive thrust generated from the hindquarters into the athletic movement of the horse. (See *Pyramid of Training* for complete explanation).

- **INSIDE, INNER, INWARDS:** 1) The direction toward which the horse should be positioned (laterally) or bent. 2) The side of the horse that is toward the center of the ring. The former takes precedence if the two are not the same (as in counter-canter or renvers).

- **IRREGULAR:** Impure, unlevel, or uneven. Can be momentary or pervasive, and may or may not be due to unsoundness. Should not be used to mean unsteadiness of tempo.

- **LATE:** Execution after the aids or after the prescribed place or letter. Usually applied to flying changes and transitions.

- **LATE BEHIND:** In flying changes, the hind legs change leads after the forelegs change.

- **LATE IN FRONT:** In flying changes, the fore legs change leads after the hind legs change.

- **LATERAL**: 1) To the side, as in flexion, bend, suppleness, or direction of movement. 2) Impurity of the gait in which the lateral pairs of legs swing forward somewhat synchronously. If the lateral pairs of legs move totally synchronously, this is called pacing.

- **LEANING IN:** The horse tilts to the inside of a turn or circle, like a motorcycle.

- **LENGTHENING OF STRIDE:** A pace at trot and canter in which the stride, frame and phase of suspension are longer than in the working pace, but the degree of uphill balance required in the medium pace is not expected. The tempo remains nearly the same as in the working pace.

- **LEVEL BALANCE:** A longitudinal balance between downhill and uphill. Same as *Horizontal Balance*.

- **LIFT:** Applied in piaffe and passage to address the height to which the forelegs are raised.

- **LIGHTNESS:** Refers to one of the following: 1) Horse's lightness on its feet. 2) Lightness of the rider's aids/horse's responsiveness to light aids. 3) Lightness/lift of the forehand.

- **LONG AND LOW:** Carriage in which the horse lowers and stretches out its head and neck, reaching forward and downward into contact on a longer rein.

- **LONGITUDINAL:** In the lengthwise, as opposed to lateral, dimension, that is from front-to-back or back-to-front.

- **LOOSENESS:** Freedom from negative physical and mental/emotional tension. Relaxation Note: "Looseness" is another translation of *"Losgelassenheit,"* the second tier of the *Pyramid of Training*.

- **MARCHING:** Taking purposeful steps in the walk.

- **MEDIUM (WALK, TROT, OR CANTER):** At trot and canter, a pace of moderate lengthening, with a longer stride than in the collected or working paces but shorter than in the extended pace. The uphill balance is greater than in the working or lengthening pace, and the length of frame and suspension are between that of the collected and extended paces. The movement produced is rounder than that of extension. The tempo should remain nearly the same as in the collected pace. At walk, a pace of moderate lengthening, with a length of stride and frame between that of the collected and extended walks, and showing the natural longitudinal oscillation of the neck.

- **METHODOLOGY:** The system that a judge uses to give scores in a consistent and standardized fashion. This results in the correct and logical placement of the competitors in each class.

- **MOBILITY:** Easy maneuverability/nimbleness of the shoulders/forehand/forelegs, made possible by a narrowing and shortening of the horse's base of support.

- **MOVEMENT:** 1) The manner in which the horse moves over the ground: way of moving. 2) Test movement: a section of a dressage test to be evaluated with one score on a score sheet. 3) Dressage Movements: these are: leg-yield, rein back, shoulder-in, travers, renvers, turn on haunches, half pass (trot or canter), flying change(s), pirouette (walk or canter), piaffe, and passage.

- **MPM OR MPH:** Meters per minute or miles per hour—measures of speed.

- **NODDING/BOBBING:** A rhythmic up-and-down or backward and forward action of the horse's head and neck which is not part of the normal mechanic of the gait. It may be caused by the past use of gadgets, by constraint, or by lameness.

- **OBEDIENCE:** Submission in reference to the accurate performance of the required exercise, in contrast to submission in regard to the basics. The horse may demonstrate resistance or evasion (lack of submission in the basics), yet still be "obedient." For example, if the horse performs a series of flying changes without mistakes and in the correct place but is behind the vertical, tilting his head and swishing his tail, he performs the exercise obediently, but is not submissive in regard to the basics.

- **ON THE AIDS:** The horse reacts to the rider's aids willingly, confidently, immediately, and correctly.

- **ON THE BIT:** Acceptance of contact (without resistance or evasion) with a stretched topline and with lateral and longitudinal flexion as required. The horse's face line is, as a rule, slightly in front of the vertical.

- **ON THE FOREHAND:** Poor longitudinal balance, with failure to elevate the withers and/or lower the haunches. Same as *Downhill*.

- **OUT BEHIND:** Hind legs operating too far behind the horse, which favors pushing at the expense of carrying.

- **OUTLINE:** The profile or silhouette of the horse, showing the horse's carriage or posture.

- **OUTSIDE, OUTER, OUTWARDS:** 1) The direction away from which the horse should be positioned or bent. 2) The side that is away from the center of the arena. The former takes precedence if the two are not the same (as in counter-canter or renvers).

- **OVERBENT/OVERBENDING:** Excessive *lateral* displacement of the neck relative to the horse's body, occurring in the neck itself or at the base of the neck, causing lack of apparent uniformity of the lateral curve of the "bent" horse. Note: In the U.S., the term overbent is based on the amount of lateral bending, and the term over-flexed is based on the amount of longitudinal flexion (rounding). In other countries, overbent is often used to indicate excessive longitudinal flexion at the poll and/or upper joints of the neck.

- **OVERFLEXED:** Behind the vertical, due to excessive longitudinal flexion at the poll and/or upper joints of the neck.

- **OVERSTEP, OVERSTRIDE, OVERTRACK:** Placement of the hind foot in front of the print of the forefoot.

- **OVER THE BACK OR TOPLINE:** The horse stretching and rounding the back or topline.

- **OVER-TURNED:** Turned more than 180 degrees in a half-pirouette or more than 360 degrees in a full pirouette.

- **PACE(S):** 1) Variations within a gait. The named paces are: at walk: collected, medium, extended, free; at trot and canter: collected, working, lengthening of stride, medium, extended. Each named pace is characterized by a given length of stride as well as by other attributes listed under their individual definitions. A horse can go at any pace on the spectrum from highly collected to fully extended (the named paces are points on that continuum), corresponding to slower or faster MPM. Optimally, any stride length is performed in the horse's ideal tempo. 2) Gait in which the lateral pairs of legs move in unison (not considered a dressage gait). If the lateral pairs move somewhat but not entirely synchronously, this is sometimes called "pacey" or "pacing tendency" or "lateral" or "lateral tendency." This faulty lateral tendency may be seen in walk or canter. Note: The U.S. uses the terms "gait and pace" where the FEI uses the terms "pace and variation."

❖ **PASSAGE-LIKE OR PASSAGEY TROT:** A trot in which there is a hesitation in the forward swing of the diagonal pairs of legs, so that they appear to hover momentarily.

❖ **PHASE:** Limb phases are part of the cycle of limb movement. Stance phase: foot on the ground. Swing phase: foot moving through the air. Support phases are differentiated according to which limbs are in the stance and swing phases. An aerial or suspension phase occurs when none of the limbs is in contact with the ground (all limbs are in the swing phase). Each gait has a characteristic sequence of support phases: the walk has 8 support phases in each stride; the trot has 2 support phases and 2 suspension phases in each stride; the canter has 5 support phases and 1 suspension phase in each stride.

❖ **PIVOTING:** Failure to pick up a foot in the rhythm of the gait, such that the horse swivels around the grounded (or "stuck") foot. Used in reference to pirouettes or turns on the haunches or forehand.

❖ **POLL:** The highest point of the horse's skull (the occipital crest). In common dressage usage, however, "flexion at the poll" refers to the longitudinal or lateral flexion at the joint between the skull and the first cervical vertebra, the atlanto-occipital joint. See *Flexion*.

❖ **POSITION:** 1) Lateral flexion at the poll so that the horse "looks" to the side, e.g. "positioned right" or "positioned left." 2) Posture of the rider.

❖ **PURITY:** Referring to the gait, the correctness of the rhythm as determined by the sequence and timing of the footfalls and phases of the gait.

❖ **PUSHING OUT:** Hind legs operating too far behind the horse, which favors pushing at the expense of carrying.

❖ **PYRAMID OF TRAINING:** To ensure that classical principles and traditions are honored and adhered to in our present day culture, the Pyramid of Training (Training Scale) evolved as a means to illustrate the different steps/concepts, which are essential ingredients in the correct training of a horse. It is important to realize that these "steps" are interrelated.

❖ **QUADRILLE:** Team riding; choreography traditionally performed by four horses, though groups may have six, eight, ten or even twelve horses. For special terminology related to this, see *Quadrille Rules and Guidelines on the USDF website*.

❖ **QUALITY (OF GAIT):** The quality of a gait refers to its freedom, elasticity, flexibility, looseness, fluency and amplitude. Not the same as purity or correctness.

❖ **QUICK:** Refers to the tempo (strides per minute) unless otherwise noted.

❖ **RAPID:** Refers to the tempo (strides per minute) unless otherwise noted.

❖ **REACH:** Refers to forward or lateral reach of the fore limbs, hind limbs, neck/poll, muzzle, or one side of the horse (as in "needs reach into outside rein"). May be used to refer to any of these individually.

❖ **REGULARITY:** Purity of the gait. At walk and trot, denotes symmetry in terms of evenness of the length of the steps, levelness of the height of the steps, and equality of the time interval between the steps of the left and right forelimbs, or the left and right hind limbs. Note: In the first collective mark on a dressage test, "Gaits (freedom and regularity)," regularity is used to address purity and soundness, not to address the horse's tempo.

❖ **RELAX/RELAXATION:** 1) Referring to the horse's mental/emotional state: calm, without anxiety or nervousness. 2) Referring to the horse's physical state: commonly used to indicate the absence of muscular contraction other than that needed for optimal carriage, strength, and range and fluency of movement. Usually the physical and mental/emotional states go hand in hand.

❖ **RELEASE:** As used in the tests, the brief release of the contact, wherein the rider in one clear motion extends the hand(s) forward along the crest of the horse's neck, then rides for several strides without contact. Its purpose is to demonstrate that, even with loose rein(s), the horse maintains its carriage, balance, pace, and tempo. This corresponds to the German expression *"Überstreichen."*

❖ **RESISTANCE:** Active or rigid opposition to the connection or to the aids of the rider (e.g. against or above the bit). Not the same as disobedience or evasion. The horse can be resistant, yet still obedient (perform the exercise). Can be momentary or pervasive, willful, or unintentional.

❖ **RESTRAINED/RESTRAINT:** Prevention (of the horse by the rider) from moving freely in any direction—usually a function of pulling backward on the reins.

❖ **RHYTHM (REGULARITY AND TEMPO):** The characteristic sequence of footfalls and timing of a pure walk, pure trot, and pure canter. The rhythm should be expressed with energy and in a suitable and consistent tempo, with the horse remaining in the balance and self-carriage appropriate to its level of training.

❖ **ROCKING/ROCKING HORSE CANTER:** A canter in which the neck/forehand goes too much up and down as a result of lack of sufficient ground coverage, lack of sufficient engagement, or interference by the rider.

❖ **ROUNDNESS:** 1) The convexity of the profile of the horse's topline, which is accompanied by concavity of the underline of the neck. 2) The circular (as opposed to linear or flat) quality characterizing the movements, action, or trajectory of the horse's limbs. 3) Shape of figure (such as a circle).

❖ **RUNNING:** Increased speed (MPM) due to quickening the tempo rather than lengthening the strides with appropriate periods of suspension. Usually used in reference to lengthened, medium or extended trot or canter, or quickening the trot tempo before a canter depart.

❖ **RUSHED:** Refers to the tempo (strides per minute) unless otherwise noted.

❖ **SCOPE:** Magnitude of range of motion. Same as *Amplitude*.

❖ **SEAT:** The rider's trunk, which includes the pelvis, spine, and rib cage, with supporting musculature. The control of the seat determines the dynamic influence and balance of the rider and harmony with the horse's movement within each gait and exercise.

❖ **SELF-CARRIAGE:** State in which the horse carries itself in balance without taking support or balancing on the rider's hand.

❖ **SLACK:** 1) Used in reference to the reins: without contact. 2) Used in reference to the condition of the musculature (e.g. "slack loin").

❖ **SNATCHING:** 1) Horse attempting to jerk the reins through the rider's hands. 2) Picking up the leg(s) jerkily and sometimes excessively high.

❖ **SPEED:** Meters per minute or miles per hour, i.e. how much ground is covered per unit of time. The horse's speed can be changed by adjusting the length of stride, adjusting the tempo, or both. Increased tempo does not necessarily mean increased speed. Not to be confused with impulsion or tempo.

- **STEP:** Referring to *either* the front *or* hind pair of legs, the movement that involves transfer from one limb to the other. Steps are measured (in time or distance) between the footfall of one hoof and the footfall of the other hoof of the pair. For counting purposes, the steps of only the front OR rear pair of limbs are counted.

- **STIFF/STIFFNESS:** Inability (as opposed to unwillingness) to flex the joints or stretch the musculature to the degree and in the way required to perform the task at hand. The opposite of suppleness. Not to be confused with tension, resistance, or bracing.

- **STRAIGHTNESS (IMPROVED ALIGNMENT AND EQUAL LATERAL SUPPLENESS ON BOTH REINS):** A horse is said to be straight when the footfalls of the forehand and the hindquarters are appropriately aligned on straight and curved lines and when his longitudinal axis is in line with the straight or curved track on which he is ridden.

- **STRIDE:** Cycle of movements that is completed when the horse's legs regain their initial positions. Length of stride refers to the amount of ground covered by the entire cycle.

- **STRUNG OUT:** Outline too elongated—horse sprawled out rather than gathered up into connection with good carriage and balance.

- **STUCK:** Instead of being raised in the rhythm of the gait, a foot remains on the ground throughout the entire stride. Usually applied to pirouette and turn on the haunches.

- **SUBMISSION:** The horse's willing cooperation and harmony with the rider, demonstrating an attentive and confident attitude. Willingness to perform the required exercise as well as operate with correct basics. (see *Basics*).

- **SUPPLENESS (ELASTICITY AND FREEDOM FROM ANXIETY):** Suppleness indicates the absence of negative muscular tension, allowing the joints to move with harmonious flexibility. Elasticity describes the horse who is able to stretch and contract the musculature smoothly and fluently.

- **SUSPENSION:** The moment or phase of the trot, canter or passage in which the horse has no feet on the ground.

- **SWINGING:** In series of flying changes, piaffe, or passage, the alternating left and right lateral displacement of the shoulders and/or haunches.

- **SWINGING BACK:** The springy motion that occurs when the thrust off the hind legs is transmitted through a stretched topline with trunk muscles that contract and release rhythmically rather than remaining either rigid or slack.

- **SWINGING HEAD:** The horse's muzzle moves left-and-right or in circles, indicating constraint or incorrect acceptance of contact/connection. Same as head wagging.

- **TEMPO:** Rate of repetition of the strides as may be measured by a metronome. Tempo is measured by counting the number of times per minute that one of the hooves touches down (indicating completion of one full stride). Alternatively, at walk and trot, both emphasized beats of the stride may be counted. Note: Tempo is often confused with rhythm, speed, pace, or cadence.

- **TENSE/ TENSENESS/TENSION:** 1) Referring to the horse's mental/emotional state -- anxious or nervous. 2) Referring to muscular tension, the state in which the muscles are contracted. Too much muscle tension or sustained muscular tension is not desirable, but a certain amount of positive tension is needed for postural support and locomotion. Often physical and mental/emotional states go hand in hand.

- **THROUGHNESS/THROUGH:** An equestrian term which means the supple, elastic, unblocked, connected state of the horse's musculature and a willing mental state that permits an unrestricted flow of energy from back to front and front to back (circle of the aids), which allows the aids/influences to go through all parts of the horse.

- **THRUST:** Propulsive forward and upward drive from hindquarters. Required at First Level to achieve improved balance and throughness; at Second Level required to be in a more uphill direction.

- **TILTING:** Tipping or cocking the head (lowering one ear)—an evasion.

- **TOPLINE:** Profile from the poll to the tail along the top of the crest of the neck and along the spine. The horse lengthens or stretches its topline by rounding its neck and back and lifting its thorax and belly. The horse can stretch its topline irrespective of the height of its neck.

- **TRACK/TRACKS:** 1) The line(s) of hoof prints laid down as the foot or feet travel their individual path(s). There are two different versions of how to count tracks: a) to address the line of travel of *each* leg in determining the number of paths of travel, as viewed by the observer as the horse approaches him (e.g. three tracks for shoulder-in, four tracks for travers). b) to address front or hind legs as *pair(s)*, such that lateral movements are considered to be "on two tracks," in contrast to when a horse tracks straight. 2) Direction of travel, as in "track right" (when all corners are right turns, and the right hand is toward the center of the arena). 3) Path next to the rail in an arena.

- **TRACKING UP:** The hind feet step into the prints of the forefeet.

- **TRAILING:** 1) In half-pass and leg-yield, refers to lack of parallelism to the long axis of the arena (as in trailing *haunches*). 2) The hind legs operating too far behind the horse, which favors pushing at the expense of carrying, especially in the lengthened, medium and extended paces (as in trailing *hind legs*).

- **TRAJECTORY:** The line of travel of the hoof from its lift-off to landing -- the reach, height, and shape of the flight arc of the hoof.

- **UNEVEN:** An irregularity in walk or trot in which the front or hind pair of legs does not move symmetrically, the right leg making a different *length* of step than the left leg.

- **UNLEVEL:** An irregularity in which the front or hind pair of legs does not move symmetrically, the right leg making a different *height* of step than the left leg.

- **UPHILL:** Good longitudinal balance, with elevated forehand and lowered croup (engaged hindquarters). The degree of engagement of the hind limbs is balanced with the degree of elevation of the forehand.

- **WAGGING:** The horse's muzzle, head and/or neck moves left-and-right or in circles, indicating constraint or incorrect acceptance of contact/connection.

- **WIDE BEHIND:** The horse travels with the hind feet further apart than the fore feet. This is an evasion of engagement which occurs most commonly in piaffe, halting, and lengthening of stride in trot.

- **WORKING (TROT OR CANTER):** A pace in which the horse goes forward energetically but calmly, with a length of stride between that of the collected and medium paces. A working trot should have at least a level balance (in contrast to the uphill balance of a collected trot).

- **ZIG-ZAG:** Three or more half passes connected by changes of direction.

Appendix II

Foundation for Critical Thinking Intellectual Standards

From *The Miniature Guide to Critical Thinking*, Eighth Edition, by Richard Paul and Linda Elder, published by The Foundation for Critical Thinking © *Linda Elder 2020*, reproduced by arrangement with The Rowman & Littlefield Publishing Group.

Some Essential Intellectual Standards for All Human Thought

Clarity	Could you elaborate further? Could you give me an example? Could you illustrate what you mean?
Accuracy	How could we check on that? How could we find out if that is true? How could we verify or test that?
Precision	Could you be more specific? Could you give me more details? Could you be more exact?
Relevance	How does that relate to the problem? How does that bear on the question? How does that help us with the issue?
Depth	What factors make this a difficult problem? What are some of the complexities of this question? What are some of the difficulties we need to deal with?
Breadth	Do we need to look at this from another perspective? Do we need to consider another point of view? Do we need to look at this in other ways?
Logic	Does all this make sense together? Does your first paragraph fit in with your last? Does what you say follow from the evidence?
Significance	Is this the most important problem to consider? Is this the central idea to focus on? Which of these facts are most important?
Fairness	Do I have any vested interest in this issue? Am I sympathetically representing the viewpoints of others? Have we fully and fairly considered all the important information relevant to the issue?
Sufficiency	Do we have sufficient information to answer the question? Are we unfairly leaving out information we would rather not consider in order to get more for our group while ignoring or downplaying the rights and needs of others?

Appendix III
Circle Templates for Dressage Arenas

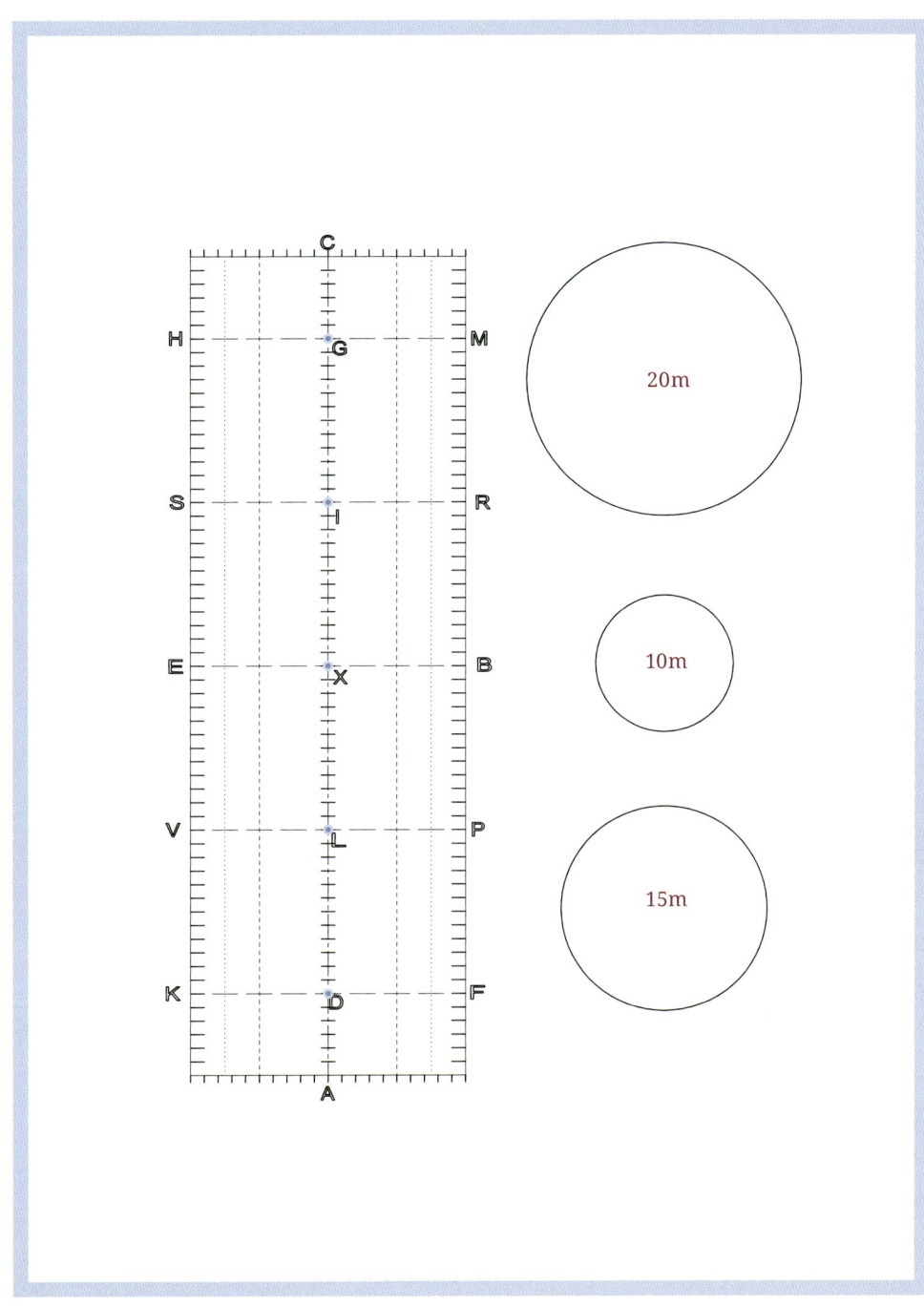

Uncertain about the precise location for executing circles in an arena? This will clarify it for you: This drawing of the large (20-meter by 60-meter) dressage arena is to-scale. Every tick mark represents one meter. The circles are 20 meters, 15 meters, and 10 meters. You can scan this, and enlarge and cut out the circles to see exactly where the circles are placed in the arena, and exactly where you need to ride to. Having them printed on see-through plastic or transparency is especially helpful.

Acknowledgements

The Untold Story

I read a lot of books, usually several per week. I read biographies because I'm fascinated by the backstory of anything. Every book has its own untold backstory, which can be found in the acknowledgments. I'm always intrigued by these mysterious acknowledgments. Who are these individuals? What did they do to assist the author? Unfortunately, I'll likely never know, but I silently honor each of their names in my mind because they have unquestionably earned their place in that book. I definitely learned about this from the people who helped me with this book! Their unending generosity of time and expertise never ceased to astound me. This book truly has a hundred authors!

Since the thanks are all equally profound, but so very different, there is no hierarchical order to this list. The book wouldn't have been possible without contributions from those who follow: Thanks to Michelle Peck Williams, my endless "go to" for everything, for decades. Thanks to my many instructors over 60 years and, specifically, to Sharon Vander Ziel, for her years of patience and guidance. Thanks to Taylor Sterry, Cindy Sither, Stacy Rector, and Emilie Goddard for their hard, hard work bringing the vitally necessary drawings to life. From them, I learned how art can, and should, tell a story. Thanks to those who participated in the demonstration videos: Paige Metcalfe, Chelsea Reyes, Taylor Sterry and, especially, Carolyn Meng for being the first video guinea pig and doing a terrific job. Thanks to Kelsey Lee for editing, voicing over, and posting the videos, plus a hundred other things! Thanks to Frank Messina, a long-time colleague, avid musician, and fellow local author, who gave me the nudge to believe I could write a book. Thanks to Becky Irwin for her incredible patience in editing early drafts. Thanks to Barry Irwin for being a great mentor for many years and making it possible for me to participate in a wide variety of extraordinary equine activities. Thanks to Laura Hornback and Felix and Jacqueline Bernard and Tulip for their determination. Thanks to Joanne Hodges for her structural advice. Thanks to Karianne Mau, a budding archivist, for generously providing a complete bibliography with citations. Thanks to the folks who agreed to be in photos: The Spanish Riding School/Rider Hannah Zeitlhofer and Siglavy Batosta, Christina Lockhart, Jim Koford, Neil Visser, Paige Metcalfe, and JP Giacomini, and to the owners of the horses who are in the photos. Thanks to the photographers who granted me permission to use their photos: Charlie Glenn from Fennell's Tack, Wendy Wooley of EquiSport Photos, Varian Arabians, Linda Grandia of Equicube, Howard Schatzberg Photography, Correct Connect LLC, Peter Rigaud, and Shelley Smith Giacomini. Thanks to everyone who gave me permissions to excerpt or quote them: Dr. Linda Elder and Rowman & Littlefield Company for Dr. Richard Paul, Vanessa Gallo for Carmine Gallo, Ruth Poulsen and Rhett Savoie for Jane Savoie, Yvonne Barteau, Karen McGoldrick, Beth Baumert, Janet Foy, Dr. Thomas Ritter, Linda Grandia, Josh Lyons for John Lyons, Jo-Ann Wilson, Anna Blake, Natasha Althoff of *YourRidingSuccess.com*, Kathy Farrokhzad, Janet Jones, and the United States Dressage Federation. Inexpressible thanks to Prince El Raff, Fenwick, Envoy, and dear Zinnie, horses that taught me so much. I only wish I had known what they taught me *before* I rode them. Thank you to my parents, grandparents, and husband, Jeff, for supporting and enduring my insatiable horse obsession. Thank you to Rebecca Didier, Martha Cook, and the entire team at Trafalgar Square Books, whose wise suggestions never failed to push me in a more productive direction. Every piece of advice was spot on! And to the countless horse people from whom I drew inspiration—just by being there, you were teaching me something.

Bibliography

- Adler, Mortimer J. and Charles Van Doren. *How to Read a Book: The Classics Guide to Intelligent Reading*. Texas: Touchstone, 1972.
- Albrecht von Ziegner, Kurd. *The Elements of Dressage: A Guide to Training the Young Horse*. Connecticut: Lyons Press, 2002.
- Backer, Horst. *The Athletic Horse: Building on Strengths, Overcoming Weaknesses*. Washington: Cadmos Books, 2010.
- Ballou, Jec Aristotle. *101 Dressage Exercises for Horse & Rider (Read & Ride)*. Massachusetts: Storey Publishing LLC, 2010.
- Barteau, Yvonne. *The Dressage Horse Manifesto: Training Secrets, Insight, and Revelations from 10 Dressage Horses*. Vermont: Trafalgar Square Books, 2016.
- Baumert, Beth. *How Two Minds Meet: The Mental Dynamics of Dressage*. Vermont: Trafalgar Square Books, 2020.
- Baumert, Beth. *When Two Spines Align: Dressafe Dynamics: Attain Remarkable Riding with Your Horse*. Vermont: Trafalgar Square Books, 2014.
- Beran, Anja. *The Dressage Seat: Achieving a Beautiful, Effective Position in Every Gait and Movement*. Vermont: Trafalgar Square Books, 2017.
- Beth-Halachmy, Eitan. *Dressage the Cowboy Way: The Complete Guide to Training and Riding with Soft Feel and Kindness*. Vermont: Trafalgar Square Books, 2018.
- Biggs, Sharon. *In One Arena: Top Dressage Experts Share Their Knowledge Through the Levels*. Maryland: Half-Halt Press, 2001.
- Blake, Anna M.. *Relaxes & Forward: Relationship Advice from Your Horse*. Missouri: Prairie Moon Press, 2016.
- Bryant, Jennifer O. *The USDF Guide to Dressage: The Official Guide of the United States Dressage Federation*. Massachusetts: Storey Publishing LLC, 2012.
- Cline, Ernest. *Ready Player Two: A Novel*. New York: Ballantine Books, 2020.
- Diggle, Martin. *Master Equitation: Collecting*. London: J. A. Allen, 2002.
- Diggle, Martin. *Masters of Equitation on Counter-Canter and Flying Changes*. London: J. A. Allen, 2002.
- Diggle, Martin. *Master of Equitation on the Canter*. Vermont: Trafalgar Square Books, 2001.
- Diggle, Martin. *Master of Equitation on Trot*. Vermont: Trafalgar Square Books, 2001.
- Dove, Peter. *Master Dressage: Ride More Beautiful Tests, Achieve Higher Marks, and Have a Better Relationship with Your Horse*. Illinois: Kenilworth Press, 2016.
- Farrokhzad, Kathy. "Horse Listening: Forward and Round to Training Success" in *The Horse Listening Collections*, Volume Two. Massachusetts: Full Circle Equestrian, 2014.
- Farrokhzad, Kathy. "Horse Listening: The Book: Stepping Forward to Effective Riding" in *The Horse Listening Collections*, Volume One. Massachusetts: Full Circle Equestrian, 2014.

- Foy, Janet. *Dressage for the Not-So-Perfect Horse: Riding Through the Levels on the Peculiar, Opinionated, Complicated Mounts We All Love.* Vermont: Trafalgar Square Books, 2012.

- German National Federation. *The Principles of Riding: Basic Training for Horse and Rider.* Illinois: Kenilworth Press, 2017.

- Gallo, Carmine. *Talk Like TED: The 9 Public-Speaking Secrets of the World's Top Minds.* New York: St. Martin's Griffin, 2015.

- Harris, Susan E.. *Horse Gaits, Balance, and Movement,* revised 2nd edition. Tennessee: Turner, 2016.

- Harris, Charles. *Workbooks from the Spanish School.* London: J. A. Allen & Co. LTD, 2004.

- Henriquet, Michel and Catherine Durand. *Henriquet on Dressage.* Vermont: Trafalgar Square Books, 2004.

- HowToDressage.com *How To Dressage: Simple 'How-To' Guides Breaking Down Dressage Movements, Helping You Avoid Costly Mistakes & Fix Common Problems.* CreateSpace Independent Publishing Platform, 2018.

- Karl, Philippe. *The Art of Riding: Classical Dressage to High School: Odin at Saumur.* Washington: Cadmos Books, 2010.

- Kohl, Julia. *Creative Dressage Schooling: Enjoy the Training Process with 55 Meaningful Exercises.* Vermont: Trafalgar Square Books, 2017.

- Kottas-Heldenberg, Arthur. *Kottas on Dressage.* Vermont: Trafalgar Square Books, 2010.

- Loch, Sylvia. *The Balanced Horse: The Aids by Feel, Not Force.* Vermont: Trafalgar Square Books, 2013.

- Marsden Hamilton, Jen. *Stride Control: Exercises to Improve Rideability, Adjustability and Performance.* Vermont: Trafalgar Square Books, 2020.

- McGoldrick, Karen. *Lessons With Margot: Notes on Dressage from the Author of the Dressage Chronicles.* Georgia: Deeds Publishing, 2017.

- McPhee, John. *Draft No. 4: On the Writing Process.* New York: Farrar, Straus and Giroux, 2018.

- Muller, Hannes, Eckart Meyners, and Kerstin Niemann. *Rider + Horse = 1: How To Achieve the Fluid Dialogue that Leads to Harmonious Performance.* Vermont: Trafalgar Square Books, 2014.

- Neindorff, Egon von. *The Art of Classical Horsemanship.* Cadmos Verlag, 2009.

- Obama, Barack. *A Promised Land.* New York: Crown, 2020.

- Paul, Richard and Linda Elder. *Instructor's Manual: Critical Thinking, Tools for Taking Charge of Your Learning and Life.* New Jersey: Prentice Hall, 2001.

- Podhajsky, Alois. *Complete Training of Horse and Rider: In the Principles of Classical Horsemanship.* California: Wilshire Book Company, 1958.

- Rachen-Schoneich, Gabriele. *Straightening the Crooked Horse: Correct Imbalance, Relieve Strain, and Encourage Free Movement with an Innovative System of Straightness Training.* Vermont: Trafalgar Square Books, 2021.

- *Ride with Your Mind Essentials: Innovative Learning Strategies for Basic Riding Skills.* Illinois: Kenilworth Press, 2002.

- Ritter, Dr. Thomas. *Dressage Principals Based on Biomechanics.* Washington, Cadmos Books, 2012.

- Sabine Schaefer, Ruth. *Feeling Dressage: How to Achieve Harmony With Your Horse.* Kentucky: Eclipse Press, 2003.

- Savoie, Jane. *Jane Savoie's Dressage 101: The Ultimate Source of Dressage Basics in a Language You Can Understand.* Vermont: Trafalgar Square Books, 2011.

- Savoie, Jane. *Jane Savoie's Dressage Between the Jumps: The Secret to Improving Your Horse's Performance Over Fences.* Vermont: Trafalgar Square Books, 2020.

- Savoie, Jane. *Jane Savoie's Guide for Training A Happy Horse.* DVD, Vermont: Trafalgar Square Books, 2007.

- Schmidt, Hubertus. *The Half-halt Simplified.* Dressage Today, 2015. https://dressagetoday.com/instruction/half-halt-simplified/.

- Schoffmann, Britta. *Dressage School: A Sourcebook of Movements and Tips.* Translated by Reina Abelshauser. Vermont: Trafalgar Square Books, 2019.

- Schoffmann, Britta. *Dressage Training Customized: Schooling Your Horse as Best Suits His Individual Personality and Conformation.* Vermont: Trafalgar Square Books, 2010.

- Schoffmann, Britta. *Klaus Balkenhol: The Man and His Training Methods.* Vermont: Trafalgar Square Books, 2007.

- Sivewright, Molly. *Thinking Riding Book 2: In Good Form.* London: J. A. Allen, 1983.

- Swartz, Krister. *Moving Freely Forward: A Handbook for Training Level Dressage.* Manor Minor Press, 2013.

- Swift, Sally. *Centered Riding.* New York: St. Martin's Press, 1985.

- Tavora, Miguel. *Dressage Principles and Techniques: A blueprint for the serious rider.* Virginia: Xenophon Press LLC, 2018.

- Wanless, Mary. *Ride with Your Mind Essentials: Innovative Learning Strategies for Basic Riding Skills.* Vermont: Trafalgar Square Books, 2002.

- Wanless, Mary. *The New Anatomy of Rider Connection: Structural Balance for Rider and Horse.* Vermont: Trafalgar Square Books, 2017.

- Wilsie, Sharon and Gretchen Vogel. *Horse Speak: An Equine-Human Translation Guide: Conversations With Horses in Their Language.* Vermont: Trafalgar Square Books, 2016.

Index

Page numbers in *italics* indicate illustrations

/ A /

- Aaron Vale Rein, 151, *151*
- Above the bit, 120, *193*, 222, *232*
- Adler, Mortimer, 5, 10
- Aids. *See also specific aids*
  analogies for, 99–101
  as communication, 97–98, *97*, 99–101
  consistency of, 98–99, 206
  effective use of, 100–101, 106–8, 154, 173, 207–8, 240, 251
  horse's responsiveness to, 10, 54, 104–7, 111, 220
  purpose of, 110, 207
  release of, 135, 173
  timing of, 10, 160–61, 173, 208, 214, 215, 251
  types discussed, 97
- Air pressure, compared to rein tension, 158–59
- Alignment
  analogies for, *146*, 207
  assessing, 219, *245*
  on bending lines, 174, 189, 196, *196*, *207*, *210*
  benefits of, *146*, 170
  on circles, 58, *63*
  development of, 112, 175, 177, 209, *210*, 248
  rein aids for, 189, 239, 246
  in transitions, 209–10
- Alphabet analogy, 77, 98
- Althoff, Natasha, 218
- Anthropomorphism, 84
- Anticipation, 217, 251
- Anxiety, 102–3, 105
- Arms, position/stability of, *137*, 148, 169, 171, 191
- Asymmetry. *See* Crookedness
- Attentiveness, of horse, 22, 35, 160, 181, 220, *224*, 235–38, 261–62

/ B /

- Back, of horse
  position of, *128*, 129, 194, *195*, 269, 273–74
  relaxation of, 121, 131, *270*
  rider's access to, 271–72
- Back, of rider, 169
- Back-to-front riding, 120–22, 129, 218
- Balance. *See also* Longitudinal balance
  of horse, 9, 54, 172, 174
  of rider, 103–4, 145, 146, 190
- Balancing lines, 177
- Balloon analogy, 122–23, 137
- Barteau, Yvonne, 242
- Baseball mitt analogy, *270*
- Baumert, Beth, 207, 248, 257
- Behavior, patterns of, 15, 251
- Behind the vertical, 109, 152–53, 193, *193*
- Bending lines
  on circles, 58
  consistency of, 189, 236–37
  vs. flexion, 232
  longeing and, 53–54, 55–57, *56–57*
  training role, 46, 174, 192–93, *245*
  transitions on, 217
- Bicycle analogy, 126
- Bits, 10, 13, 59, *59*, 100–101, 194, 253
- Body awareness, in horses, 64, 76, 77
- Body language, 21
- Books. *See* Reading
- Bracing, 103–4, 110, 150, 234, 235, 250
- Breed characteristics, 223–24
- Bridles, 10, 193–94, 253
- Buchanan, Anne, 3
- Bungee cord contact exercise, 157
- Burch, Noel, 3, 212–13

/ C /

- Calmness, 63, 196, 235
- Canter, 64, 139, *214*, 215–16
- Carpal tunnel gloves, 191
- Cavalletti, 66, *66*
- Caveats, about, 7
- Chains, on lead shanks, 34, *34*
- Circle of energy, 118, 127–28
- Circles
  - accuracy of, 61–62, *62*, 195–96
  - benefits of, 147–48, 178, 194, 238, 274
  - connection in, 186, 236–37
  - counting strides on, 106–7
  - halts on, 111
  - longeing and, 53–54, 60
  - marking quarters of, 106–7
  - size of, 54, 62–63, *64*, 192–93, 196
  - transitions on, 204, 210, *210*, 217
- Circuit theory, of connection, 119–23
- Clarity/State, Elaborate, Illustrate, Exemplify technique, 162–63
- Collection, 77, 248
- Color-coding, of texts, *4*
- Communication, 5, 21, 99, 261–62, 266, 272
- Compass analogy, 170
- Compassion, for self, 248, 272
- Competence, 3, 12, 212–13
- Cones, 106
- Conformation, 173, 223–24
- Conformation pose, *81*, 83
- Connection. *See also* Getting connected; Staying connected
  - analogies for, 122–23, 126, 137, 145, *145*, 203
  - circle of energy in, 118, 127–28
  - consistency of, 155, 191
  - vs. contact, 124–26, 193, 203
  - flexion in, 234–35
  - half-halts and, 269–70
  - head height and, 221–24, *222*
  - horse's role in, 150, 152–53
  - rider feel for, 125, 148, *182*, 186
  - "sweet spot" of, 189
  - in transitions, 211–13
  - unique to each horse, 166, 171, 193
- Consistency
  - of horse's movement, 48, 63 (*See also* Rhythm; Tempo)
  - in riding, 98–99, 133, 248
  - Contact
    - analogies for, *145*
    - connection and, 123, 124–26, 203
    - consistency of, 138, 147–48, 153, 155
    - establishing, 54–55, 60–61, 129–32, 167–68
    - evasion of, 109, 152–53, 193, *193*
    - exercises for, 135–36, 139–46, 155–57, *155*
    - horse's role in, 140, 144, 146, 150, 152–53, 156
    - rider's role in, 109, 125, 148, 156, *182*, 269
    - seeking of, by horse, 128, 139–46, *223*
    - softness and, 135–39
- Coordination
  - of horse, 37, 55, 91, 101
  - of rider, 107, 137, 243, 275
- Core, of rider, 114–15, 160, *161*, 264
- Corners, of arena, 46, 181
- Correct Connect Aaron Vale Rein, 151, *151*
- Corrections, *35*, 57, 83, 110, 217, 251
- Counterbend, *56*, *57*, 172, 186–87, 239–40
- Counting strides, 106–7, 174
- Crawling demonstration, 194
- Crest, flipping of, 232, 254, 255
- Critical thinking, 72, 140–42, 162–63, 276–77
- *Critical Thinking* (Paul and Elder), 72, 162–63
- Crookedness
  - caused by rider, 273
  - contact and, 172–73
  - effects of, *146*
  - exercises for, 58, *58* (*See also* Widen and squeeze technique)
  - sidedness in, 36, 190, 217–18, 243–44, 251–52
- Crowding, by horses, 33–38
- Cup-and-string phone analogy, 145, *145*
- Cyr Stokely, Christine, 45–46

/ D /

- Data cable analogy, 170
- Dental problems, 218
- Devices, 65, 152, 194
- "Diagonal sprawl," 172–73
- Direction changes, 61, 178, 195
- Discovery learning, 5–6, 198
- Displacement behavior, 21, *21*, 33, *33*
- Dogs, 8, 87
- Dominance, defined, 35
- Dover, Robert, 270–71
- Downhill balance, 102, *102*, 108–9, *206*, 221
- Draw reins, 194
- *Dressage 101* (Savoie), 269
- *Dressage for the Not-So-Perfect Horse* (Foy), 236
- *The Dressage Horse Manifesto* (Barteau), 242
- Drifting out, 56, *57*, 172
- Drilling, avoiding, 10, 218
- Driving hold, 155–56, *155*
- Driving pressure, 54, 120–22, 130–31

/ E /

- Education. *See* Learning
- Elbows, position/stability of, 169, 171, 211–12, *212*, 239, 241
- Elder, Linda, 72, 162
- Emotions, managing, 61, 83–84, 149, 250
- Energy
  - of horse, 114–15, 118, 121–23, 125, 127–29, *128*
  - of rider, 168–69
- Engagement, 65–66
- Equicube, 160, 161
- Equitation. *See* Rider position
- Equus Academy, 46
- Evasion, 244–45. *See also* Resistance
- Expectations, 248, 263. *See also* Non-negotiables
- Extension activities, about, 11–12, 26
- Eye, training of, 44, 45, 86–87
- Eyes, closing, 157

/ F /

- Falling in, 53, 56, *56–57*, 61, 172, 189, 246
- Fatigue, 11, 213, 246–47
- Feel, 133–39, 161, 257, *269*, 279
- Feet, movement/placement of, 33–36, 38, 81–83, 208, *209*
- Feldenkrais Method, 12
- Fight/flight/freeze responses, 235–36
- Figure eights, 178, 220, *220*
- Figures, 8, 176, 178, 220, *220*. *See also* Circles
- Fishing reel analogy, 157
- Fitness
  - of horse, 9, 55, 63–64, 108, 153–54, 213, 253
  - of rider, 9
- Flexibility
  - of horse, 56
  - in training, 4
- Flexion
  - vs. bend, 232
  - caveats regarding, 249–54
  - described, 230, 231–32, *231*, 242–43, *242*
  - different in each direction, 251–52
  - establishing, 242–45, 247–50
  - extension activities, 254–55
  - fatigue and, 246–47
  - of joints, 231
  - as Non-negotiable, 91, 235, 272
  - quality of, 251, 254
  - rein aids in, 190, 235–36, 243–46
  - troubleshooting, 240–42
  - uses of, 150, 177–79, 233–35, 238–40, 244, 262–63
  - warm-up and, 236–38
- Footing, 64
- Fore, Lilo, 174
- Forehand, falling onto. *See* Downhill balance
- Forelegs
  - crossing over of, 37, *37*, 53, *78*, 236–37
  - in forward energy, 108
  - posing of, *81*, 82
- Forward movement. *See also* "Go"
  - balance in, 101–4
  - in connection, 122, 127–28, 153, 166, 192
  - groundwork for, 45–46
  - half-halts and, 264–65, 273, 274
  - horse's responsibility for, 111–12
  - in leg-yield, 178
  - longeing and, 53–54, 60
  - resistance to, 108, 111
  - vs. speed, 108
  - in transitions, 211, 220
- *Four Stages of Competence* (Burch), 3
- Foy, Janet, 236
- Frame, artificial, 125, 129, 145, 224, *224*. *See also* Longitudinal balance
- Frisbee analogy, *203*
- Front-to-back riding, 120, 121–23, 129, 152

/ G /

- Gaits, generally, 55, 213
- Gallo, Carmine, 16, 197–98
- Getting connected
  - analogies for, 119–23
  - balance and, 125–28
  - caveats regarding, 153–55
  - challenge of, 127–28
  - contact in, 124–26, 129–34
  - energy in, 128–29
  - exercises for, 54, 147–53 (*See also* Widen and squeeze technique)
  - as Non-negotiable, 91, 119, 272
  - rider feel for, 133–39, 147
  - softness in, 134–46
- Giacomini, Jean-Philippe (JP), 35, 46, 78,

- 102–3, 131, 135, 241, *281*
- Gloves, 59
- "Go." *See also* Forward movement
    - aids in, 97–101
    - balance and, 101–4
    - caveats regarding, 104–9
    - extension activities, 110–12
    - as Non-negotiable, 91, 97
    - during transitions, 203–4
    - "Whoa" and, 110
- Go Away Button, 38
- Ground poles, 153
- Groundwork. *See also* Longeing
    - benefits of, 21–22, 84–85, 221
    - developing flexion in, 254–55
    - exercises, 33–38, 45–46, *45*
- Gymnastic exercises, 63, 65, 66

/H/

- Hacking, 181, 221
- Half-halts
    - aids for, 264–67
    - caveats regarding, 272–74
    - extension activities, 274
    - flexion in, 262–63
    - intensity of, 266, 269, 273
    - as Non-negotiable, 91, 261, 272
    - release in, 262, 266
    - stages of, 268–70
    - timing of, 263–64, 266–68, 273
    - as universal tool, 261, 267, 273
    - uses of, 110, 160, 214–17, 260, 269, *269*, 271–72
- Halter pose, *81*
- Halts
    - aids for, 99–100, 110
    - on circles, 111
    - energy in, 173–74
    - foot placement in, 6–10, 81–83, *81*
    - in groundwork, *34*, 61
- Handler position, in longeing, 60
- Hands. *See also* Rein aids
    - belong to the horse, 124, 137–38, 158
    - "flipping" of, 155–56, *155*
    - giving/following with, 124, *124*, 138–46, 157, 274
    - position of, 154, 158, *160*, 161, 241
    - refined use of, 144–46, 148, 149, *158*, 161, 190–91, 241
    - stability of, 211–13, *212*
    - *A Happy Horse Study Course* (Savoie), 100
- Haunches, turn on, 77–79, *78–79*. *See also* Hindquarters
- Head, of horse
    - bobbing of, *156*, 216
    - dropping/lowering of, 66, 131–33, 154, 192–95, *193*, 210
    - raising of, 139, 194, *195*, 205, 224, 235, 274
    - rider positioning of, 125, 129, 145, 221–24, *222*, 241
    - tilting of, 252, *252*
    - "wagging" of, by rider, 241, 251
- Head, of rider, 168
- "Head down" cue, 235
- "Head" half-halt, 264, 274
- "Head Position Matters" (Lyons), 235
- Headset. *See* Frame, artificial
- Hess, Christoph, 119

- Hill work, 153
- Hind legs
    - crossing over of, 80
    - engagement of, 65–66, 126
    - half-halt effects on, 269, *269*
    - longitudinal balance and, 77–79, 108, 205, *206*, 274
    - pushing power of, 121–22, 152, 160, 166
    - restriction of, 194, *195*, 208, *209*
    - tension in, 154
    - trailing of, 102, *102*, 206
- Hindquarters
    - lowering of, 77, 223
    - mobility of, 79–80
    - in straightness, *210*, 236–37, 239, 246, 253
- Hips
    - of horse, 253
    - of rider, 112, 131, 170
- Hollowness, 55–57, *56–57*, 143–44, 154
- *Horse Brain, Human Brain* (Jones), 224
- *Horse Speak* (Wilsie and Vogel), 38
- Horsemanship, elements of, 6
- *How to Read a Book* (Adler), 5, 10

/I/

- Ice skating analogy, 236–37
- Impulsion, 111, 122–23, 127, 174, 203–4, 241, 274
- "Inside," defined, 233, *233*
- Inside rein
    - "opening" of, 245–46, *246*
    - overreliance on, 241
    - uses of, 100, 169, 187–90, 243–44, 264–66
- Inside/outside aids, balance of, 106, 187–90
- Intellectual standards, 113–15, 162. *See also* Learning
- Intentions, 4–5, 8, 91, 105, 174, 217, 248
- Interference, avoiding, 240–41
- Inversion, vs. flexion, *232*

/J/

- Jackknifed neck position, 240–41, *241*, 249
- Jaw, suppling of, 170, 178, 254
- Joints
    - of horse, 210, *210*, 231
    - of rider, 170
- Jones, Janet, 224

/K/

- *Kata*, in marital arts, 77–78
- Kehr, Fran, 189
- Keller, Helen, 99
- Kicking, by rider, *97*, 131
- Koford, Jim, *119*, 219, 261
- Kryptonite analogy, 233

/L/

- LaCroix, Ray, 35
- Lancastre Tavora, Miguel de, 163
- Latent learners, 48, 133
- Lateral balance, 102, *103*, 219
- Lateral work, 175–79
- Lead shanks, 34, *34*, 65
- Leadership, 21–22, *33*
- Leading exercises, 33–38, *33–34*, *36–37*

- Leaning, by rider, 99. *See also* Falling in
- Learning
    - assessing competence, 3, 5, 12, 212–13
    - discussion in, 12, 28–29, 40
    - exercises, 3–4, *4*, 72, 86–87, 92, 162–63, 197–98, 276–77
    - from experience, 5–6, 13, 96, 161
    - intellectual standards and, 113–15, 162
    - kinesthetic, 134
    - latent, 48, 133
    - lesson plans and, 23–29, 47–48
    - paradigm shifts, 11, 275
    - patterns in, 14–16
    - questions in, 225–26
    - by reading, 3–7, *4*, 10, 12–13, 39–40, 276
    - reflection in, 47–48, 67–72, 174–75, 248
    - rephrasing and, 39–40, 256–57
    - review in, 6–7, 12
    - self-directed, 5–10, 198
- Leg aids
    - on circles, 239
    - in connection, 123, 143
    - in half-halts, 264–66
    - hands and, 188, 191, 208, 255, 257
    - horse's responsiveness to, 97, 107, 131
    - reinforcement of, 106
    - in steering, 155, 169–70
- Legs, position/control of, 79–80, 148, 170, 208
- Leg-yield
    - benefits of, 175–77, 274
    - caveats regarding, 179–81
    - exercises for, 182–85
    - extension activities, 181
    - preparation for, 177–79
    - uses of, 153, 175–79, 220, *220*
- Lesson plans, 23–29, 47–48
- Lessons, 5–6, 11–12
- Lightness, vs. softness, 134
- Listening, 12, 268, 271
- Long and low, 221
- Longe lines, 59–61, *59*
- Longeing
    - areas for, 59
    - benefits of, 52, 54–57, 108–9
    - caveats regarding, 59–64
    - equipment for, 59, *59*
    - exercises, 53–54, 63
    - "fake," 156
    - of rider, 156, 161, 187–88, 245
    - session duration, 63–64
- *Longissimus dorsi*, 129
- Longitudinal balance, 102, *102*. *See also* Downhill balance; Uphill balance
- Lunge whip connection analogy, *128*, 129
- Lyons, John, 235

/M/

- Mane flip, 232, 254, 255
- Manners, 21–22
- McDonald, Debbie, 250
- Mechanical devices, 152
- Messina, Frank, 276
- Mirrors, 103, 155, 211–12, *212*, 218–19
- Mistakes, correcting, 109, 152
- Monorail on tracks analogy, 146, *207*, 209
- Morse Code analogy, 100, 205, 261–62
- Mounting/mounting blocks, 26–28
- Movement, of horse, 44, 77–84, 209.

See also Forward movement
- Movements. *See* Figures

/ N /

- Nagging, by rider, *97*, 267
- Neck
  bracing of, 150
  conformation of, 121–22, *121*, 173, 250
  in fight/flight/freeze responses, 235–36
  height of, 120, *121*, *193*, 221–24, *232*, 273
  mane flip, 232, 254, *255*
  movement of, 139–46
  overbending of, 58, 188, 194, *196*, 240–41, 249, 273
- Nerve cells, 107
- Nervous horses, 21, 235–36
- Neutrality, 61, 83–84, 251
- Non-negotiables, 91, 92, 272, 279
- Nose
  centering of, 130, 143, *168*, 189, 194, 209
  stretching down with, 66, 147–48, 153, 221–24
- Nose to Rail Leg-Yield, 182–83, *182–83*, 274
- Noseband adjustment, 194
- Nosich, Gerald, 276
- Nuchal ligament, 232, 253–54, *253*, 255

/ O /

- Observation, of horse, 44, 55, 86–87
- "Off" side, working on, 36
- "On the bit." *See* Connection
- "Opening" rein, 245–46, *246*
- Out behind, 102, *102*, 206
- "Outside"
  aids, generally, 58, 106, 187–90
  defined, 233, *233*
- Outside rein
  connection role, 175, 186–87, *188*
  evasion of, 192, 236–37, 239
  flexion role, 235–36
  following with, 251
  in half-halts, 263–65, 266, 268, *270*, 272
  inside leg and, 187–89, *188*
  in suppling, 238–39, 243–44
- Ovals, 54, 195
- Overwork, 11, 152

/ P /

Pain, 152, 218, 253
Painting analogy, 129
Pantographs, 138, *138*
Parade (half-halt), 262
Paradigm shifts, 11
"Pass the Pulse" game analogy, 123
Patience, 4, 8–9, 105, 132, 147, 247–48, 271
Paul, Richard, 72, 162
Pelvis, of rider, 38, 169, 170, *171*
Pendulum analogy, 247–48
Persistence, 247–48, 253
Petting/patting, *35*, 104, 171, 250
Phone dialing metaphor, 101
Physical issues, 44, 101, 108, 126, 252. *See also* Fitness; Pain
Piano hands, 154
Pivot points, 78–79
Poll
  connection to hips, 253
  flexion of, 150, 230, 231–32, *231*, 245
  mobility of, 171–72, 194, 247, 253
  neck position and, 245–46
"Popping out," of outside shoulder, 240–41, *241*, 249, 250
Posed stances, 81–83, *81*
Posting, at trot, 211–12, *212*, 221
Practice, 6–7, 13, 25, 35–36, 147
Predator/prey behaviors, 8, 35
Pressure
  moving away from, *80*
  release of, 101, 132–33, 142, 187–88
- Problem-solving, 6, 55–57. *See also* Learning
- Proprioception, in riders, 12
- Pulling, by horse, 102–3, 108–9, 144–45, 154
- Pulling, by rider
  analogies for, 249
  avoiding, 107, 110, 124–25, *124*, 145, 241
  effects of, 120, 121, 142
  vs. "opening" of rein, 245–46, *246*
  as "steering," 189–90
- Pushing power, 121–22, 152, 160, 166

/ Q /

- Questions, power of, 225–26

/ R /

- Rail, of arena, 111, 155, 189
- Reaction times, 107–8
- Reading, 3–7, *4*, 10, 12–13, 39–40, 276
- Reflection, 47–48
- Refractory period, for nerve cells, 107
- Rein aids. *See also* Contact; Hands; Pulling, by rider; Reins
  analogies for, 99–101
  in connection, 120–23
  effective use of, 107, 110, 144–46, 249
  legs and, 188, 191, 208, 255, 257
- Rein lameness, 190
- Reins. *See also* Rein aids
  in connection, 170–72
  holding of, 155–56, *155*, 170–71
  horse's responsiveness to, 154, 167–68, *168*, 170
  length of, 170, 223, 244, 250
  slack in, 121–22, 129–31, *130*, 141–42, 149, *156*
  tension on, 140, 156–59, 187
- Relationships, between horse and rider, 21–22
- Relative motion, in physics, 139
- Relaxation, *22*, 46, 55, 195, 220
- Release
  in half-halts, 262, 266
  as reward, 104, 142, 167, 172, 246, 269–70
  timing of, 147, 152
- Rephrasing, 39–40, 256–57
- Resistance
  anticipating, 251
  causes of, 102–3, 150, 152–53, 218
  flexion and, 233–34, *234*
  overcoming, 46, 142, 144, 247–48
  persistence of, 247–48, 253
  to suppling, 171–72, 244–45, 249
  during warm-up, 236–38

- Respect, for space, 21–22, 33–38
- Rest, 11, 48
- Review, in learning, 12, 25
- Rewards
  patting/petting as, *35*, 104, 171
  release as, 104, 142, 167, 172, 246, 269–70
  timing of, 147
  verbal, 104
- Rhythm, 63, 106, 190, 191–92
- Rib cage
  hind leg movement and, 208, *209*
  outward positioning of, 159, *159*, 178, 181, 186, 188, *188*
  in suppling, 238
  in transitions, 204, *209*
- Rider position
  on circles, 193
  in contact/connection, 148, 168–70
  correction of, 11, 104–5, 149
  in half-halts, 264–65, 273
  in posting trot, 221
  stability of, 103, 168–69, 279
  in transitions, 203–4, 214
- Riders
  breakthroughs by, 275
  mentality of, 248, 272, 279 (*See also* Learning)
  responsibilities of, 107, 114–15, 148, 168–70
  self-carriage of, 114, 125, 195
  stiffness in, 273
- Riding
  benefits of, 1
  incorrect, consequences of, 213
  intellectual aspects, 4–5, 16, 174–75, 248
  as problem-solving, 6
  systematic aspects of, 91, 105
  vs. training, 143
- Ritter, Thomas
  on aids, 240
  on contact, 170, 174
  exercise suggestions, 6–10, 220
  on learning, 13, 275
  on neck conformation, 250
  on rider interference, 105, 169, 205
  on transitions, 204
- Running through the bit, 109, 150, 193, *193*
- Rushing
  by horse, 55, 101, 108, 127, 193, 210–13
  by rider, 205

/ S /

- Saddles, 148, 253–54
- Salivary gland, 254, *255*
- Savoie, Jane
  on communication, 77, 98, 100
  on half-halts, 261, 268, 269–70
  on use of hands, 122, 123, 137
- Schmidt, Hubertus, 263
- Schoolmasters, 134
- "Scoop Into the Mitt" analogy, *270*
- Seat
  aiding with, 111, 191
  in connection, 123
  in half-halts, 264–65, 273–74
  "pumping" of, 97, *97*
  in slowing down/halts, 110

- stability of, 114, 125, 146, 148, 161
- steering with, 155
- USDF definition of, 113–15
- SEIE technique, 162–63
- Self-carriage
  - of horse, 167, 193
  - of rider, 114, 125
- Self-perception, 86–87
- Serpentines, 178
- *7 Non-Negotiables of Winning* (Williams), 92
- Shanking exercise, 33–36
- Shoulders
  - alignment of, 56, *210*
  - mobility of, 77–79, *78–79*
  - popping out of, 240–41, *241*, 249, 250
  - steering of, 55–57, 58
- Shoulders facing pose, 82, *82*
- Side-pass, *184*
- Side-reins, 65
- Sign language analogy, 99
- Singing, to maintain tempo, 109, 192
- Slowing down, 145
- Snaffle bits, 13
- Sobering, Denise, 169
- Social media post exercise, 197–98
- Softness, 134–39, 150, 233–34, 236–38
- Soundness issues, 126
- Space, respect for, *21, 32–33*, 33–38, 61
- Spanish Riding School, 161, *167*
- Speed, 101, 108
- Spine, poll and, *234*. See also Back, of horse
- Spinning plates analogy, 204
- Spiraling in/out, on longe, 63
- Spring puppet analogy, 233, *234*
- Sprocket and gear analogy, *269*
- Spurs, 97, 106–7
- Square pose, *81*
- "Staircase" exercise, 179, 181
- Standing still, *81*, 111
- Staying connected
  - aids in, 170–72, 186–90
  - caveats regarding, 179–81, 190–94
  - challenge of, 166, 167–68, 174, 186
  - exercises for, 175–79
  - extension activities, 181, 194–96
  - flexion in, 234–35
  - head height and, 221–24, *222*
  - horse's responsibility for, 172–74
  - as Non-negotiable, 91, 167, 272
  - rider's responsibility for, 168–70, 174–75
  - sweet spot of, 189
  - through transitions, 203–7, 209
- Steering, 154–55, 169–70, 186, 189–90, 246
- Stepping over, in leg-yield, 182–83, *183*
- Stiffness. See also Tension
  - connection and, 143–44, 154
  - exercises for, 55–57, *56–57*
  - in poll, 171–72, 194, 247, 253
  - in riders, 103, 195, 273
- Stirrups and stirrup leathers, 112, 160–61, 179
- "Stopping into All Four Feet" exercise, 6–10
- Straight lines, 9, 174, 195. See also Alignment
- Strength, 108. See also Fitness
- "Stretchy" circle exercises, 66, 147–48, 153, 221–24
- Stride, length of, 194

- Strides, counting, 106–7, 174
- "Stuck" legs, 38, 78
- Stud chains, 34, *34*
- Study buddies, 28, 40
- Study guides. See Learning
- Stumbling, 154
- Sucking back, 109, 152–53, 193, *193*
- Suppleness, 54, 238–42, 243–44, 249
- Supraspinous ligament, 253–54, *253*
- Swift, Sally, 194
- Symmetry, 56, 105, 109, 154, 160. See also Alignment; Crookedness

/ T /

- Tail to Rail Leg-Yield, 184–85, *184–85*
- *Talk Like TED* (Gallo), 16
- Tap Tap exercise, 45–46, *45*, 53–54
- Teachers, horses as, 13. See also Learning
- Tempo, 55, 106, 109, 111–12, 174, 191–92, 222
- Tension, 170, 172, *193*, 233–34, *234*
- Terminology, standardization of, 7, 113, 262
- Texts. See Reading
- Think Pair Share Compare activity, 28–29
- Thinking about thinking, 67–72. See also Learning
- Thousand Rule, 247, 271
- Throughness, 115, *270*, 271
- Thumbs up hand position, 154
- Tilting of head, vs. flexion, *252*
- Tongue, of horse, 257
- Topline, *121*, 122, *128*, 129
- Torso, centering of, 168
- Tracking up, *195*
- Trail riding, 181, 221
- Train on tracks analogy, 146, *146*, 153–54, *207*, 209
- Training
  - on both sides of horse, 36, 190, 217–18, 243–44, 251–52
  - caveats regarding, 83–84
  - general tips for, 4, 7, 152
  - horse's understanding of, 22
  - repetition and review in, 46, 61
  - rewards in, 11
  - vs. riding, 143
  - time required for, 25, 105
- Transitions
  - aids for, 110, 205–7, 209
  - benefits of, 153
  - canter, 215–16
  - caveats regarding, 216–18
  - on circles, 204, 210, *210*, 217
  - connection in, 173
  - downward, 110, 173–74, 213–16
  - extension activities, 218–21
  - within gaits, 110
  - goals for, 202, 204–5, 274
  - half-halts and, 266
  - horse's position in, 205, 218, *219*, 247
  - during leg-yield, 181
  - on longe, 55
  - as Non-negotiable, 91, 203, 214, 272
  - preparing for, 211, 217, 220, *220*
  - quality of, 210–13, 218
  - upward, 174, 203–13, 215
  - walk-trot, 203–15
- "Trit, trot" rhythm exercise, 206
- Trot, 66, 111, 203–16, 221

- Trust
  - in contact/connection, 135, *136*, 138–40, 144, 224
  - of horse for rider, 22, 224
- Tug of war analogy, 150
- Turn on the haunches, 79–80, *80*
- Turns and turning, 36–38, *37*, 192–93. See also Bending lines
- Twerking motion, 169, 273
- "Two minutes past noon," 242, *242*
- Two Whips exercise, 158, *158*

/ U /

- United States Dressage Federation (USDF), 7, 113
- Uphill balance, 102, 139, 211, 269

/ V /

- Vale, Aaron, 151
- Van der Schaft, Rien, 125, 129
- Vander Ziel, Sharon
  - on communication, 98
  - on flexion, 232, 240, 254
  - on horse's personality, 35
  - on rein aids, 186, 187, 243
  - on rider attitude, 209
  - on tension, 233
- Varian, Sheila, 84
- Vaulting, 52
- Verbal cues, 55, 104
- Videos, 86, 155, 212, 215
- Viking ship ride analogy, *159*, 178, 208
- Vision, of horse, 224, *224*
- Vogel, Gretchen, 38

/ W /

- "Wagging" of horse's head, 241, 251
- Walk, 8, 64, 81, 109, 139, 203–15
- Wanless, Mary, 168, 169, 209, 212–13
- Warm-up, 108, 142, 156, 175, 236–38, 255
- Water skier analogy, 127–28, 193
- Weaknesses, working on, 109
- Weight, of rider, 10
- *When Two Spines Align* (Baumert), 207, 248, 257
- Whips
  - aiding with, 97, 106
  - connection analogy, *128*, 129
  - exercises using, 45–46, *45*, 158, *158*
  - for longeing, 60
- "Whoa," "Go" and, 110
- Widen and squeeze technique
  - in developing feel for contact, 135–46, *136*
  - how-to, 129–31, *130*, 156, 160–61
  - with one rein, *168*
  - vs. opening rein, 246
  - uses of, 167–68, *168*, 223
- Williams, David, 92
- Wilsie, Sharon, 38
- Wilson, Jo-Ann, 233
- Withers, 38, 188
- Wrists, 158, 191, 240, 264

/ X /

- X post exercise, 197–98